UNDERSTANDING EQUAL OPPORTUNITIES AND DIVERSITY

DATE DUE FOR RETURN

The loan period may be shortened if the item is requested.

Also available in the series

Understanding global social policy

Nicola Yeates, The Open University

"Nicola Yeates has brought together an impressive, coherent collection of contributors providing comprehensive coverage of developments in global social policy across a wide range of policy areas. The relationship between globalisation and social policy is one that is rapidly evolving and differentiated. This collection successfully captures these dynamics whilst at the same time providing empirical substance to developments at a particular point in time."
Patricia Kennett, Department of Applied Social Sciences, The Hong Kong Polytechnic University
PB £19.99 (US$32.50) ISBN 978-1-86134-943-9
HB £60.00 (US$80.00) ISBN 978-1-86134-944-6
240 x 172mm 352 pages June 2008

Understanding poverty, inequality and wealth
Policies and prospects

Edited by Tess Ridge and Sharon Wright

"This volume provides a timely and much-needed critical account of the inter-relationship between 'the problem of poverty' and 'the problem of riches'. Combining both conceptual, empirical and policy perspectives and a UK and global focus, it offers rich pickings for students and all who are concerned about poverty and inequality."
Ruth Lister, Loughborough University, author of *Poverty* (Polity Press, 2004)
PB £19.99 (US$34.95) ISBN 978-1-86134-914-9
HB £60.00 (US$80.00) ISBN 978-1-86134-915-6
240 x 172mm 360 pages June 2008

Understanding immigration and refugee policy
Contradictions and continuities

Rosemary Sales, Middlesex University

"This book provides a much-needed overview to the key concepts and issues in global migration and the development of immigration and asylum policy. The book is thought provoking and deserves to be read widely."
Alice Bloch, City University London

PB £19.99 (US$34.95) ISBN 978-1-86134-451-9
HB £60.00 (US$80.00) ISBN 978-1-86134-452-6
240 x 172mm 296 pages June 2007

Understanding health policy

Rob Baggott, De Montfort University

"This book by a leading commentator on health policy breaks new ground in understanding how health policy is made and implemented."
Martin Powell, University of Birmingham
PB £18.99 (US$34.95) ISBN 978-1-86134-630-8
HB £60.00 (US$80.00) ISBN 978-1-86134-631-5
240 x 172mm 292 pages June 2007

Understanding health and social care

Jon Glasby, University of Birmingham

"This is an ambitious and wide-ranging book which provides a valuable historical perspective, as well as a forward-looking analysis, based on real experience. It will be a valuable tool for leaders, policy makers and students." **Nigel Edwards, Policy Director, The NHS Confederation.**
PB £18.99 (US$34.95) ISBN 978-1-86134-910-1
HB £60.00 (US$80.00) ISBN 978-1-86134-911-8
240 x 172mm 216 pages June 2007

For a full listing of all titles in the series visit www.policypress.org.uk

www.policypress.org.uk

INSPECTION COPIES AND ORDERS AVAILABLE FROM:
Marston Book Services • PO Box 269 • Abingdon • Oxon OX14 4YN UK
INSPECTION COPIES
Tel: +44 (0) 1235 465500 • Fax: +44 (0) 1235 465556 • Email: inspections@marston.co.uk
ORDERS
Tel: +44 (0) 1235 465500 • Fax: +44 (0) 1235 465556 • Email: direct.orders@marston.co.uk

UNDERSTANDING EQUAL OPPORTUNITIES AND DIVERSITY

The social differentiations and intersections of inequality

Barbara Bagilhole

First published in Great Britain in 2009 by

The Policy Press
University of Bristol
Fourth Floor, Beacon House
Queen's Road
Bristol BS8 1QU
UK

Tel +44 (0)117 331 4054
Fax +44 (0)117 331 4093
e-mail tpp-info@bristol.ac.uk
www.policypress.org.uk

North American office:
The Policy Press
c/o International Specialized Books Services
920 NE 58th Avenue, Suite 300
Portland, OR 97213-3786, USA
Tel +1 503 287 3093 */o 05982521*
Fax +1 503 280 8832
e-mail info@isbs.com

© The Policy Press and the Social Policy Association 2009

British Library Cataloguing in Publication Data
A catalogue record for this book is available from the British Library.

Library of Congress Cataloging-in-Publication Data
A catalog record for this book has been requested.

ISBN 978 1 86134 848 7   paperback
ISBN 978 1 86134 849 4   hardcover

Barbara Bagilhole is Professor of Equal Opportunities and Social Policy at Loughborough University. She has carried out extensive research in the field of equal opportunities and diversity, both nationally and internationally.

The right of Barbara Bagilhole to be identified as author of this work has been asserted by her in accordance with the 1988 Copyright, Designs and Patents Act.

Cover design by Qube Design Associates, Bristol.
Front cover: photograph kindly supplied by www.alamy.com
Printed and bound in Great Britain by Hobbs the Printers, Southampton

For Beth, Orli, Leo and Maya – our four shining stars

Contents

Detailed contents

List of tables and boxes

Tables

Boxes

Acknowledgements

I would like to thank my friends and colleagues in the Criminology and Social Policy teaching group at Loughborough University for supporting and enabling my study leave. This has given me time to reflect and complete this book, which contains my thoughts and ideas developed over two decades of working in the field of equal opportunities and diversity, both as a practitioner and an academic. More recently, I have been involved as a working group coordinator in the European Union-funded Advanced Thematic Network of Women's Studies in Europe (ATHENA). Since 1997, our aim has been to unite scholars, teachers and stakeholders from civil society and public institutions in the field of gender and diversity. Started in 2006, ATHENA thematically focuses on 'Gender, Culture and European Diversity' and 'Women, Access and European Citizenship'. Involvement with ATHENA has brought with it the joy of meeting, exchanging ideas and working with many highly committed and knowledgeable women experts across Europe, whom I now count as friends as well as valued colleagues. This has allowed the development of my ideas into a much wider context and has become one of the strengths of this book. I would particularly like to acknowledge my joint coordinators and friends Martha Franken, Chris Zwaenepoel and Anna Cabo. I should like to thank staff at The Policy Press for their encouragement and friendly, positive communications. Finally, I would like to thank Rupert for his steadfast love and support, and George, Elli, Ben and Nicky for producing and sharing Beth, Orli, Leo and Maya, who give us a warm glow inside and bring a smile to our faces whenever we think of them.

Glossary

Defining the following terms is both complex and controversial but also essential. Other writers will use different definitions and terms, but if the terms used in this book are clearly defined, it will at least allow the reader to contrast and compare the analysis with other work in the field. Therefore, some of the terms used in this book are explained below to try to help the reader to a clearer understanding.

Disability

The way that disability is defined is very important as it affects the way that disabled people are viewed and the way that they are treated. Definitions of disability have moved from ones that were based on a medicalised, individualistic approach to ones that emphasise the social dimensions of disability. The Disabled People's International definition is: the loss or limitation of opportunities to take part in the life of the community on an equal level with others due to physical and social barriers.

Despite the recognition of the need to move to a social definition, the World Health Organization offers definitions of impairment, disability and handicap that continue to concentrate on an individual's condition. Impairment is defined as any loss or abnormality of psychological, physiological or anatomical structure or function. Disability is seen as any restriction or lack (resulting from an impairment) of ability to perform an activity in the manner of, or within the range considered as normal for, a human being. Finally, handicap is viewed as a disadvantage for a given individual resulting from an impairment or disability that limits the fulfilment of a role for that individual.

Disabled people

This is the preferred term for people who are disabled and one that highlights the fact that they are 'disabled' by society.

Diversity

The concept of diversity has come about through researchers', policy makers' and politicians' recognition of the important reality of the different experiences of disadvantage that can occur between and even within social groups. For example, the experiences and consequences of racism and racial discrimination differ in important ways for black women and black men, and the experiences and consequences of sexism and gender discrimination differ in important ways for white women and black women.

Equal opportunities

The concept of equal opportunities in policy making was originally based on the now disputed premise of treating everyone the same. It is both a complex and contested concept. Although the term was widely used, there is often an assumed shared meaning, which may be seen to be somewhat superficial and at times erroneous when analysed further. The difficulty of definition is pursued in Chapter Three.

Equal opportunities and diversity

The later and more sophisticated coupling of the concepts of equal opportunities and diversity emphasises the recognition of difference, the possibility of 'multiple disadvantage', and different treatment, which can be legitimate in the pursuit of social equality, fairness and justice. The idea of 'multiple disadvantage' has moved from a rather crude idea of 'adding up' disadvantages to a more sophisticated level still, of thinking that disadvantages are not cumulative but interactional – that is, their effect runs more than one way. For example, racism is infected and changed by sexism for black women, and vice versa – the sexism they encounter is infected and changed by racism.

Ethnicity

is the recognition of a group's shared identity based on country of origin, culture, language or religion.

Gender

Sociology has for two decades made a clear distinction between sex and gender. It was argued that the relatively fixed nature of sex based on biological determinants could be compared to the variability of gender as a cultural product that refers to the social classifications of 'masculine' and 'feminine'. However, the clarity of the distinction between sex and gender has been challenged. The declared fact that sex is natural, biologically clear and divided into two groups is now being reappraised. The biological understanding of the determinant of sex difference is in fact still being investigated through medical research work in the area of chromosomal theory, and it is argued that this work is influenced by notions of gender.

Glass ceiling

was originally coined to describe the situation common to women where they are blocked from progressing up an organisational hierarchy. 'Ceiling' describes the highest level that women may reach, and 'glass' indicates that they can see through it but not break through it.

Intersectionality

is both a theory and methodological tool. It acknowledges and stresses the importance of the intersections of disadvantage between and within social groups. Hill Collins (2000: 180) writes: 'Intersectionality refers to particular forms of intersecting oppressions, for example, intersections of race and gender, or of sexuality and nation. Intersectional paradigms remind us that oppression cannot be reduced to one fundamental type, and that oppressions work together in producing injustice'.

Minority ethnic groups or ethnic minorities

These terms are broadly applied and widespread in official and academic publications, often with an implication of difference in colour. They are sometimes qualified by being linked with black, that is, black and minority ethnic (BME) groups. The use of the term minority ethnic groups emphasises the different ethnic groupings within the black community, and may be used to avoid a false and imposed homogeneity of black people when the heterogeneity in the different communities needs drawing out to differentiate forms and experiences of racism. We need to bear in mind that minority ethnic communities may not necessarily have much else in common than adverse treatment and experiences, and that both treatment and experiences may differ between groups. For example, although Black Caribbean children continue to underachieve in schools and experience the highest exclusion rates, Indian children are now achieving better than Whites and have lower exclusion rates than them. Therefore, groups have to be disaggregated to provide a clearer understanding of differentiation of experience and treatment within broader classifications. For instance, minority ethnic communities may be differentiated by two broad groups, Asian and Black, or classified by country of origin, for example, Indian, Pakistani or Bangladeshi, or even religion where this is relevant, for example, Hindu, Muslim or Sikh. We need some reasonably understood and flexible ways of identifying and categorising groups in the area of race, when discussing the differentiated experiences of certain groups.

Official categories

are not without problems and contradictions. While there is considerable overlap between them they are not consistent. The Labour Force Survey contains a category that specifically signifies a 'mixed-race' classification, which since 1992 has been further subdivided, whereas the Census only offers a Black/Other or Other category. This may pick up people of mixed descent but does not allow their quantification. This omission is important because this is the fastest growing community of all minority groups, and those in this group may experience racial prejudice and discrimination that is either the same as, or different from, that experienced by other visible groups. Also, in both the Labour Force Survey and the Census, the White category is not subdivided into ethnic or national categories. Looking at the categories on offer in the Census, it is not clear where Black British-born people would put themselves. They may choose 'Black Other', or their parental decent such as 'Indian' or 'Pakistani', or if they do not identify with the political classification of Black, they may choose 'Other'. All these official categories confuse social, national and political affiliations, ignore religion and do not differentiate between White groups that may experience discrimination.

Multiculturalism

was an approach adopted in the 1980s, particularly in schools, that emphasised the need to understand, accept and respect the cultural aspects of other groups within society to facilitate good race relations.

Multiple disadvantage

The idea of 'multiple disadvantage' has moved from the rather crude idea of 'adding up' disadvantages to a more sophisticated level still, of thinking that disadvantages are not cumulative but interactional – that is, their effect runs more than one way. For example, racism is infected and changed by sexism for black women, and vice versa – the sexism they encounter is infected and changed by racism.

Non-disabled people

This term is preferred over 'able-bodied' to describe people without a disability because it does not imply a monopoly on ability.

People with learning difficulties

This term is used to describe someone with an impairment of their intellectual abilities. It used to be called mental handicap.

Political correctness

This concept is controversial. It is mostly used in a pejorative way to denounce language that is designed so as not to cause offence to certain groups (for example, women, disabled people, minority ethnic groups and so on) and ideas and policies to counter disadvantage in those groups.

Prejudice
This may take the following forms:

- Ageism: stereotyping, prejudice or discriminatory practice or policies based on age.
- Disabilism: stereotyping, prejudice or discriminatory practice or policies based on the assumption that disabled people are inferior to non-disabled people.
- Heterosexism: stereotyping, prejudice or discriminatory practice or policies that assume heterosexuals are superior to homosexuals.
- Homophobia: fear of, aversion to or discrimination against homosexuals.
- Islamophobia: a relatively new term used to refer to fear, prejudice or discrimination against Muslims.
- Racism: in its simplest definition, the belief that race is the primary determinant of human traits and capacities and that racial differences produce an inherent superiority of a particular race.
- Sexism: the belief or attitude that women are inferior to men, and includes practices or policies stemming from this belief.

Race
is now recognised as a social construction denoting a particular way in which communal differences come to be constructed, rather than a biological, genetic or physical concept. However, it still has significant currency in both sociological analysis and official publications and classifications. The Labour Force Survey has classified its data by official definitions of race since the mid–1980s, and from 1991, an 'ethnic' question was included in the Population Census, which asked for self-categorisation of ethnic identity. Race is used in British legislation to refer to such things as ethnic or national origins, nationality or citizenship, and skin colour. In practice, references to race focus on visibly identifiable groups, such as Asian, African and Black Caribbean communities, but it is important to recognise that discrimination is also directed against White groups. For example, there is a long history of prejudice against Irish and Jewish people in Britain, and more recently against European Unions from former Eastern bloc countries who have entered the UK legitimately to work.

Stereotypes
are over-generalised, misinformed or false beliefs about a group that are applied broadly to each member of the group.

Introduction

This book examines and offers an understanding of the complex and often misunderstood concept of **equal opportunities and diversity** (EO&D). It analyses disadvantage and discrimination experienced by certain groups in Britain, and policies and legislation to combat them. There is a lack of understanding about what EO&D means, and what is required or permitted in its pursuance under the law by individuals and organisations. As the Equalities Review (2007: 93-94) pointed out:

> Some people still view equality as being about 'political correctness' – for example, preventing competitive sport at school so as not to allow anyone to win or lose. Some associate equality with oppressive petty bureaucracy, while others think that pursuing equality means advancing some groups above others – rather than improving opportunities and narrowing the gaps for groups who are disadvantaged, and thus improving society as a whole.

There is a parallel tradition of research and publications on the extent of and reasons for disadvantage among specific social groups that has influenced the introduction of new policies and legislation. However, there has been less research providing an integrated view of the experience of all such groups. This book is different as it is based on all the major social differentiations within society on which EO&D legislation in the UK is based: gender, race, disability, sexual orientation, religion or belief, and age.

The discourse around this area of social policy was originally conceptualised as **equal opportunities** (EO) (see Bagilhole (1997) for a full discussion of this discourse). The later and more sophisticated coupling of the concept of **diversity** to this area of policy making has come about through researchers', policy makers' and politicians' recognition of the important reality of the different experiences of disadvantage that can occur between and even within a social group. For example, the experiences and consequences of racism and racial discrimination differ in important ways for black women and black men, and the experiences and consequences of sexism and gender discrimination differ in important ways for white women and black women.

The concept of EO in policy making was originally based on the now disputed premise of treating everyone the same, whereas the concept of EO&D emphasises the recognition of difference, the possibility of **multiple disadvantage**, and different treatment, which can be legitimate in the pursuit of social equality, fairness and justice. The idea of 'multiple disadvantage' has moved from a rather crude idea of 'adding up' disadvantages to a more sophisticated level still, of thinking that disadvantages are not cumulative but interactional – that is, their effect runs more than one way. For example, racism is infected and changed by sexism for black women, and vice versa – the sexism they encounter is infected and changed by racism.

Therefore, underpinning this book's arguments is the acknowledgement that the social differentiations of gender, race, disability, sexual orientation, religion or belief, and age do not create homogeneous groups. Where possible, the concept of **intersectionality** is used to run as a coordinating thread throughout the book. Intersectionality is both a theory and methodological tool and, where appropriate and relevant, it is used to develop the understanding of EO&D.

As examples:

- Chapter Two uses intersectionality as a methodological tool to analyse and expose the complex nature of both the homogeneity and heterogeneity of disadvantage between and within social groups;
- Chapter Three uses intersectionality as a theory to further understand the concept of EO&D;
- Chapter Six tests the usefulness of intersectionality as a policy-making tool;
- Chapter Seven examines the consequences of intersectional discourse in EU policy making.

The aim of the book is to clarify and develop the concept of EO&D as it has changed to incorporate not just gender, race and disability equality, but the further three strands of equality that include sexual orientation, religion or belief, and age. EO&D policy in the UK, as in other EU member states, has moved from the 'big two strands' of gender and race, through the inclusion of disability policy, finally to incorporate all the 'six strands' now required by the EU social policy agenda. During this development, and particularly since the 1980s, the concept of intersectionality has emerged and been adopted in the discourse around legislation and policy. It is seen as a possible way forward that recognises the heterogeneity of social groups while at the same time taking the EO&D agenda forward.

The scope of the book

Chapter Two includes evidence of the extent and nature of disadvantage across, between and within social groups. Chapter Three provides and examines different definitions of, and theoretical and ideological approaches to EO&D. Chapter Four exposes the historical, political and economic background to the concept. Chapter Five lays out and examines the legislation in the area. Chapter Six follows the policy process through national and regional agencies, and at organisational and institutional level through case study analysis. Chapter Seven considers the influence and effect of the European Union (EU) on UK EO&D legislation and policy. Chapter Eight includes a cross-national comparison of approaches to EO&D between EU member states. Chapter Nine addresses some issues on the future agenda for EO&D policies.

The dilemma of equality versus difference

Feminism and the women's movement have always struggled with the dilemma of equality and difference: equality with men versus being different from them. Benhabib (1994: 2) saw the dilemma as 'preserving a woman's separate sphere versus becoming full members of existing society by giving up women's traditional spaces' – the traditional spaces for women being in the private sphere and particularly in the caring role. This dilemma is now compounded by the contemporary agenda of the heterogeneity and diversity of the different strands of EO&D policy. Diversity can pose particular challenges to gender theory and gender equality policies and legislation. It highlights that it is not enough to focus on gender equality or discrimination, but that there is a need to understand and study inequalities and discrimination in plural, across gender, race, disability, sexual orientation, religion or belief, and age.

Feminist theory has tackled this with the concept of intersectionality that acknowledges and stresses the importance of the intersections of disadvantage between and within the social groups covered by policies prohibiting discrimination, promoting equal opportunities and valuing diversity. In this way, EU policies on EO&D and feminist theories of intersectionality can be seen to be pointing in the same direction. Intersectionality as a theory and methodology for research could be a springboard for the operationalisation of a social justice agenda.

Initially, Crenshaw (1989, 1991) defined the concept of intersectionality to denote the various ways race and gender interact to shape multiple dimensions of black women's employment experiences, moving away from what was perceived as a mono-focus approach on white middle-class women's interests. This concept could offer a theoretical base and policy tool that usefully illuminates the multiple, intersecting, interlacing nature of complex social relations both between and within socially disadvantaged groups in society. However, its very complexity must in some way be contained to allow its utility for the reality and practicality of EO&D policy making. This concept of intersectionality needs to be analysed and understood to assess its potential for facilitating genuine social policy change in an area that has in the past been beset with mainly bureaucratic lip-service and paper trails.

Box 1.1: Intersectionality

Neither the concept of, nor the interest in, intersectionality is new for researchers: for a decade, 'multiple discrimination' has been addressed through an intersectional approach. It reflects the interest of feminist scholars and activists in looking at the different inequalities and identities that intertwine in women's lives, contributing to experiences of exclusion as well as unique ways of resistance.

Some of the voices and needs to first create an interest in challenging the supposed uniformity and universality of women's demands represented by feminism were those of black and lesbian women – see, for instance, Angela Davis' work concerning gender, social class, race and sexuality (1981); Audre Lorde's exploration of systems of oppression (1984); and the framing of margin/centre in the work of bell hooks (1981).

There was a general dissatisfaction with the assumption of the homogeneity of the group women, and the consequences of separating race and gender studies. hooks (1981) cautioned against assumptions that all women experienced common oppression, and raised the feminist question of 'equal to whom?'. Do black women want to be equal to black men or white women?

There is a need for an analysis that looks at whole people rather than breaking them up into component parts (for example, race separate from gender). Individuals possess identities that encompass multiple, intersecting oppressions that are complex and shifting. However, in order to prevent impotence in EO&D policy making, it is also necessary to acknowledge that some disadvantages are persistent and maintained. Also, intersectionally informed policies can address issues that may be only relevant for people at a certain period in their lives, for example, policies for lesbian mothers with small children, or for young black men.

Women's different experiences of exclusion help us to understand that there are power relationships based not only on gender, but also on sexual orientation, age, disability, race, and religion or belief. Sex is only one of the many inequalities that construct gender; gender is constructed through and by the distinctions of race and ethnicity, sexuality, disability, religion or belief, and age. These experiences of exclusion and inequality also interact and may conflict with each other.

UK policy makers in the past used a mono-focus approach on one social group at a time, reflecting the demands of mono-focused social movements. However, the discourses of intersectionality and identities have now emerged from politicians and policy makers both nationally and in the EU. Therefore, the main theoretical underpinning of this book is to look at the issue of intersectionality as it arises in new structures, legislation, policies and processes.

It starts from the premise that people live in multiple, layered identities derived from social relations, history and the operation of structures of power. Intersectional analysis aims to reveal both these multiple identities and the inequalities that arise from them. It exposes the different types of discrimination and disadvantage that occur as a consequence of either the foregrounding of one identity or the combination of two or more identities at different moments in time, for example, black women, disabled women, gay men, Muslim women, elderly men and so on. It acknowledges that social groupings on the grounds of gender, race, disability, religion or belief, sexual orientation and age are simultaneously socially constructed, and concern social positioning and everyday practices.

In the past, EO&D policies, legislation and enacting agencies have enforced a public assertion that the interests of different social groups are inherently non-conflicting. However, there is no longer a uniform story of blanket disadvantage for any of these groups in the UK. Therefore, it is time to acknowledge, confront and deal with the actual problems of separate and relative multiple deprivation, and sometimes conflicting experiences and interests, both between different categories of disadvantage and even within these categories themselves.

Statistical evidence of disadvantage

Overview

This chapter:

- includes an examination of some of the available statistical evidence of the extent and nature of advantage and disadvantage on the grounds of gender, race, disability, religion or belief, sexual orientation and age. Some statistics are gathered for the United Kingdom (UK) as a whole and some only for Great Britain (GB), or even its separate constituent countries[1];
- identifies some areas of continuing and consistent disadvantage, particularly in the social differentiation of gender;
- investigates and analyses some of the data available across different strands of equal opportunities and diversity (EO&D), which can lead to the examination of the interaction and amplification of disadvantage across and within different social categories in an attempt to use an intersectional approach, for example, gender and race, gender and disability, and so on.

Key concepts

Measures of disadvantage; statistical analysis; intersectionality; social categories

Introduction

Britain has changed considerably since some types of discrimination were originally outlawed. Since the 1970s, the population of GB has grown from less than 55 million to over 57 million. This includes:

- one million more men and 0.6 million more women aged 65 or over. There were 9.4 million adults over 65 in 2005 (16% of the population) and this figure is predicted to rise to 12.4 million by 2021 (20%);
- 24 million households, and seven million families with dependent children. These include just over five million families headed by couples, over one and a half million headed by a lone mother, and 180,000 headed by a lone father;
- 10 million disabled people (those people reporting a long-term illness or disability that restricts daily activities);
- over four and a half million minority ethnic communities, an increase of over 50% between the 1991 and 2001 Censuses;
- just over three million people belonging to a non-Christian religion;
- an estimated just over two to just over three million gay, lesbian or bisexual adults (EOC, 2006b).

Continuing disadvantage

Britain is in many ways a fairer and more equal society than at any time in living memory, and many of us enjoy a lifestyle far richer and less restricted than ever. However, there are still ingrained disadvantages for some groups. As the Equalities Review (2007: 12) points out, 'deep inequalities persist. In some cases they have widened. Some kinds of disadvantage have resisted all efforts to reduce them'. For example, in all communities there are marked differences in the experiences of women and men.

It is important to acknowledge that women are not an homogeneous group. Gender is one basis of inequality that intersects with other areas of inequality. Gender segregation is mediated by other patterns of disadvantage. Women have identities formed in gendered processes that vary according to age, marital and parental status, whether they are white or black (including differences between minority ethnic groups), whether they are lesbian or heterosexual, and whether or not they experience disabilities.

Feminist theorists therefore often find themselves struggling with the risk posed by a relativist stress on **difference and diversity**. While the experiences of women originating from different locations within a society cannot be the same, it is possible to identify common interests and common experiences of disadvantage among women. The Women and

Work Commission (2006) demonstrated this by looking at general statistics on gender disadvantage, focusing only on the interaction between gender and age, not on any of the other social differentiations such as disability and ethnicity. While the arguments against essentialism are accepted, of either a biological or social constructionist nature, it must be acknowledged that gender is a key constitutive part of the social, cultural and economic divisions in society. While it is acknowledged that women's experiences of disadvantage are tempered and altered by other social divisions, women do have considerable shared experiences, still suffer systematic modes of discrimination, and share distinct patternings that relate to gender.

Overall:
- the gendered domestic division of labour and time is still skewed firmly in men's favour, so that women enter the public spheres of the labour market and politics at a disadvantage;
- in the labour market, occupational segregation, the greater concentration of women in part-time work and the gender pay gap mean that women remain more likely than men to be low paid;
- a **glass ceiling** (discussed in Chapter Six) still governs women's lack of access to top jobs;
- women are still dramatically under-represented in all key areas of public, political and economic life. In some areas the situation is static, while in others women's representation is actually decreasing (EHRC, 2008a). The majority of public appointments, senior civil servants, members of the legal profession, directors of companies, key actors in the media and individuals holding senior positions in universities are men;
- women are more likely than men to be poor and to carry the main burden of managing poverty;
- domestic violence still stunts the lives of many women.

Employment and gender

In Great Britain:

- 79% of men of working age are in employment compared with 70% of women;
- 42% of women employees work part-time compared with 9% of men.

Despite the dramatic increase in women's participation in the labour force during the 20th century, women are concentrated in a narrow range of occupations, often seen as 'women's work'. Occupational segregation by sex is 'extensive and pervasive and is one of the most important and enduring aspects of labour markets around the world' (Anker, 1998: 3). Not only is it extensive in all countries, it exists no matter how those countries are organised economically and politically, whether they are industrialised, capitalist countries, former communist countries or less industrialised countries.

The persistence of sex segregation across different types of occupation and between high and low status occupations has been extensively documented, and continues despite technological advances in work organisation. The sex segregation of occupations has two dimensions: horizontal and vertical. On the whole, women and men have different types of occupation (horizontal segregation), but where women and men are found in the same occupation, even if women predominate, they are most commonly found in the lower grades (vertical segregation). Both forms of occupational segregation have different consequences for women than for men. Women's situations are characterised by low wages, intermittent employment and subordination to men in the workplace. Men's situations are characterised by higher wages, lifelong employment and either dominance over women or little contact with them in the workplace.

This is crucially important because over half of women working in low-paid, part-time jobs are 'working below their potential', that is, they are not using either their skills or experience, or their qualifications, in their current job. Despite strong growth in the number of part-time jobs, large numbers of women cannot find jobs that use their abilities; there are simply too few part-time jobs available at an appropriate level. The distribution of part-time and full-time jobs in workplaces tends to be reproduced year on year, as managers usually replace 'like with like'. Many managers are resistant to part-time working in jobs at senior levels, and within workplaces opportunities for advancement for part-time workers are often limited. Thus women find themselves trapped in low-paid jobs if they wish to work part-time.

Pay and gender

UK women workers on average earn only 83 pence for every pound that is earned by a man for full-time work. The full-time pay gap is even starker for weekly and annual earnings (23.4% and 27.1% respectively). Part-time women workers earn 41% less per hour than men who work full-time (see *Table 2.1*). Since 1975 (when the Equal Pay Act was implemented; see Chapter Five), the overall full-time gender pay gap has decreased by 12% from 29.4%, but the part-time gender pay gap by only 3%. As the Equalities Review (2007) pointed out, at the present rate of progress it will take over 75 years for women to gain equal pay to men.

It is striking that men start to earn more than women almost as soon as they enter the labour market, and this gender pay gap exists not only for lower-paid workers. For example, just three years after graduating, women earn 15% less than their male counterparts (Women and Work Commission, 2006). Also, the pay gap rises with age and time in employment. In 2005, the gender pay gap for full-time workers aged 18-21 was 3.7%. For those aged 40-49, the age group for whom the gap is widest, the pay gap was 21.7%. Manning and Swaffield (2005) found only small differences between women and men in the early years of their careers. However, a woman continually working full-time experiences a pay gap of 12% compared with an equivalent man after ten years. About half of this gap was explained by different pay rates in different gendered occupations, but the other half remained unexplained.

Table 2.1: *Gender pay gap, UK (%)*

Hourly earnings	
Full-time	17.1
Part-time	41
Weekly earnings	
Full-time	23.4
Annual earnings	
Full-time	27.1

Source: EOC, 2006b

Lower lifetime earnings for women mean lower contributions and lower pensions. Rake et al (2000) estimated that the difference in the lifetime earnings of men and childless women was just under £250,000 for mid-skilled workers. This is 37% less than those of an equivalently skilled man, of which 16% is due to fewer hours in the labour market and 18% due to differences in hourly pay.

Education and gender

On average, girls in the UK gain higher qualifications than boys:

- 59% of girls but only 49% of boys gain five or more high-grade GCSEs or equivalent;
- 44% of young women but only 35% of young men gain two or more A levels or equivalent.

However, disadvantageous segregation in education for women is seen in the different subjects taken by female and male students. These choices have important consequences for gendered inequality in the workforce. At age 16 many subjects are taken by similar numbers of girls and boys (due to the introduction of the compulsory national curriculum), but this changes at A level/**Higher Grade where**:

- 71% of students taking examinations in English Literature are young women;
- 76% of students taking physics are young men.

More extreme segregation of young women and men is seen in apprenticeship figures for England:

- 97% of early years care and education and 91% of hairdressing apprenticeships are taken by women;
- 97% of engineering, 98% of automotive industry, and 99% of construction, plumbing and electrotechnical apprentices are taken by men.

Subject segregation in further education (FE) and higher education (HE) in GB is almost as extreme:

- in engineering and technology, 87% of FE and 86% of HE students are male;
- in HE, only 24% of computer science students, 22% of physics students and 32% of architecture students are women.

The subjects studied have major implications for different careers and wage structures for women and men, and a knock-on effect on pension entitlement. Consequently, in 2005, the then Pensions Minister, Alan Johnson, described women's pensions as a 'scandal' (Thane et al, 2007).

Power and gender

In the public sector:

- seven in 10 head teachers in secondary schools and FE college principals are men, and eight in nine university vice-chancellors are men;
- three-quarters of Civil Service top managers, 90% of senior police officers, 91% of the senior judiciary, and more than 99% of senior ranking officers in the armed forces are men (EOC, 2007).

The Equality and Human Rights Commission (EHRC) has carried on the tradition of the former Equal Opportunities Commission (EOC) annual reports. Each year since 2005, the EOC estimated the number of years it would take for women to achieve equality in key areas of power in society at the current rate of progress. The 2008 report indicated (EHRC, 2008a) that, compared with the previous year's report, it would now take 15 years longer (55 years in total) for women to achieve equal status to men at senior levels in the judiciary, and women directors in FTSE 100 companies could be waiting eight years longer (73 years in total).

The Equalities Review (2007: 99) described our democratic institutions as 'shockingly unrepresentative'. Women's representation in Parliament increased from 27 women elected in October 1974, to 126 women MPs. This was an increase from 4% to 20% in 2006, the highest ever proportion. However, this subsequently declined to 19.3% (EHRC, 2008a). There are only two minority ethnic women MPs at Westminster, and 13 men. All four Muslim MPs are men. In 2006, only 29% of local councillors in England were women. At the current rate of progress, it will take over 75 years for parity of women's political representation with men (Equalities Review, 2007).

This contrasts markedly with:

- the Scottish Parliament (40% women); and
- the National Assembly for Wales (50% women).

In Scotland and Wales, more equal representation has been achieved through **positive action** on gender by some political parties (see Chapter Five for a discussion of this).

In the private sector, in the FTSE100 companies, there are:

- 78 women directors, up 13% on 2004;
- 11 women executive directors, down from 13% in 2004;
- one woman chief executive officer and one woman chair (Singh and Vinnicombe, 2005).

Caring responsibilities and gender

Parenthood affects women and men in GB to different extents, with mothers of younger children being most negatively affected (see *Table 2.2*). Despite women with children increasing their participation in paid work more than any other group during the past 20 years, they continue to have the main responsibility for childcare, other unpaid care and domestic work. According to analysis of the UK Time Use Survey, mothers do three-quarters of childcare during the week and two-thirds at weekends (Women and Work Commission, 2006).

However, attitudes to paid work and caring roles within families are changing. Increasingly, both partners in a couple are in paid work, though not necessarily full-time, and men are stating a desire to take a more active role in caring for children. Hatten et al (2002) found that a substantial minority of fathers would like to be more involved in looking after their

Table 2.2: Employment profile of mothers and fathers by youngest child, GB (%)

	Employment rate	% full-time	% part-time
All mothers	67	42	58
Youngest child 0-4	55	36	64
Youngest child 5-10	71	39	61
Youngest child 11-15	77	50	50
Youngest child 16-18	79	56	44
All fathers	90	96	4
Youngest child 0-4	90	96	4
Youngest child 5-10	90	96	4
Youngest child 11-15	90	97	3
Youngest child 16-18	88	95	5

Source: EOC, 2006b

children. O'Brien and Shemit (2003) found that about one-third of active parental childcare was carried out by fathers.

Adult caring is becoming increasingly necessary due to the ageing of the British population. Women in the UK are most likely to care for elderly or disabled relatives and friends and are most likely to be carers in all age groups under 75 years. Almost one in eight women and one in 12 men aged 25-44 have unpaid caring responsibilities. A quarter of all women aged 50-59 provide unpaid care, compared with about one in six men. Both women and men carers have lower employment rates than non-carers, but again the impact is gendered, especially around the full-time/part-time employment dimension (see *Table 2.3*). Women with caring responsibilities are much more likely than men to work part-time or not at all. The majority of men with caring responsibilities in paid work have full-time jobs (Sheffield Hallam University, 2005).

Caring rates are highest between the ages of 45 and 64, having a knock-on effect on differential accumulated pension rights for women and men. The gender income gap is widest in retirement, where women receive 47% lower weekly income than men. While retired men get nearly half

Table 2.3: Employment profile of carers by sex, UK (%)

	Employment rate	% full-time	% part-time
Women carers	65	54	46
Men carers	72	89	11

Source: EOC, 2006b

their income from non-state pensions, retired women get only a quarter of their income from this source.

Diverse and intersectional disadvantage

Given this general continuing disadvantage based on gender, there are nevertheless differences between women that are only now being exposed as more data become disaggregated by the other strands of EO&D. Despite this, these data continue to be mostly inadequate and inaccessible. However, diverse inequality and multiple disadvantage are increasingly being recognised between and within different social groups.

There is no uniform story of blanket disadvantage among social groups. Inequalities and disadvantage exist among as well as between socially differentiated groups. Gender, race, disability, religion or belief, sexual orientation and age are differentiating factors that apply to all people, influencing their experiences and opportunities. All communities are increasingly heterogeneous and changing, and all are complex, with internal diversity and even disagreements. For example, as the Runnymede Trust Commission (2000: 30) report pointed out, in the area of race, ethnicity and religion, 'the conventional terminology of Asian blurs critical distinctions between Bangladeshis, Gujaratis, Pakistanis and Punjabis; between South Asians, East African Asians and Chinese; and between Hindus, Muslims and Sikhs. South Asians vary significantly not only in terms of nationality and religion but also in terms of language, caste and class, and of whether they have come to Britain from urban or rural backgrounds'.

Importance of disaggregated data

Good evidence-based policy making requires the use of both up-to-date quantitative data, collected across a wide sample base, and qualitative information to help refine our understanding of it. Looking specifically at the interaction between gender and race, the Runnymede Trust Commission (2000) highlighted and emphasised the importance of disaggregated data. It specifically gives examples of where gender and race data on disadvantage can complement each other and further illuminates issues that need to be tackled. As it argued, 'in most contexts the experiences, interests and perceptions of women are different from those of men.... If the likelihood of different impacts is not recognised it can happen – notoriously – that race equality initiatives benefit mainly black and Asian men, and that gender equality initiatives benefit mainly white women' (Runnymede Trust Commission, 2000: 68).

However, there is still a considerable lack of comprehensive British data disaggregated by the 'six equality strands'. As the Equalities Review (2007: 10) states:

> Poor measurement and a lack of transparency have contributed to society and governments being unable to tackle persistent inequalities and their causes. The data on inequality are utterly inadequate in many ways … even where data do exist, they are not consistently used well or published in a way that makes sense.

The Review's experience of both analysing specific sectors and reviewing the quantity, quality and availability of data more generally highlighted difficulties in compiling a complete picture of inequality in Britain. The general problems it encountered included:

- the fragmentary nature of official data;
- inadequate recording of data relevant to equality in certain areas;
- inadequate cross-referencing and consistency of data;
- devolved and different arrangements for collecting data, which can make it difficult to compare data between different departments and between England, Scotland and Wales;
- the use of proxy measures of disadvantage that do not always accurately reflect the underlying inequality;
- lack of historic data; and
- the failure of official statistical publications generally to report on even those equality groups for which data do exist.

Specifically:

- There is a particular lack of comprehensive data on minority ethnic communities in Wales and Scotland, and for the new equality strands of religion or belief, and age for the whole of GB.
- Statistics on sexual orientation are non-existent. There is a lack of robust statistical evidence concerning the proportion of the population who identify as lesbian, gay or bisexual (LGB).

The Department of Trade and Industry's regulatory impact assessment suggested that between 5% and 7% of the population is LGB (DTI, 2005). Stonewall (2008) estimates that there are 1.7 million gay people in the workforce, and 150,000 gay university students. The fundamental problem is the lack of baseline robust data. The national census has never asked about sexual orientation and there is no intention to include a question on it in the future, and general national attitudinal studies do not include questions about homophobia and attitudes to gay people.

Some examples of ways forward

The phrase **multiple disadvantage** has drifted into popular use and policy makers' vocabulary in recent years. It is taken to mean that having more than one characteristic typically associated with a disadvantage increases an individual's likelihood of experiencing that disadvantage and may even increase its intensity. In the name of exposing 'political correctness', some media and political commentators have lampooned ideas about the most 'oppressed' person, for example the fabled black, disabled lesbian. However, available data show that the concept does have some validity, and may even take us towards a more sophisticated intersectional approach to policy making. National and EU politicians and policy makers are beginning through the use of the term EO&D to move their discourse from the idea of 'multiple disadvantage' to intersectionality, although it seems they often lack an understanding of this complex concept. Therefore, it may be useful to examine some of the data available in the field of employment for a better understanding of the diverse nature of disadvantage in Britain.

Age and gender

Age is a mitigating factor in employment rates for both women and men in GB (see *Tables 2.4* and *2.5*), despite gender remaining an important factor in terms of rate of employment, particularly in part-time working. Both women and men in the 25-44 age group experience the highest rate of employment, but still show differences by gender:

- 74% for women;
- 88% for men.

Also, there is a difference in the proportion of those working part-time:

- 40% of the women are part-timers;
- 4% of the men work part-time.

Even in the youngest age group – 16- to 24-year-olds – where the employment rate is closest for women and men (57% and 60% respectively), the proportion working part-time is different:

Table 2.4: Women's employment profile by age, GB (%)

Women	Employment rate	% full-time	% part-time
16-24	57	56	44
25-44	74	60	40
45-64	63	55	45
65 or over	4	18	82

Source: EOC, 2006b

Table 2.5: Men's employment profile by age, GB (%)

Men	Employment rate	% full-time	% part-time
16-24	60	72	28
25-44	88	96	4
45-64	77	91	9
65 or over	9	37	63

Source: EOC, 2006b

- 44% of the women are part-timers;
- 28% of the men work part-time.

Disability and gender

The Disability Rights Commission (before its integration into the Equality and Human Rights Commission; see Chapter Five) produced some figures for GB that showed an improvement in disabled people's position in society:

- 51% of disabled people were in work in 2005 compared with 46.6% in 2000;
- in HE the number of disabled students rose from 86,250 in 2001/01 to 121,080 in 2003/04;
- by 2005, 2.9% of senior Civil Service employees were disabled compared with 1.5% in 1998.

However, both disabled women and men each have lower employment rates than those who are not disabled (see *Table 2.6*). The difference is largest for men: 52% of disabled men work compared with 85% of men who are not disabled.

Table 2.6: Disabled women's and men's employment profile, GB (%)

	Employment rate	% full-time	% part-time
Disabled women	49	54	46
Disabled men	52	87	13

Source: EOC, 2006b

However, disabled women still have a lower rate than disabled men overall, only 49% of disabled women work, and disabled women are much more likely to work part-time (46% compared with 13% disabled men).

Ethnicity and gender

Studies of ethnicity have revealed patterns of segregation by race and occupation. Many studies particularly identify a general tendency for minority ethnic women to be concentrated among the lowest-status occupational groups. There has been a small rise in the share of minority ethnic women in higher-grade employment, but they continue to be under-represented in this group relative to white women. However, importantly, there is also a wide variation between the employment rate for different ethnic groups in GB, especially for women, with 69% of white women and 64% of African Caribbean women working, compared with only 23% of women from Pakistani and 18% from Bangladeshi origins (see *Table 2.7*).

Part-time employment is less common for minority ethnic women than white women. On the other hand, proportionately more minority ethnic men than white men work part-time. Bangladeshi men at 39% have the highest part-time rates compared with other men (see *Table 2.8*).

Table 2.7: Women's employment profile by ethnic group, GB (%)

Women	Employment rate	% full-time	% part-time
White	69	57	43
Black Caribbean	64	73	27
Mixed	64	66	34
Indian	61	68	32
Chinese	55	74	26
Black African	48	73	27
Pakistani	23	55	45
Bangladeshi	18	52	48

Source: EOC, 2006b

Table 2.8: Men's employment profile by ethnic group, GB (%)

Men	Employment rate	% full-time	% part-time
White	80	91	9
Indian	75	91	9
Black Caribbean	71	87	13
Mixed	63	85	15
Black African	63	78	22
Pakistani	63	80	20
Bangladeshi	54	61	39
Chinese	49	82	18

Source: EOC, 2006b

Motherhood also differentially affects the employment profiles of women in different ethnic groups. White, Indian and African Caribbean mothers have the highest employment rates of between 65% and 70%. Pakistani mothers have the lowest rate at 15%. The conventional British pattern of women's employment (the interrupted pattern including a part-time period) is, in fact, a pattern most often seen in white women and cannot be generalised to all other ethnic groups. Simplistic, monocausal explanations of ethnic differences in women's employment based either on cultural differences or economic necessity are inadequate. Black feminists have criticised traditional cultural explanations for minority ethnic women's employment profiles, arguing that cultural values should not be treated as entities separate from social, economic and spatial factors, nor from the agency of women themselves. Qualitative research has shown that, while minority ethnic women do ascribe to distinctive culturally defined gender roles, the manifestation of those roles may not be straightforward. Thus women's employment patterns may be contingent on social and economic factors, such as the structure of the local labour market, timing of immigration and knowledge of English, all of which mediate culturally ascribed gender roles.

The gender pay gap is also mediated by ethnicity. Average full-time hourly earnings for white men and men of Indian origin are relatively high, and so full-time gender pay gaps are large in these ethnic groups. On the other hand, full-time earnings are mostly low for both women and men in other minority ethnic groups, with Pakistani and Bangladeshi women at the highest risk of disadvantage. The low economic activity level of Pakistani and Bangladeshi women may suggest that cultural factors are playing an important role, but those women in this group with higher educational qualifications are much more likely to be economically active than those without. Thus cultural factors alone are not pre-eminent. White women, and minority ethnic women and men (except those of Indian origin), are particularly likely to be concentrated in low-paid jobs.

Religious belief

The Home Office Report, *Religious discrimination in England and Wales* (Weller et al, 2001), sought to analyse religious discrimination separately from the issues of race. It found that one-third of Muslims and one-quarter of Jews and Hindus had suffered unjust treatment in the workplace and elsewhere compared with 16% of Christians. The government then decided to include a question on religion in the 2001 Census, which provided comprehensive data on religious affiliation for the first time. Muslims form the largest group belonging to a non-Christian religion: 1.5 million. They have the lowest employment rates of all religious groups; only 24% of women and 58% of men aged 16-64 are in employment.

Unemployment rates for Muslims are higher than those for people from any other religion, for both men and women. Muslim women were more likely than other women to be economically inactive. About seven in 10 Muslim women of working age (69%) were economically inactive, compared with no more than four in 10 women in each of the other religious groups. In 2004, the unemployment rate for Muslim women, at 18%, was about four times the rate for Christian and Jewish women (4% in each case). Unemployment rates for women in the other religious groups were between 6% and 9%. Muslim men had the highest male unemployment rate, at 13%. This was about three times the rate for Christian men (4%). Unemployment rates for men in the other religious groups were between 3% and 8%. Within each religious group, women were more likely than men to be economically inactive. The main reason was that they were looking after family and home. Christian women were least likely to be economically inactive (25%) (ONS, 2004).

An intersectional approach?

Integrated view of disadvantage in employment

Berthoud and Blekesaune (2006) unusually attempted to provide an integrated view of the extent of disadvantage in employment of all groups that have data collected on them in the General Household Survey: statistics broken down by age, sex and motherhood, disability, ethnicity and religion. They also refined their analysis by making a distinction between percentage differences between social groups and **employment penalties**. Penalties refer to social group differences that remain after all other factors that can be are controlled for, such as age, education level, family composition and local unemployment rates. Penalties are therefore a more accurate measure of disadvantage that excludes measurable characteristics, but importantly includes unmeasurable characteristics such as discrimination, aspiration and constraints (such as childcare). The employment penalty is therefore different from, and in most cases smaller than, the overall percentage difference in employment rates of different groups. Although Berthoud and Blekesaune's (2006) analysis of employment penalties was useful, it is important to point out that we also need to be aware of actual employment rate differences, since the fact that part of the employment penalty is attributable to factors such as different educational achievements does not make it any less real or needful of attention.

Berthoud and Blekesaune's (2006) analysis of employment rates showed that:

- women as a group generally faced an employment penalty of about 23% compared with men as a group;
- mothers were much less likely to have a paid job than either childless women or men (with or without children). The employment penalty for mothers with children below 11 years rose to around 40%;
- employment penalties varied widely between minority ethnic groups. African Caribbean women were even more likely to have a paid job than equivalent white women. All other minority groups were worse off than whites, but Pakistani and Bangladeshi women were by far the most disadvantaged by over 30%;
- disabled people were about 29% less likely to be in work than non-disabled people; and
- people in their fifties were disadvantaged compared with younger adults, by 14%. Older women were more disadvantaged than older men in addition to the overall disadvantage of all women.

Prioritising policy through an intersectional approach?

Although Berthoud and Blekesaune (2006) showed that all social groups considered were disadvantaged, they identified three that stood out with particularly large employment penalties: mothers, Pakistani and Bangladeshi women, and disabled people. These groups were also more likely to suffer from disadvantage in the workplace, in terms of limited career progression, large pay gaps and discrimination. So by this intersectional approach, we can see that these groups may be the ones to target as priorities for specialised policy making.

They concluded by trying to address the question: which social groups faced the largest disadvantage in employment? They argued that, despite the fact that mothers are in a disadvantaged employment position, their situation has improved during the past five decades and as most mothers moved into employment as the children grew older their disadvantage was not as persistent as that of the other groups. At the current rate of progress, it was estimated that their employment penalty would disappear in 2025 (Equalities Review, 2007). There were other intersectional issues that made a difference. The mothers of disabled children faced worse disadvantage, being twice as likely not to be working as mothers of non-disabled children (Equalities Review, 2007). So an even more sophisticated intersectional analysis may place them in one of the persistent categories of disadvantage and demand policy attention and priority.

In contrast to mothers generally, Berthoud and Blekesaune (2006) showed that Pakistani and Bangladeshi women, the largest group of Muslim women, have remained in a constantly disadvantaged position as compared with white women. Very few non-employed Pakistani and Bangladeshi women, or Muslim women generally, moved back into employment once out of it. It was only disabled people who were equally as unlikely to move back into employment as Muslim women. Thus it appeared that Muslim women and disabled people were the two most persistently disadvantaged social groups in employment terms, and at the rate of progress so far their employment penalties would never disappear unless specialised positive action policies were devised (Equalities Review, 2007).

It would appear that Berthoud and Blekesaune's (2006) example may give us a fruitful and more sophisticated method for analysing data and using this to target EO&D positive action policies. However, evidence suggests that this is not a simple phenomenon and does need highly sophisticated analysis, including, importantly, qualitative research, which gleans the voices and views of the particular group being targeted. For example, as the Equalities Review (2007) pointed out, it is tempting to attribute the high employment penalty of Pakistani and Bangladeshi women entirely to reasons of ethnicity or country of origin. However, given increasing availability of disaggregated data, there is emerging evidence that Indian and white Muslims also experience employment disadvantage when compared with Indian and white Christians. This could mean that being a Muslim in itself carries a negative impact on the employment prospects of Pakistani and Bangladeshi women. However, the available evidence does not allow us to make firm conclusions, particularly because almost all Pakistani and Bangladeshi women are also Muslims, making it hard to separate the two factors for them.

The majority of economically inactive Pakistani and Bangladeshi women say they do not want to work because they are looking after the family and home. This was the reason given by almost two in three economically inactive Pakistani women (63%) and nearly three in four economically inactive Bangladeshi women (72%). There is evidence that the reasons for Pakistani and Bangladeshi women's employment penalty arise from a belief that good motherhood involves women staying at home and providing their own childcare (Dale et al, 2006). Set against this, however, research on employment for Pakistani and Bangladeshi young women found that they have a positive attitude to work. They want to balance the desire to work with the need to care for their children (Institute for Employment Studies, 2006). Also, attitudes to working women seem to be changing faster among Bangladeshi communities than Pakistani communities.

The same research (Institute for Employment Studies, 2006) also identified barriers to employment, including Pakistani and Bangladeshi women's lack of high-level educational qualifications, vocational skills and real-world work experience. Language is also a barrier to employment. The manner in which aspirations can be destroyed by external factors is clearly demonstrated by research showing that young Pakistani and Bangladeshi women with the same ambitions, training and level of skills as their white peers are three to four times more likely to accept a job for which they are over-qualified (EOC, 2006a).

The Equalities Review (2007: 71) summed up that, in spite of signs of change, 'the employment penalty associated with this group remains exceptionally high, with consequent social costs for the whole community. It is still a matter of contention to what extent this penalty is driven by historical factors, cultural preference or by discrimination. But to decide how best to tackle this particular gap, there needs to be further research and deeper consideration, not least involving the women themselves'.

Conclusion

The British population is becoming more diverse and to reflect this the collection and analysis of EO&D data is improving and becoming more sophisticated, although there is room for much improvement. Of particular note is the complete lack of data on sexual orientation.

Within this diverse society there are still important signs of continuing disadvantage for women generally, but particularly in the field of employment and in terms of pay, education and the impact of caring responsibilities, and in the powerful arenas in society. Alongside this there are indications that other social differentiations are having an important impact. Statistics on the effect of disability, age and minority ethnic status show their important influence, and that disadvantage is not homogeneous in any social group.

New theoretical and practical challenges such as the recognition of intersectional disadvantage are required to address an increasingly complex range of inequalities. Some researchers are beginning to try to tackle the areas of multiple disadvantage and come up with more useful measures of disadvantage for policy makers. However, there is a need to engage further with EO&D using both quantitative statistics and qualitative research methods to gain a clearer insight to enable the targeting of positive action measures for the most disadvantaged groups within society.

Note
[1] Great Britain consists only of England, Scotland and Wales; the United Kingdom also includes Northern Ireland.

Summary

- Britain's population has changed considerably over the last four decades.
- The population has diversified in terms of age, make-up of households, disability, ethnicity, religion, and recognition and visibility of homosexuality.
- Despite being a heterogeneous group women's continuing disadvantage persists, particularly around employment segregation, pay, educational subject segregation, positions of power and caring responsibilities.
- Alongside women's continuing disadvantage, differences between women are being exposed with more disaggregated data available across the other strands of EO&D.
- However, there is still a considerable lack of disaggregated data, which is crucial for EO&D policy making.
- EO&D policy makers at both national and EU level are beginning to move from the concept of 'multiple disadvantage' to an intersectional approach, which allows prioritisation of policies.

Questions for discussion

- Does racial discrimination amplify sex discrimination?
- How far is racial discrimination tempered by religion?
- How many social divisions are there and which ones should be incorporated into an intersectional analysis of disadvantage?
- Should it concern us that the list may be boundless?

Further reading

Berthoud, R. and Blekesaune, M. (2006) *Persistent employment disadvantage, 1974 to 2003*, Institute for Social & Economic Research Working Paper 2006-9, Colchester: ISER, University of Essex.

Equalities Review (2007) *Fairness and freedom: The final report of the Equalities Review*, London: Equalities Review.

EHRC (2008) *Sex and power*, London: Equality and Human Rights Commission.

Women and Work Commission (2006) *Shaping a fairer future*, London: Women and Equality Unit.

three

What do we mean by equal opportunities and diversity? Theoretical approaches and ideologies

Overview

This chapter:

- explores some of the myths and realities behind the concept of equal opportunities and diversity (EO&D);
- examines the concepts of prejudice and discrimination and gives some examples of prejudice that still exist in Britain today, including racism, sexism, disablism, homophobia, Islamophobia and ageism;
- discusses and analyses definitions of EO&D;
- considers some theories and ideologies that are linked to EO&D;
- examines the concepts of individual and institutional discrimination;
- investigates the concept of social justice.

Key concepts

Prejudice; individual and institutional discrimination; stereotypes; racism; sexism; feminism; disablism; homophobia; Islamophobia; ageism; social justice

Myths and realities

To answer the question in the title of this chapter, we must consider the area of theory and ideologies attached to EO&D. EO&D as a concept is complex, contentious and controversial. It is linked to other important values such as social equality, social rights and social justice, which some would argue are fundamental underpinnings to liberal democratic societies. However, it is important to acknowledge that in highly stratified, modern industrial societies any move towards EO&D would involve a fundamental change in power and reward differentiated by race, gender, disability, sexual orientation, religion or belief, and age, and the implications these categories have for people's life chances and social and economic positions (see Chapter Two for an analysis of disadvantage for these categories). Even at an institutional level, EO&D can stoke up conflicts and expose difficulties within organisations that were previously dormant. EO&D means different things to different people, and those members of society and particular organisations who have already benefited from inequality, usually white, non-disabled, middle-aged, heterosexual males, may resist EO&D policies, if they feel that their opportunities and prospects are threatened.

Everyone has an opinion and often a deeply held and emotional viewpoint on EO&D, and people are often keen to share their opinions. Some people are passionately in favour of EO&D and some passionately against. When this author worked as an Equal Opportunities Officer in local government, she soon learnt not to admit to it at social gatherings to avoid either confrontation or lectures on how to do it better. The historical, ideological and political background to EO&D still influences people's perception of it and their attitude towards it (see Chapter Four for a discussion of this background). It still creates confusion, apprehension and suspicion in many people's minds, and is still associated by some with what they picture as 'political correctness' of the political left. Others who were once committed to EO&D and were early champions of its introduction into their own organisations have become disillusioned by a lack of success or the slow progress towards change, as the realisation of the complexity, intricacy and long-term nature of the animal dawns.

EO&D has certainly spawned many myths that camouflage the facts. The following list is not exhaustive, but includes some commonly held opinions about EO&D:

• It is for black people only.
• It is anti-white.
• It helps minorities at the expense of majorities.
• It means not employing the best people so that standards drop.

- It is left-wing propaganda.
- It leads to conflict.
- It does not work.

These examples can all, of course, be countered with more dispassionate and logical statements:

- It aims for equality for all.
- It upholds social justice.
- It says no to discrimination.
- It makes the best use of human resources.
- It wants services to be accessible to everyone.
- It gives people a fair chance in getting jobs.
- It is a legal obligation.

As the Equalities Review (2007) so clearly pointed out, equality is not a 'minority business'. There are, in fact, substantial economic and social rewards to be gained for everyone by ensuring a just, fair and equal society. And not all disadvantaged groups are minorities. For example:

- women form more than half the population;
- most of us will become older people;
- we may have children who are mixed race;
- we might become disabled.

Despite all the controversy, many people would agree that, at least in theory, at both a societal and organisational level, EO&D is desirable. The concept can be seen as conjuring up and building on the commendable cornerstones of fairness, justice, morality, impartiality and accountability.

Prejudice and discrimination

Britain is a more tolerant society today than it has ever been and there is strong support for equality, fairness and justice for all in our society. So where does the threat to a more equal society come from? Prejudices still exist that are based on stereotyped perceptions of different groups. As the Equalities Review (2007: 3) argued, 'we are not yet a nation at ease with our diversity – ethnic, religious, disability and other differences are still the cause of genuine anxiety'.

Prejudice has serious negative consequences for the treatment of women, minority ethnic people, people of different ages, disabled people, people with particular religious beliefs, and lesbian and gay people. Studies have shown that prejudice and stereotyping can even psychologically undermine individuals on the receiving end. People to whom a negative group stereotype has been applied can react by under-performing in accordance with this stereotype. For example:

- Black people may perform below their true ability when competing with white people.
- Women may under-perform when competing with men, and older people when competing with younger people (Steele and Aronsen, 1995).

The Equalities Review (2007: 93) argued that 'if we do not act to address prejudice and negative stereotyping explicitly, whatever other action we take to reduce inequality in areas such as education or employment can have only partial success'.

Both prejudice and discrimination are fundamental concepts that underpin the unequal treatment of both individuals and groups within society. **Discrimination** is differential treatment of people ascribed to particular social categories. Different judgements and distinctions are not necessarily unfair or unjustifiable discrimination, but they may be. To decide whether discriminatory behaviour is just or unjust, we need to know the grounds used for it, that is, whether there is an objective or reasonable justification. British EO&D legislation outlaws and penalises discriminatory behaviour based on sex, marital status, colour, race, ethnicity, national origins, disability, sexual orientation, religion or belief, and age.

Prejudice often informs unjust discrimination. Although it must be acknowledged that there can be positive prejudice towards a particular group, it is more frequently defined as holding hostile or negative attitudes towards individuals 'solely on the basis of their group membership, rather than their own merits' (Hilgard et al, 1979, 20). Prejudices are based on the perceived 'threat', whether social, cultural, physical or economic, posed by each group. Hence older people and disabled people, who may be perceived as less threatening, may experience what could be seen as 'benevolent' prejudice based on kindly intent. However, this can be experienced as patronising and demeaning to the person subjected to it. Even apparently mild 'benevolent' forms of prejudice can translate into attitudes that negatively affect the treatment and prospects of such groups.

People's prejudiced attitudes towards other groups also differ according to the type of interaction taking place. For example:

- people are generally more comfortable with a black boss than a female one, but would prefer a female boss to a black in-law (Adams and Houston, 2006);
- most people would not be concerned to have a blind person as an in-law, but they would be very concerned if a person with (managed) schizophrenia moved in next door (Rigg, 2007).

The Equalities Review (2007) also pointed out that prejudices can grow and diminish over time in society in line with the growing assertiveness of their rights by different groups of people, who previously might have been content to suppress aspects of their identity. Accordingly, attitudes to women, minority ethnic people, disabled people, gay men and lesbians, people with particular religious beliefs, and younger and older people have waxed and waned in part because more and more people in these groups refuse to be silent and/or invisible.

People often generalise about both individuals and groups. As Hilgard et al (1979: 548) explained, this is a necessary part of life:

Generalizing from a set of experiences and treating individuals as members of a group are common and necessary practices. It is simply not possible to deal with every new person as if he or she were unique.

However, when generalisations concern groups they are often called **stereotypes**, especially when beliefs about a group are over-generalised, if not misinformed or false, and applied too broadly to each member of the group.

In trying to explain negative prejudice, the first theories looked at personality types. It was felt that the more dogmatic, conservative, closed-minded personality would be more prejudiced (Adorno et al, 1950). Then came theories that emphasised social variables. A relationship was found between a person's dissatisfaction with their financial position and the general political state of their country, and prejudice against certain groups. As part of this process, 'scapegoating' was recognised as a substitution of targets for aggression and hostility (Hilgard et al, 1979). Prejudice can be reduced through contact between different groups, but contact is not enough on its own, as many studies concerned with white people's prejudice to minority ethnic people have shown (Cook, 1978). Certain conditions need to be present to reduce prejudice; the contact must be between those of equal status and with individuals who counter our stereotypes, there must be potential for personal acquaintance, support for intergroup contact, and pursuit of common goals (Cook, 1978).

Continuing prejudice

Although it has become increasingly unacceptable to express prejudiced views in public, old attitudes persist and new ones emerge. They may be unspoken, but registered in increasingly subtle and insidious ways. Adams and Houston (2006) showed that prejudice is still widespread in Britain, against both old and new targets. Their survey revealed that 69% of respondents had experienced some form of prejudice in the past year and 25% were unconcerned about showing prejudice themselves. Table 3.1 shows the level of prejudice in society and that people's willingness to show it varies according to the social group concerned. Muslims, gay men and lesbians, and black people experience the highest levels of prejudice. However, people are less concerned about showing prejudice against Muslims and gay men and lesbians than against black people. They are less likely to be prejudiced and most concerned about being seen to be prejudiced against older people or disabled people.

Table 3.1: Expressions of prejudice towards different groups within society

Group	Some prejudice, try not to show it %	Prejudiced, do not mind if show it %
Muslim people	26	9
Gay/lesbian people	23	10
Black people	20	5
Women	14	7
People aged 70+	9	4
Disabled people	7	3

Source: Adapted from Equalities Review, 2007, Figure 4.1.

So it would seem that prejudice persists in Britain against some groups, from a substantial minority of the population. However, many of those who hold such prejudices are now much less likely to express their negative feelings publicly. Britain continues to be infected with racism, sexism, disablism, heterosexism, homophobia, Islamophobia and ageism. These prejudices will be examined and defined where evidence is available. Newer, emerging areas for EO&D legislation (sexual orientation, religion or belief, and age) have less of a history of research on the forms, origins and levels of prejudice and discrimination. For example, whereas the issues of racism, sexism and even disablism have been thoroughly examined and analysed, homophobia, Islamophobia and ageism are relatively 'new kids on the block'.

Racism

For black people, racism is a day-to-day experience.

> The first time my son was called a nigger, he was about 16 months old. The insult, delivered by an old man in an overcoat, stomping through the park, was directed at Marcus in his pushchair but intended for me to hear. (Ware, 1985: 21)

> This isn't as serious or as bad as being hit by the teachers and stuff, but in classes the teacher, because of my colour, will talk to everyone else but me because I'm the only black person in my maths class. She tells us to put our hand up and what she did to me once was that I put my hand up and she looked all the way around the room and then looked at me and then walked to me, but she checked every opportunity to avoid answering to my question. It's happened quite a few times. I think it's because of the colour of my skin. (unnamed case study from *Walking in my shoes: Personal experiences of inequality in Britain*, Equalities Review, 2007)

There is an enormous literature on the issue of racism. Hesse et al (1992) cited Gilroy as arguing that: 'The word racism has become too easy to say and too difficult to explain'. The term was introduced in the 1930s to refer to doctrines of racial superiority. In the 1960s, it was given a wider connotation. Racism consists of structures within society, policies and procedures within institutions **(institutional racism)** and prejudice among individuals **(individual racism)** that maintain and encourage inequality and discrimination on the grounds of race, when certain racial categories are imbued with negative meaning (Benedict, 1968; Miles, 1989). The Commission for Race Equality (CRE, 1991: 7) warned us that 'the pervasiveness and deep rootedness of racism requires us to be continually vigilant and to understand that, simply because it no longer finds the same expression, it has not been erased'.

Throughout the 1980s, **multiculturalism** was adopted particularly in schools, where it emphasised the need to understand, accept and respect the cultural aspects of other groups within society to facilitate 'good race relations'. This has been labelled in a somewhat derogatory way as the 'three Ss approach' – saris, samosas and steel drums. The approach was criticised for its lack of analysis of power, which, it was argued, obscured and obfuscated racism.

It has been argued that an emphasis on racism as a uniting oppression of black people can limit thinking by ignoring difference and diversity within minority ethnic communities (Rattansi, 1992; Gilroy, 1993).

However, Anthias and Yuval-Davis (1993: 15) argued for the retention of the concept of racism, maintaining that power and racist effects were central to its definition: 'racism is a set of postulates, images and ... practices which serve to differentiate and dominate ... serving to deny full participation in economic, social, political and cultural life'. They in fact used the concept of 'racisms' to acknowledge difference and diversity: 'These are all differently experienced by different class, ethnic and gender categories' (Anthias and Yuval-Davis, 1993: 2). They argued that there was neither a 'unitary system' of racism, nor a 'unitary perpetrator or victim' (Anthias and Yuval-Davis, 1993: 2). They understood 'racisms' as modes of exclusion, inferiorisation, subordination and exploitation, in different social and historical contexts. Extreme examples were given as extermination, slavery and segregation.

There has been a long-standing historical link between Europe and Asia, Africa and the Americas characterised by 'economic exploitation, gross inhumanity and political subjugation, which relied on the use of military force and racist ideology to legitimise and perpetuate "white" supremacy' (Lester and Bindman, 1972: 23). Hartmann and Husbands (1974: 20) stated:

> [The] main ideas about race and colour that have been current in Britain developed as a result of colonial expansion from the late sixteenth century onwards. Since that time the essential character of relations between the British and the indigenous inhabitants of other continents has been the domination of the non-white by the white.... As the colonial period progressed, these ideas became elaborated and more and more widely diffused, until by the end of the nineteenth century the idea of white superiority held central place in British national culture.

However, racism today is its own animal. Even though the new form builds on the old, it is also importantly connected to present-day social, economic and political factors.

If we look at post-1945 black immigration, we find that it is 'littered with periodic short term crises over immigration', and, in pointing this out, Saggar (1991: 27) asked us 'to remember that this was the backdrop to the genesis of race-related public policy-making in British central and local government'. Social policy towards minority ethnic people has been shaped and determined by the tenor of a series of immigration Acts over the past four decades, serving to reinforce, legitimise and perpetuate racist assumptions and stereotypes (see Chapter Five). All political parties agreed on discriminatory controls at the point of entry in the name of racial harmony. In 1978, Margaret Thatcher stated that her party (the

Conservatives) in power would see an end to immigration for the sake of 'race relations' and to preserve the 'British way of life' (Brandt, 1986). As Crewe (1983: 263) pointed out, 'there are votes for the picking in fanning the flames of racial resentment'. Certain events have proved very worrying in this area, such as the victory of British National Party candidates in local elections, the threat of support for certain far right political groups in Europe, and the ever-present and widespread incidence of racist attacks. As the Runnymede Trust Commission (2000: 36) argued:

> Britain continues to be disfigured by racism; by phobias about cultural difference; by sustained social, economic, educational and cultural disadvantage; by institutional discrimination; and by a systematic failure of social justice or respect for difference.

Sexism and feminism

Women can explain the influence of sexism on their lives, as the following examples show.

> Five years in the Civil Service have changed me from a career woman. I think, like most other women, I have realised that unless I am prepared to make quite disproportionate sacrifices, I will not succeed in the Civil Service. Having accepted that, you can either seek satisfaction elsewhere, in the home, or in your family, or seek to change the existing structures. Unless you are extraordinarily ambitious, the sexism and sexual harassment soon puts you in your place. (Bagilhole, 1994a: 182)

> Joining the Royal Air Force (RAF) was something I had wanted to do since I was about 12 years old. As I got older my interest in the RAF grew until I joined in January 1990. I was only the third woman to become a RAF police dog handler. If anything went wrong for me I was told that it was because I was a woman, yet if I did well I was told that I'd only done well because they were being easy on me because I was a woman. I often felt that for a woman to succeed and do well she had to be better than the men! I did get a lot of sexist remarks and came across men who believed that women should not be in the RAF ... most of them made their feelings quite clear to me. (Catherine Brumfitt, who brought a successful case against the Ministry of Defence in 2004; case study from *Walking in my shoes: Personal experiences of inequality in Britain*, Equalities Review, 2007).

Employers' prejudice and discrimination continues against women. The Women and Work Commission (2006) cited a survey by the Recruitment Employment Confederation of 122 recruitment agencies that revealed that more than 70% of them had been asked by clients to avoid hiring pregnant women or those of childbearing age.

As with racism, sexism consists of structures within society, policies and procedures within institutions **(institutional sexism)** and prejudice among individuals **(individual sexism)** that maintain and encourage inequality and discrimination – this time on the grounds of sex: 'Sexism occurs at different levels from the individual to the institutionalized, but all forms combine to preserve inequality' (Marshall, 1994: 35). Cook and Watt (1987: 70) defined sexism as 'a process of systematic oppression directed towards women who are defined as inferior to men'. The recognition and identification of the sexist nature of society and women's subordination to men, coupled with the desire to change this situation, led to the feminist movement, which 'argues that sexist social beliefs and practices not only limit the activities of women, but are an impertinent way of making distinctions between the sexes, because they are not founded on evidence' (Humm, 1995: 15).

Offen (1992: 68) asked the questions: 'What is feminism? Who is a feminist?' She answered herself in the following way:

> Everyone seems to have different answers, and every answer is infused with a political and emotional charge. The word 'feminism' continues to inspire controversy – indeed, even to evoke fear among a sizeable portion of the general public. (Offen, 1992: 69)

Two of the central aspects of feminism are: the struggle for effective access to political rights, and the struggle for women to have full ownership of their bodies (Pruvot et al, 2008).

Feminist analysis draws on different traditions, different feminisms. Dale and Foster (1986) identified liberal feminism, radical feminism and socialist feminism, while others have expanded the list. Williams (1989) included libertarian feminism, welfare feminism and black feminism. Certainly, one thing that all types of feminism share is an awareness of the disadvantage and inequality that women experience and that 'women's subordination must be questioned and challenged' (Abbott and Wallace, 1990: 10).

Historically, the main planks of feminist thinking have been liberal feminism, socialist feminism and radical feminism. Where these approaches differ is in their identification of the causes of women's disadvantage and therefore in their proposed solutions. For example, liberal feminism has a concern with equal rights, equal treatment and equal access in education, employment and politics, associated with the EO&D legislation in the 1970s. Socialist and radical feminists see the cause as stemming from the social structure of society and social relations within it, predominantly and centrally either capitalism for the former or patriarchy for the latter.

Walby (1990: 4) argued as a socialist feminist that 'class relations and the economic exploitation of one class by another are the central features of social structure and these determine the nature of gender relations'. These relations are seen as important both in determining material conditions for women and creating an ideological explanation for them. George and Wilding (1994: 132) explained these relations from the material position of women's traditional role as mother and wife: 'Unpaid labour in the home is a subsidy to capitalism because it reduces the cost of reproducing the next generation of workers and servicing male breadwinners'.

Radical feminists look to patriarchy as an explanation for women's oppression within society. **Patriarchy** has been defined as male domination and the power of men to control women. It is:

> … a system of social structures and practices in which men dominate, oppress and exploit women. The use of the term social structure is important here, since it clearly implies rejection both of biological determinism, and the notion that every individual man is in a dominant position and every woman in a subordinate one. (Walby, 1990: 20)

Male social power is seen as located in and derived from two separate arenas: 'private' relations within the household or family and 'public' relations of economic, ideological and political power. In the household, women's labour is expropriated by their partners. In the labour market, women are excluded from the better forms of paid work and are segregated into the worst jobs, which are classified as less skilled and are therefore less well paid.

These different strands of feminism share the common theme of the search for universal explanations of women's subordination, and the emphasis on the universalism and commonality of the women's cause. This has now been challenged and there is a growing recognition of difference and diversity within the category 'women', and the way women's oppression is experienced. To begin with, the challenge came mainly from black feminists (see hooks, 1981), but has been reiterated by working-class women, lesbians, disabled women and older women.

These challenges have led to radical changes in feminism, an acknowledgement of difference among women and, some would argue, more relevant, inclusive and comprehensive feminist thinking. However, some commentators have highlighted the dangers of following the diversity argument too far. For example, ultimately, it could logically lead to the fragmentation of feminism into so many small parts and causes that would make it untenable, if not as a theory then certainly as a political force for change. As Soper (1994: 14-15) argued:

> One is bound to feel that feminism as theory has pulled the rug from under feminism as politics. For politics is essentially a group affair, based on the ideas of making 'common cause', and feminism, like any other politics, has always implied a banding together, a movement based on the solidarity sisterhood of women, who are linked by perhaps very little else than their sameness and 'common cause' as women.

Despite the fact that feminism has changed, society has not changed very much (see Chapter Two for an analysis of the continuing nature of gender disadvantage). As Evans (1994) pointed out, this means that the position of women remains in some senses common. Women:

> ... are paid less, have less social power and are still assumed to have the primary, if not exclusive, responsibility for the care of children and dependant relatives.... Women in some Western societies may have made some inroads in some portions of junior/middle management, but to all effects and purposes the public world, of institutional power, remains dominated by men. (Evans, 1994: 1)

Soper (1994: 19) also argued that there are 'some concrete and universal dimensions of women's lives'. She cited the example of the reality of men's violence and the threat of men's violence against women, describing the way in which 'women live in a kind of alertness to the possibility of attack and must to some degree organize their lives in order to minimise its threat' (1994: 19). An example of this might be a self-imposed curfew of not walking on the streets alone after dark. Finally, then, we see a call for feminist thinking to move forward in two ways at the same time, always recognising and acknowledging the importance and value both of diversity and difference, but also of gender-specific issues and at times the universal category of women.

The Runnymede Trust Commission (2000: 68) illustrated the complexity of this way forward for both the feminist and anti-racist movements:

> Asian and black women bring distinctive insights and experience to both feminism and anti-racism. But they frequently find that they have to struggle not only against sexism and racism

within society generally but also against racism within white feminism and sexism within anti-racist projects. They have to counter the view that all women are affected by sexism and gender inequality in the same way, regardless of issues of race and ethnicity. At the same time, they have to counter forms of anti-racism which assume, explicitly or implicitly, that men are affected more seriously by racism than women are. They are also affected by processes within Asian and black communities that involve perpetuating traditional gender roles and traditional stereotypes relating to womanhood and manhood. Lastly, they are affected indirectly, but nonetheless powerfully, by the racism encountered by their partners, fathers, brothers and sons. Similarly, men in these communities are affected by the racism experienced by women.

Disabilism

'Disabilism is the operation of attitudinal, environmental and institutional barriers to deny disabled people full human and civil rights' (Begum, 1994: 19). Only disabled people can voice its true experience, as the following examples illustrate.

> This leg, not me you understand, had polio when I was one year old and it is not normal. If I cover it up perhaps they won't realize for a while, at least until I get up. This leg was my passport to being bullied in school, to being called names like 'spastic' and 'cripple', to being both hated and feared as well as over-protected to shield me from both. (Finger, 1992: 9)

> Pupils at school make fun of me because I have Asperger's Syndrome, and call me horrible names. I feel ashamed of myself because I'm different. I'm stressed out and don't know how to cope. (Jonathon, aged 11; case study from *Walking in my shoes: Personal experiences of inequality in Britain*, Equalities Review, 2007)

Disabled people are in an extremely disadvantaged position compared with non-disabled people in terms of housing, employment, finance, transport and education (Equalities Review, 2007). Disabled people have also been denied access to key political, educational and cultural institutions that could enable them to participate fully in society. Oliver (1990) argued that this exclusion of disabled people has had profound effects on social relations, resulting not only in the marginalisation of disabled people within labour markets, but from society as a whole. Bullying is also an issue in the workplace. In a national survey, more than one in 10 employees with a disability or long-term illness, and one in seven disabled women employees, reported experiencing bullying (Grainger and Fitzner, 2006).

Finkelstein (1980) argued that disabled people's disadvantage was not only because of their perceived or real impairments, but because changes in the work system have excluded them from the work process. He developed an evolutionary model linked to the history of disability as follows. Historical changes in the work process through the rise of capitalism from feudalism have led to the changing needs of the labour market. In Britain, before the industrial revolution, feudal society's economic base was agriculture or small-scale industry, which did not preclude the great majority of disabled people from participating in the production process or making at least a contribution. Disabled people were regarded as individually unfortunate but not segregated from society. However, the process of industrialisation shifted the place of work from the home to the factory. Under capitalism, many more disabled people were excluded from the production process because speed, enforced discipline and time keeping became production imperatives, alongside a growth in formal educational requirements. As a result, disabled people came to be regarded as a social and educational problem and more and more were segregated in workhouses, asylums and special schools out of the mainstream institutions.

Is this explanation an over-simplification? It highlights the role of the mode of production in significantly influencing perceptions and experiences of disability. It certainly implies that Britain before capitalism was some kind of idealised society where minority groups were treated more benignly, which is questionable. It does not explore negative attitudes towards disability, such as fear or hostility, or ideas commonly held in society that disabled people are incapable of running their own lives. Within institutional settings and outside in the community, disabled people's lives are often controlled by professionals in power over them. However, although a labour market explanation cannot adequately contain these elements, it can and does usefully move the analysis away from individual impairment and clinical conditions to structural explanations of disabled people's disadvantage.

The 'new kids on the block' in legislation

Work is beginning on research to provide evidence of discrimination on the grounds of homophobia, Islamophobia and ageism. A few examples follow.

Homophobia

Qualitative and case study research is needed to record everyday experiences of homophobia and its effects.

> It feels like everyone at school is picking on me. They shove me in the corridor and call me 'gay boy'. It happens in almost every lesson, too. My so-called friends don't stand up for me, and the teachers don't do anything to help, even when half the class is calling me names. I was bullied in my last school for being gay – that's why I left. Here it's even worse. I don't know what to do. (Jason, aged 15; case study from *Walking in my shoes: Personal experiences of inequality in Britain*, Equalities Review, 2007)

> I am 35 and work in the public sector. I am also a gay man but am too concerned about unknown consequences to out myself at work, and am ashamed to say that my partner of four years is invisible even for pensions purposes.... I was brought up in a rural area in the South West in a Christian family and there was no one I felt I could talk to about my sexuality until I was 25. I didn't know anyone else in the same situation at school and in fact didn't really know what sexuality meant until I started looking at where I might go to university. I was academically able ... but I was very frightened about the prospect of living away from home and being 'found out'.... This was cemented in my mind when I read the 'alternative' (Student Union) prospectus of a university which had a half page 'comic' article about what they thought of gay men and how any that came to university would be exposed very quickly. As a result I formed lots of excuses about why I wasn't going to university. (Christopher, London; case study from *Walking in my shoes: Personal experiences of inequality in Britain*, Equalities Review, 2007)

In 1806, more men were executed for homosexual offences than for murder. In 2006, gay men and lesbians could register civil partnerships and were granted legal protection from discrimination (Porter, 2007). However, bullying at school remains a serious issue for many children and young people. A survey of adult lesbians and gay men found that over half had considered self-harm as a result of being bullied at school (Rivers, 2001).

Research has revealed the persistence of popular prejudice against gay men and lesbians, with 17% of respondents saying they felt 'less positive' towards gay or lesbian people than towards heterosexuals (Stonewall, 2003). This research also showed that respondents' attitudes tended to be based on old fears and perceptions articulated throughout the 20th century, which were used to justify social and legal inequalities, for example:

- 'a grudging and conditional acceptance' founded on the belief that 'they can't help it' or an acceptance of the 'right to choose' a gay or lesbian way of life, although 'both forms of acceptance are usually conditional upon lesbians and gay men keeping a low profile in public spaces';
- gendered prejudice, with heterosexual men fearing overt homosexuality, 'which they describe as "disgusting" and "repulsive"', while heterosexual women do not have the same fear of Lesbians';
- a belief that 'gay men's sexuality is also elided with paedophilia', while 'there is some concern that Lesbian mothers deprive children of a father or male figure in their lives'.

Islamophobia

Individual experiences of Islamophobia tell a poignant story.

> I'm getting bullied at school. People in the neighbourhood are calling my family 'terrorists' and say, 'Go back to your own country'. I'm worried they'll start these things at school. Muslim boys are getting beaten up at school. (Fatima, aged nine; case study from *Walking in my shoes: Personal experiences of inequality in Britain*, Equalities Review, 2007)

> Selina, a social worker, visited a Muslim woman whose husband was in hospital with a broken leg. Selina was told that the woman was close to a nervous breakdown. Selina was instructed to start the procedure which would take the children of this family into care. On visiting the family, Selina found little evidence to suggest the woman was on the verge of a nervous breakdown. On reviewing the case notes, Selina found that the assessment was made on the basis that the woman prayed regularly and this was taken as a sign of extreme anxiety. (unnamed case study from *Walking in my shoes: Personal experiences of inequality in Britain*, Equalities Review, 2007)

The Equalities Review (2007) showed that the emergence of British Muslims as a group that is systematically disadvantaged predates any concerns about security. Muslims account for a disproportionate number of people living in areas of multiple deprivation; more than two in three Bangladeshis and more than half of all Pakistanis live in the areas in the bottom decile for deprivation.

This disadvantage could be attributed to reasons of ethnicity or country of origin. But there is emerging evidence that Indian and White Muslims also experience employment disadvantage when compared to Indian and White Christians (Berthoud and Blekesaune, 2006). This could mean that being a Muslim in itself confers a negative impact on the employment prospects of Pakistani and Bangladeshi people. Legislators have responded with new protections against discrimination on the grounds of religion or belief, (2003 Employment Equality (Religion or Belief) Regulations), more recently in the provision of goods, facilities and services or public functions (as an amendment to the above legislation; see Chapter Five).

Ageism

Ageism is particularly prevalent in the labour market, and health and social care services:

> During 1991, when I was 56 years of age, I was unable to find work. After some time and, realising that job advertisements suitable to my background stipulated age ranges, I resigned myself to registering with private agencies (a total of 65 in number). It was only after a period of 11 months and some hundreds of applications that I finally acquired a short term contract. (unnamed case study from *Walking in my shoes: Personal experiences of inequality in Britain*, Equalities Review, 2007)

> Her meal would be on the tray cold and hardly touched. More often than not her teeth would be on the locker at the other side of the bed, well way from the chair on which she was sitting. At no time was she encouraged to eat, the food was not cut into bite-size pieces, and no person seemed to be responsible to see that the patients received nourishment. (As described to Help the Aged's Dignity on the Ward campaign; unnamed case study from *Walking in my shoes: Personal experiences of inequality in Britain*, Equalities Review, 2007)

A national sample survey conducted by Age Concern in late 2005 reported that more people (29%) reported experiencing age discrimination than another form of discrimination. Those over 55 were nearly twice as likely to have experienced age prejudice than any other form of discrimination.

One-third of people surveyed viewed people over 70 as incompetent and incapable. Nearly 30% believed that age discrimination was more serious than five years before (Age Concern, 2006).

Making the case for EO&D

The identification alone of existing negative prejudices and their dire consequences for individuals may seem sufficient to prove the case for EO&D and justify their elimination. However, it is useful to examine the issue further by examining three separate but interlinking arguments that have been put forward as justifications for EO&D policy. There is the traditional **moral case**, with its foundations in social justice and fairness, which is a reaction to prejudice and discrimination. Then come two arguments that are in some part reactions to the political agendas and preoccupations of their time, but remain valid today. The **economic or business case** was first seen as a way of expediting EO&D during the 1980s, when the then Conservative governments were predominantly extolling the virtues of the private market. This case has continued to be attractive and successfully persuasive in some quarters, but has also been joined by the **social cohesion case**, which gained favour in political circles after the Bradford and Oldham disturbances of the early 2000s, which were blamed partly on social divisions within society. The Equalities Review (2007: 19) summed these ideas up:

> Objectively we can also show that greater equality will make our society better off, our economy stronger, our social fabric more cohesive, and reassert the moral values which underpin the British tradition of fairness.

The moral case

There is traditionally a strong moral case for tackling inequality, summed up by a belief in social justice. Some of the important historical achievements in the name of social justice are as follows:

- equal franchise for all women and men;
- the right for women to own property;
- the right to practise any religion or belief and to be free from discrimination in civic life for doing so;
- a fair and universal system of social welfare and healthcare.

Important philosophical debates have addressed the concept of **justice**. Rawls (1971) claimed that the principles of 'justice' were those that would be chosen by persons located behind a veil of ignorance that rendered them ignorant of their own future position in the world, that is, how rational and impartial individuals would reason. Deprived of any knowledge of their own economic interests, rational people would favour the difference principle, according to which inequalities are only just if they work to the advantage of the least well-off. Therefore, 'justice' is concerned with ensuring that every person receives what is due to them (Cohen, 1986) on the basis of their particular characteristics and circumstances (Buchanan and Mathieu, 1986), even if this means unequal treatment. As Buchanan and Mathieu (1986: 18) put it: 'People should be treated as equals in the proportion that they are equals ... [and] ... people should be treated as unequals only to the extent that they are unequal'.

In other words, people should be treated in ways that enable them to enjoy the same level of wellbeing or quality of life as everyone else:

> In this way, the principle of equality does not prescribe positively that all human beings be treated alike.... To act justly, then, is to treat all men [sic] alike except where there are relevant differences between them. (Benn and Peters, 1959: 111)

Where relevant differences between cases are identified, Frankena (1962) argued that it was not unjust to treat different cases in different ways.

If the most general definition of justice is that each person should have what they are entitled to according to personal characteristics and circumstances, how do we decide on that entitlement? Miller (1976) put forward three main principles of distributive justice, **'rights, deserts and needs'**, none of which dictates an 'equal treatment' approach to EO&D. The first principle of 'rights' is relatively straightforward: an individual receives justice according to the rules and regulations within their society. Second, in terms of 'deserts', individuals are rewarded in terms of such things as their moral virtues, productive efforts, capacities and merit. The principle of selecting people on merit is enshrined in the EO&D legislation, where, even when legitimate positive action is taken either in the form of advertising or training, final selection for posts is to be made on what was generally termed the principle of the 'best person for the job'. As Pitt (1992: 282) argued, 'positive action is not committed to the preference of a less-qualified candidate'. However, the 2008 Equality Bill suggests that in future, when selecting between two equally qualified candidates, employers will be able to choose one of them on the basis of the under-representation of disadvantaged groups in their organisation, for example, women or minority ethnic groups (see Chapter Five).

The merit approach is not unproblematic, however. There is the assumption that 'merit's claim to reward is morally self-evident and needs no justification', whereas in reality 'what constitutes merit is a social decision and a matter of social policy' (Parekh, 1992: 276). One has to question what traditional definitions of merit actually expound. The accepted criteria for merit are maintained by the established and the powerful, which may yield them a false veneer of objectivity. Parekh (1992: 275) also asks us to consider whether holding traditionally defined merit, such as the highest qualifications, does always by itself confer rights to employment: 'It views merit as the sole basis of desert, which it is not ... it is an important source of claim, but not the only one'.

We need to accept that EO&D based on the concept of 'deserts' is complex. For example, some disabled people and women may have lower productive capabilities in certain areas of paid work, but contribute different qualities. In the case of women, a wider societal approach would lead to recognition of other contributions to society, such as caring for dependent children. And, importantly, some groups in society that do not hold conventional qualifications may have other skills, such as knowledge of a foreign language or empathy with a particular culture that means that they are 'the best person for the job'.

Finally, the needs-based approach maintains that individuals are entitled to the things they lack or are necessary to them. This appears to be the most rational argument and one that favours the more radical 'equality of outcome' approach to EO&D by treating people differently where it is warranted (see Chapter Six for a full discussion of this approach). However, the great difficulties in defining need should not be underestimated. Blakemore and Drake (1996: 46) argue that what they coined as this 'humane justice' approach to equality, 'despite its great potential, is beset with unresolved questions'. This can be illustrated in the area of disability, where Oliver (1996) argued strongly against a needs-based approach because the power relations between disabled people and professionals, be they medical practitioners or social workers, determine that they interpret and define the needs of disabled people rather than disabled people themselves.

The business or economic case

The business or economic case argues that EO&D brings greater efficiency and economic growth to organisations and society in general. Opportunity Now (2001), which was set up to increase the quantity and quality of women's work, argued that EO&D can increase effectiveness and reduce costs.

Box 3.1: Business case for EO&D

Increasing effectiveness
- Attracting the best employees – organisations that champion equality are employers of choice.
- Staff commitment – staff who feel that they are treated fairly and that their contribution is valued will be more committed.
- Increased quality and productivity – staff who are happy at work will be more productive and the quality of products and service will improve.
- Organisational flexibility – having both women and men involved in problem-solving will introduce different perspectives and improve the quality of decision-making.
- Satisfying customers, shareholders and other stakeholders – better products and services, which meet diverse clients and customers' needs, will satisfy customers. This in turn will satisfy shareholders.

Reducing cost
- Reduced staff turnover – the cost of losing staff who feel unhappy and discriminated against can be up to 150% of their annual salary.
- Reduced absenteeism – stress is a major cause of absence. Staff who feel unfairly treated and who struggle to balance work and personal commitments are liable to be absent with stress.
- Legislation – the costs of failing to comply with quality legislation can be high, not just in financial terms but in terms of lost reputation.

Source: Opportunity Now, 2001.

The following economic benefits of EO&D policies for society have been quantified:

- If women move into higher-paid occupations, the productive potential of the economy will increase by between £2 billion and £9 billion (Women and Work Commission, 2006).
- Just over a million women who are currently not working would like to work and nearly 15% of the 5.1 million women working part-time would like to increase their hours – this would raise the employment rate for women from 70% towards 75%. Increasing women's employment could raise output in the economy by between £13 billion and £14 billion (Women and Work Commission, 2006).
- The total potential economic benefits of removing barriers to women working in occupations traditionally done by men, and increasing

women's participation in the labour market, would be worth between £15 billion and £23 billion, equivalent to 1.3% to 2% of gross domestic product (Women and Work Commission, 2006).

- Disabled people are 30% more likely to be out of work than non-disabled people with the same qualifications, age, place of residence and so on. This costs the government almost £9 billion annually (including unemployment-related benefits) in lost revenue (Equalities Review, 2007).

The social cohesion case

The links between equality and social cohesion are well documented. Violence, conflict, insecurity and political instability are all more likely to occur in more unequal and socially divided societies (Benabou, 1997). In the poorest areas of unequal societies, the quality of social relations and the social fabric are stretched to breaking point (Wilkinson, 2005). The report of the Community Cohesion Review into the disturbances in Bradford, Burnley and Oldham in 2001 argued that equality and social cohesion were closely intertwined (Home Office, 2001).

Definitions of and theories for understanding EO&D

Equal opportunities and diversity is a normatively charged umbrella term. In order to give EO&D a scientific basis and to pursue good EO&D policy, it is imperative to define this concept as best we can. Despite the difficulties of definition, we do need a reasonably clear and agreed idea of what the term EO&D means – that is, a working definition – to enable us to carry the discussion further. Perhaps we can begin by examining one of the original and simplest definitions of equal opportunities (EO), that is, before its later and more sophisticated coupling with the concept of diversity in policy making. This definition is founded on the premise of not acting or treating anyone in a blatantly discriminatory manner. Collins (1992: 3) offered us just such a definition: 'Basically equal opportunities is about treating everybody fairly and equally regardless of background or lifestyle'.

As discussed earlier, however, the idea that everyone should be treated in the same way is a questionable one. It is important to note that different treatment can be meted out, not only in an unjust way, but also as part of the furtherance of EO. The later and more sophisticated coupling of the concept of **diversity** with this area of policy making has come about through researchers', policy makers' and politicians' recognition of the important reality of the different experiences of disadvantage that can occur between and even within social groups. For example, the experiences and consequences of racism and racial discrimination differ in important ways for black women and black men, and the experiences and consequences of sexism and gender discrimination differ in important ways for white women and black women. As the Runnymede Trust Commission (2000: xv) pointed out:

> All communities are changing and all are complex, with internal diversity and disagreements, linked to differences of gender, generation, religion and language, and to different stances in relation to wider society.

The challenge of diversity and multiple disadvantage

Social divisions in society can be seen to be manifested in individuals in different ways and with a different impact at different times and in different circumstances. When we look at the relationships between gender, race, disability, sexual orientation, religion or belief, and age, we must see them as dynamic and interactive. It is not enough to add mixed categories such as minority ethnic women or disabled women to existing frameworks. At first, terms like 'double' then 'triple' oppression were used to try to conceptualise the complexity of people's experiences and disadvantage. For example, Crenshaw (1991) presents a graphic analysis of who can make it through the 'trapdoor' to promotion, which tends to imply a multiplication factor in disadvantage:

> Imagine a basement which contains all people who are disadvantaged on the basis of race, sex, class, sexual preference, age and/or physical ability. These people are stacked – feet standing on shoulders – with those on the bottom being disadvantaged by the full array of factors, up to the very top, where the heads of all those disadvantaged by a single factor brush up against the ceiling.... A hatch is developed through which those placed immediately below can crawl. Yet this hatch is generally available only to those who – due to the singularity of their burden and their otherwise privileged position relative to those below – are in a position to crawl through. Those who are multiply-burdened are generally left below. (Crenshaw, 1991: 1242)

Definition of diversity

Diversity as a concept slipped into use at the end of the 1990s and was, initially, primarily a code word for race. Public debate in the European Union (EU) about living together with difference was constructed in terms of 'multiculturalism'. Choices regarding definitions of concepts in social sciences are political as well as academic and scientific. Therefore, for the expediency of the EO&D project, it is important to conceptualise diversity in terms not only of 'being different', but also having been systematically discriminated against (Konrad et al, 2006: 1226). In fact, in the EU, the diversity approach is being promulgated in a format directly linked to the word 'discrimination'. The slogan used is 'for diversity, against discrimination' (Woodward, 2004).

Savoie and Sheehan (2001: 2) offer a useful and comprehensive definition of diversity:

> Diversity includes all characteristics and experiences that define each of us as individuals.... A common misconception about diversity is that only individuals or groups with particular attributes are included under its umbrella. Exactly the opposite is true. Diversity encompasses the entire spectrum of primary attributes of individuals, including Race, Ethnicity, Gender, Age, Religion, Disability, and Sexual Orientation.

From diversity to intersectionality

The coupling of the concept of diversity (in its broadest sense) with EO can be useful for the development of EO&D policy, as it raises important points concerning the fact that subject positions are multiple and questions the complacent assumptions about the homogeneous nature of disadvantaged groups. However, this can also be fundamentally difficult for EO&D if it only functions to deconstruct groups and categories of disadvantage and does not reconstruct them in some way. McCall (2005: 1773) categorised this approach as 'anticategorical':

> Social life is considered too irreducibly complex — overflowing with multiple and fluid determinations of both subjects and structures — to make fixed categories anything but simplifying social fictions that produce inequalities in the process of producing differences.

Joseph and Lewis (1981) offer a fairytale analogy to explain this phenomenon. Three minority ethnic women assume the role of Snow White, rather than the Black Queen. They each in turn respond to the question: 'Mirror, mirror on the wall, what is the greatest oppressor of us all?'. The first woman argues that, being black, racism is the main cause of her oppression. The second explains that her life is dominated and controlled by men. Therefore, sexism is her greatest oppressor. The third woman says that it is not possible to respond because her gender, race and class are all causes of her oppression. In this third case, it would be impossible to develop EO&D policies to rectify her situation.

This success in satisfying the need to recognise heterogeneity among and between social groups is also a failure of the EO&D project if it rejects its traditional foundational conceptions of social equality, fairness and justice. Despite evidence of diverse (in)equality among different socially disadvantaged groups in the UK, there are also common patterns of continuing disadvantage for these groups and an 'anticategorical' approach creates impotency for policy makers.

What we have to deal with is multiple layers of identity and the intersection of factors. Terms like 'double' then 'triple' oppression were initially used to try to conceptualise the complexity of people's experiences and disadvantage. More sophisticated analyses referred to the way that race, like other social divisions, reconstituted altogether the way in which oppressions were manifest and experienced rather than just adding an extra layer (Williams, 1989; Anthias and Yuval-Davis, 1993). As Begum (1994: 17) pointed out:

> Potentially the list [of oppressions] is endless, but simply counting the different types of oppression will not tell us anything. Notions of 'double disadvantage' or 'triple jeopardy' do nothing to facilitate understanding of multiple and simultaneous oppression.

Feminist theory has tackled this with the concept of **intersectionality**, which stresses the importance of the intersecting nature of the various prohibited grounds of prejudice and discrimination. In this way, EU policies on diversity and feminist theories of intersectionality can be seen to be pointing in the same direction. Intersectionality as a theory and methodology for research could be a springboard for the operationalisation of a social justice policy agenda. The term intersectionality, which was first highlighted by Crenshaw (1989, 1991), could offer a theoretical base for the potential of trans-issue mobilisation, as it usefully illuminates the multiple, intersecting, interlacing nature of complex social relations both between and within socially disadvantaged groups in society. However, its very complexity must in some way be contained to allow its utility for the reality and practicality of EO&D policy making.

McCall (2005) usefully addressed this complexity by delineating the two most useful approaches to the acknowledgement and recognition of the heterogeneous nature of disadvantaged groups. These approaches are delineated by the possibility of categorising socially disadvantaged groups for the purposes of research to inform EO&D policy. The first is the **intracategorical** approach, which really inaugurated intersectional studies by strategically using categories to focus 'on particular social groups at neglected points of intersection'. Second is the **intercategorical** approach, which strategically adopts existing categories to investigate the multiple and conflicting dimensions of inequality among them.

EO&D policy development has to function in the context of the 'Realpolitik'.

Therefore, it is argued that the intracategorical and intercategorical approaches to intersectionality, as both theories and methodological tools for EO&D policy making, may be the way forward. These last two approaches acknowledge and illuminate where disadvantages interplay and coincide or conflict between and within groups where new policy approaches need to be considered. Thus intersectionality alerts us to the need to fine-tune policy in a more sophisticated manner than in the past, once we have assessed its impact on people with more than one social differentiation that creates disadvantage, for example, disabled gay men, lesbian mothers and so on.

How to apply intersectional EO&D

An example of how intersectionality has been used as a methodological research tool for unearthing evidence to inform EO&D policy is useful to further our understanding, as seen in the following example from Canada:

Intersectional discrimination

The Canadian experience shows that in the market for rental housing, single, black women may have a particularly difficult time in finding apartments, especially if they are recipients of social assistance and/or single parents. Many landlords buy into various stereotypes and believe them to be less dependable.

On the basis of sex alone, this discrimination would not be apparent. Similarly, if considering race alone, this discrimination would not be evident. Thus using standard discrimination analysis, courts would fail to see that there is discrimination against those who are single, black and female. It is the singular identity of 'single-black-poor-single parent-woman' which is the subject of discrimination in the housing market. (Symington, 2004: 7)

Working definition of EO&D

Acknowledging the importance and usefulness of the concept of equal opportunities coupled with the concept of diversity, and approached through the theoretical lens of intersectionality, we can adopt a working definition of EO&D policy as seeking to achieve an equal society. This is usefully defined by the Equalities Review (2007, 16) as follows:

> An equal society protects and promotes equal, real freedom and substantive opportunity to live in the ways people value and would choose, so that everyone can flourish.

An equal society recognises people's different needs, situations and goals and removes the barriers that limit what people can do and can be.

Such a working definition recognises that some people may need more and different resources to enjoy genuine freedom and fair access to opportunities, in different ways and at different times. It recognises that equality does not mean sameness or same treatment.

Conclusion

As we have seen, EO&D as a concept is extremely complex and at times controversial. Although Britain is a more tolerant and fair society than ever, old prejudices still exist and new ones emerge, such as sexism, racism, disabilism, ageism, homophobia, heterosexism and Islamophobia. These prejudices are the underpinning of discriminatory practices. For this reason, different cases have been made for introducing or strengthening EO&D policies at different times and in different political contexts. The concept of diversity was added to the original concept of equal opportunities in recognition of the heterogeneity between and even within social groups. This has been further developed with the advocacy of intersectionality as a theory and methodological tool for EO&D policy development. The basic premise is that individuals possess multiple identities simultaneously and that subsequent multiple oppressions based on these are not additive, but mutually constitutive. Most studies of disadvantaged groups have in the past analysed them along one, or possibly two or three, dimensions, but have not been informed by theoretical understandings of the effects of intersection.

As with all approaches and tools, the usefulness and impact of intersectionality to EO&D policy making will depend on how it is used. Its complexity must not make policy makers impotent, but must be unravelled to provide a useful tool for informing EO&D policy. As the example from Canada shows, it certainly has potential for uncovering complex disadvantage and allowing positive action measures to be developed and targeted towards particular groups.

Summary

* EO&D is a complex, contentious and controversial concept surrounded by many myths.
* Britain is a more tolerant society today than it has ever been but prejudices still exist that are based on stereotyped perceptions of different groups and these can lead to discriminatory behaviour.
* People form generalisations about groups and they are often called stereotypes, especially when beliefs about a group are over-generalised, if not misinformed or false, and applied too broadly to each member of the group.
* Britain continues to be infected with racism, sexism, disabilism, heterosexism, homophobia, Islamophobia and ageism.
* Three separate but interlinking arguments that have been put forward as justifications for EO&D policy; the moral case, the economic or business case, and the social cohesion case.
* Defining EO&D presents a challenge, which feminist theory has tackled with the concept of intersectionality.

Questions for discussion

* Should we treat everyone the same?
* What is the most convincing case for EO&D?
* What does diversity add to the concept of equal opportunities?
* What would your definition of EO&D look like?

Further reading

Adams, D. and Houston, D.M. (2006) *Equalities, diversity and prejudice in Britain: Results from the 2005 National Survey*, Report commissioned by the Equalities Review, Centre for the Study of Group Processes, University of Kent.

Equalities Review (2007) *Fairness and freedom: The final report of the Equalities Review*, London: Equalities Review.

Parekh, B. (2006) *Rethinking multiculturalism. Cultural diversity and political theory* (2nd edn), Basingstoke: Palgrave MacMillan.

Runnymede Trust Commission (2000) *The future of multi-ethnic Britain*, London: Profile Books Ltd.

Women and Work Commission (2006) *Shaping a fairer future,* London: Women and Equality Unit.

four

Equal opportunities and diversity: the history, politics and economics

Overview

This chapter:

- sets out and examines the historical development of EO&D policies and legislation in the context of the major driving forces and catalysts;
- considers the ideological background within this analysis;
- highlights the politics of EO&D by charting and exploring their development in the UK through five distinct eras.

Key concepts

Ideology; historical development; driving forces; catalysts; social movements

The ideological and historical background to EO&D policies

Equal opportunities and diversity (EO&D) policies are a political phenomenon even though they affect most people only as organisational or bureaucratic procedures, and there are many factors that create the motivation for their introduction and development. EO&D policies did not simply arise because governments decided to legislate or employers to improve their personnel policies. The radical heritage of EO&D should not be forgotten. EO&D, like any other rights in society and in the workplace were not given on a plate, but came about because people campaigned and struggled for them. Social movements have played an important part in the recognition of EO&D. These include the civil rights movement, the women's movement, anti-racist movements, the disability rights movement, gay rights activism, campaigns for the rights and recognition of religious belief, and activism around issues of age. Sivanandan (1976) demonstrated early political action in the area of race:

The fact of the matter was that laissez-faire immigration and laissez-faire discrimination had thrown up social problems which after the riots of 1958 and the growing militancy of a Black underclass, were taking on political proportions that the government – irrespective of party – could not ignore. (Sivanandan, 1976: 352)

The five eras of EO&D

This chapter charts and explores the development of EO&D policies in Britain through what can be seen as five distinct eras:

- the 'moral era' – 1940s and 1950s;
- the 'liberal legislative era' – 1960s and 1970s;
- the 'politically hostile era' – 1980s;
- the 'public relations and professional era' – 1990s;
- the 'fairness tempered with economic efficiency era' – 2000s.

This analysis of the historical development is set in the context of the major driving forces and catalysts for EO&D in the different decades, which have changed in dominance over time. The major forces can be categorised respectively as morality, liberal legislation, political opposition, economic and professional interests, and finally a combination of supranational, political will and economic drivers. Although we can see that there is often a combination of forces acting on the development of EO&D in the different eras identified, on the whole it is possible to speculate about the dominant force.

The moral era: emphasis on disability

The 1940s and 1950s saw a post-war burst of egalitarianism inspired by the Attlee government and its introduction of the welfare state, which has been described as the greatest revolution in British social policy (see Thane,

1996 for a full discussion of this). The thinking on EO&D at this time was based on morality, and ideas of social equality and justice. After much lobbying, the earliest EO&D legislation came into being throughout the 1940s and 1950s. This was designed to assist returning disabled soldiers from the Second World War to obtain work. The Disabled Persons (Employment) Act (DPEA) was passed in 1944 and amended in 1958. One of the things it set down was a quota system of 3% for disabled workers in workforces of over 20 (the details of the Act are discussed in Chapter Five). As Oliver (1990: 89) stated, the DPEA was influenced by the 'collective guilt of seeing ex-servicemen disabled while fighting for their country'.

The liberal legislative era: gender, race and gay men's issues

During the 1960s and 1970s, the painstaking struggles of grassroots organisations gained recognition and the voices of long-neglected groups were heard in the political and public arena. Social movements formed in the 1960s, such as the women's movement, the Disablement Income Group, Help the Aged, and the Campaign against Racial Discrimination, articulated alongside the trade unions a range of political demands for action against discrimination, improved workplace conditions and equal access to public services.

Throughout the 1950s and 1960s, an array of groups had cooperated to keep the gender equality agenda alive. In 1966, an alliance of women's groups produced a set of election demands concerning equality at work, in pensions and other benefits and taxation (Meehan, 1990). Lobbying by the Abortion Law Reform Association founded in 1935 by women with the support of doctors who had witnessed the damage done by illegal abortions, eventually succeeded in getting the 1967 Abortion Act passed. This was done in alliance with backbench MPs, notably David Steel, and the tacit support of Roy Jenkins, Labour Home Secretary, 'one of a remarkable series of pieces of liberalizing legislation which characterized this period' (McCarthy, 2007: 99).

In 1974, the London Trades Council issued a 10–point Charter for Working Women adopted by the Trades Union Congress in 1975, which formed the basis for a widespread campaign by women's groups. It included demands for equal pay and equal opportunity, 18 weeks' paid maternity leave, a minimum wage, an increase in family allowances and an end to social security and tax discrimination (Lovenduski, 1986).

The Women's Liberation Movement (WLM) formed in 1968 was focused less on influencing government and changing legislation, and more on extending lifestyle choices and achieving cultural change, in particular protesting about the sexual exploitation of women and violence against them. Women openly took to the streets, or used their public image, to challenge the existing social structures that made them second-class citizens with restricted access to certain rights (Pruvot et al, 2008). McCarthy (2007: 102) argued that the Equal Pay Act passed in 1970 and the Sex Discrimination Act passed in 1975 (see Chapter Five) 'would almost certainly have still occurred if the Women's Liberation Movement (WLM) had not existed, given the strength of other drivers of change. However, the WLM was a significant assertion of the independent voices of women and it brought new issues onto the public agenda and new groups of women into activism'.

In terms of race, the West Indian Standing Committee (WISC), formed in 1958, coordinated the activities of associations based on separate islands of origin. A federal Indian Workers' Association (IWA), with its roots in the struggles for independence in India, was created in 1958 largely in response to increasing immigration from Asia (Kimber, 2007). The IWA concentrated on organising Indian workers into trade unions and on anti-racist campaigning. It allied itself with other minority ethnic organisations in the 1960s such as WISC and the Campaign Against Racial Discrimination (CARD), which was formed in 1964 as a broadly based group of black and white activists focusing mainly on lobbying for race relations legislation. CARD had close informal links with the Labour Party and developed more ties with government officials, MPs and public bodies than any other race-based group (Shukra, 1998). The late 1970s saw the continued rise of the National Front (NF) on a platform of opposition to immigration and multiculturalism. The NF performed particularly well in by-elections in 1972 and 1973 and in local elections in 1977. Anti-racist organisations such as the Anti-Nazi League (ANL) and Rock Against Racism campaigned in opposition (Renton, 2006). Black people were involved but did not predominate. Kimber (2007) argued that by the early 1980s the ANL's street tactics were important in exposing and publicising the racism of the NF.

In the 1970s, women from minority ethnic communities shared the cause of the WLM to campaign for gender and race equality. Organisations founded during the 1970s and later – such as the Organisation of Women of Asian and African Descent, Southall Black Sisters, Brixton Black Women, Liverpool Black Sisters, Baheno Women's organisation in Leicester and other groups throughout Wales, Scotland and England – campaigned in particular against immigration restrictions, virginity tests imposed on women arriving in Britain (see Chapter Five), police brutality and domestic violence. These organisations continue to campaign on a wide range of issues affecting minority ethnic women and their communities (Kimber, 2007).

The 1960s and 1970s also saw the formation of new activist groups focusing on age issues and homosexual rights. In the area of age, professionals began to work with, not for, excluded groups. Existing groups began to change along similar political lines, often changing their names in the process, for example, the National Old People's Welfare Committee, which became Age Concern in the early 1970s. Help the Aged also shifted from being an essentially philanthropic activity to lobbying government to improve pensions and services for older people (Thane, 2007).

The Homosexual Law Reform Society (HLRS) was founded in 1958 to campaign for the Wolfenden reforms (see Chapter Five for details of these reforms). It aimed for a respectable public image, and was 'a classic single-issue pressure group of a type which flourished in the 1960s' (Weeks, 1990: 171). The HLRS 'saw itself as the main instrument of the process of public education which the report and the government had advocated' (Holden, 2005: 86). HLRS's first public meeting in London in 1960 attracted more than a thousand people. After the first legislation that legalised homosexual acts in 1967 (see Chapter Five for details), support for HLRS decreased, though it was reincarnated as the Sexual Reform Society in 1970. But the North West Branch (which later became the Committee for Homosexual Equality) continued to flourish and the Albany Trust continued to provide counselling (including for lesbians), receiving a £30,000 government grant in 1974 (Porter, 2007).

The catalyst for the formation of the Gay Liberation Front (GLF) in 1970 was the Stonewall riots in New York, sparked in 1969 by a police raid on a known gay bar. The GLF's first meeting involved nine people, but just a few months later, about 500 people were attending weekly meetings. The GLF rejected the leadership and organisational models of the HLRS as well as its more cautious aims. It defined itself as 'a revolutionary organisation' and 'aimed to confront the persecution, discrimination and oppression of the gay community' (Weeks, 1990: 186). As well as establishing new mass tactics such as Gay Pride marches, the GLF was also actively involved with other contemporary organisations campaigning for women's rights, against racism, in industrial relations disputes, and in protest against the Vietnam War. But the unstructured and diverse nature of the movement soon caused divisions and it broke up in 1971.

Within these supposedly single-issue campaigns, **intersectional issues** of multiple disadvantage began to emerge at this time. For many lesbian women, sexism appeared as prevalent in the male gay community as in wider society, and they found their interests were taken more seriously by the WLM. In early 1972, the women in London's GLF formed a separate group. New organisations and support groups emerged for lesbians during the 1970s, including Sappho in 1972, a lesbian social group and magazine that became the focus of regular meetings, and Action for Lesbian Parents in 1976, which campaigned for lesbian's rights to custody of their children (Weeks, 1990). By the 1980s, race and ethnicity were also more prominent issues, with a particularly strong black lesbian and gay presence. Minority ethnic groups sometimes found the GLF's 'anti-family rhetoric' unhelpful, as family often provided their only support against racism (Weeks, 1990: 236).

These social movements marked the beginning of a new period of action towards EO&D, in which policies began to be understood in terms of anti-discrimination and equality instead of protection (Pruvot et al, 2008). Then a wave of legislation attempted to fill the gaps in discrimination law and to widen its scope (Equalities Review, 2007).

During the 1960s and the 1970s, major legislation to outlaw race and sex discrimination was laid down. In 1967, during this mood of legislative change and liberalisation, the Sexual Offences Act was passed, which sanctioned sexual relations between consenting adult men (21 years and over) in private, although no similar legislation on same-sex relations between women has ever been passed. The different provisions of the Sexual Offences Act are discussed in more detail in Chapter Five.

Patterns of labour market segregation and disadvantage experienced by women and minority ethnic people were an important part of the context in which anti-discrimination legislation developed in this period. More women were entering the labour market, but they were highly concentrated in certain industrial sectors through vertical segregation and at the bottom of organisations through horizontal segregation (Bagilhole, 1994a). In addition, large-scale immigration of people from the New Commonwealth and Pakistan had been encouraged and they were highly concentrated geographically, industrially and occupationally (Brown, 1984).

Pressures from women's organisations converged in campaigns for equal pay and anti-discrimination legislation, culminating in the 1970 Equal Pay Act and the 1975 Sex Discrimination Act. For minority ethnic communities, the successful passing of the 1976 Race Relations Act owed much to the momentum in the EO&D field established by the legislation on sex discrimination. This Act built on and strengthened the previous Acts of 1965 and 1968, which had sought to give minority ethnic communities the same rights of access to housing, public places and services as the white majority.

However, all the Race Relations Acts were presented as part of a double-edged package. The promotion of 'good race relations' through legal prohibitions on discrimination was balanced by the increasingly restrictive regulation of minority ethnic immigration. In 1968 came Enoch Powell's famous 'rivers of blood' speech in Birmingham, for which he was dismissed from the Conservative Party. Powell went beyond the advocacy of strengthening immigration controls to introduce the idea of sending minority ethnic British citizens back to their country of origin:

> As I look ahead, I am filled with foreboding. Like the Roman, I seem to see the River Tiber foaming with much blood. The tragic and intractable phenomenon which we watch with horror on the other side of the Atlantic, but which there is interwoven with the history and existence of the States itself, is coming upon us here by our own volition and our neglect. (*Observer*, 1968)

The underlying philosophy behind EO&D in the area of race was based on what has been called a 'colour-blind approach': policies and practices that gave equal access and equal treatment, but failed to recognise the historical and contemporary reality of minority ethnic people's experiences and to acknowledge their different needs. This approach rested on the premise that the 'problem', identified as resting in minority ethnic people themselves, would disappear over time. The focus of attention for academics was the internal make-up of minority ethnic groups, such as culture, social lifestyles and means of adaptation. Parmar (1981) described how pathological perspectives informed such investigations. The purpose of such research was 'to explain black cultures to white people so that white people could learn to become more tolerant, and secondly, the "objective" "race" expert and sociologist sought to inform policy-makers about the ways in which state policies could be implemented in order to aid the task of integration' (Parmar, 1981: 22).

Some of the remnants of the moral force driving EO&D in the 1940s and 1950s remained as an influence. When white people behaved in a racist manner there were perceived to be two sets of victims, both minority ethnic people and the white people themselves, who were also seen as victims of their own inhumanity. Clifton Robinson, Chair of the Commission for Racial Equality, wrote at the time:

> We should see more clearly that racism is a problem created by whites with more direct and dire consequences for Blacks but in a more general sense also affecting whites. Prejudice, discrimination, the denial of opportunities, injustice and hate not only affect the victims, but also the perpetrators. It lessens the humanity of both, Black and white. (Beauchamp, 1979, 3)

This led to the creation of 'racism awareness training' in the 1980s, which had the aim of exposing whites to the racist nature of their own behaviour with the assumption that they would reform in the light of this revelation. It has been argued that this form of training was both questionable in its effectiveness and counterproductive, in that it took up the energies of activists and diverted resources away from minority ethnic groups themselves (Sivanandan, 1985).

EO&D policy in the workplace was in its infancy and consisted of ad hoc responses to special needs rather than systematic reviews of the recruitment and selection process as a whole. For example, in the area of race, any special provisions tended to be one-off arrangements specific to minority ethnic employees who were perceived, because of their culture or the fact that they were migrants, to require and be entitled to exceptional treatment. There was an emphasis on extended leave, and the provision of interpreters and time off for religious observance (Department of Employment, 1995). Discrimination was predominantly seen as a product of prejudiced individuals and there was little appreciation of the existence of systematic structural disadvantage and discrimination.

The politically hostile era: threats to gender and race, no hope for disability

Even during the legislative era of the 1960s and 1970s, EO&D developments were a political response to campaigning and political pressure both nationally and locally. However, in the late 1970s and early 1980s, there was a sea change in political outlooks, policy objectives and economic organisation. The election of Margaret Thatcher in 1979 heralded a decisive rejection of Keynsianism and 'welfare statism'. This led to a polarisation of political philosophies that had direct implications for EO&D. As Cheung-Judge and Henley (1994: 3) argue: 'Within a decade the idea of equal opportunities changed from a sleepy ideological abstraction to a controversial and high-profile fact of life'.

The urban disorders of 1980, 1981 and 1985 effectively signalled to both sides of the political spectrum the deficiencies of the previous notion of the 'colour-blind approach' to race issues. Mobilisation and pressure group action ensured the take-up of recommendations concerning action on racial discrimination that resulted from the inquiry into the unrest (Virdee, 2006). On the political left, the 'riots' were seen as evidence of the revolutionary potential of 'racialised' minorities (Jewson, 1990). Traditionally, political action by the left had taken the form of promoting solidarity within horizontally defined strata, predominantly the working class. Now alternative sources of collective identities and interest groups were recognised as important. These included women, minority ethnic people and disabled people. This recognition was reflected in policies adopted by a number of Labour-controlled local authorities, particularly in the London boroughs, but also in the provinces (Bagilhole, 1993, 1994b). One of the primary actors in the field was the Greater London Council (GLC), which was responsible from 1965 to 1986 for running many public services for the whole of the Greater London area. In 1980, a Labour majority came to power with a major priority to further equality for all oppressed groups in terms of employment and service delivery. It introduced many radical policies in this area and became a left-wing beacon of the EO&D movement. Debates within local authorities over EO&D had a pivotal role in changing local authority structures and cultures, and attacks on their power by central government were fuelled in part by hostility to the prominence they gave to these issues.

The campaign for anti-discrimination legislation for disabled people intensified nationally and internationally. In 1981, Disabled People International was established and led to the formation of the British Council of Organisations of Disabled People. In 1982, the first attempt to place anti-discrimination legislation for disabled people on the statute books was made unsuccessfully by Labour MP Jack Ashley, who was himself deaf. In 1985, Voluntary Organisations for Anti-Discrimination Legislation was formed, later becoming Rights Now! At its heart were organisations set up and run by disabled people but with the active support of charities (Millar, 2007).

The emergence of AIDS into political and public consciousness generated fear and panic that led to 'an explosion of homophobia' (Weeks, 1990: 244). Gay men were mainly affected and the disease was considered a 'gay plague', known initially as 'Gay-Related Immune Deficiency'. After the splintering of the gay and lesbian movement in the 1970s, the AIDS crisis became a unifying force. The first self-help and support groupings were set up by the gay community, including the Terrence Higgins Trust founded in 1982 in memory of the first Briton known to have died of AIDS. Stonewall was founded in 1989 to fight for the repeal of Section 28 of the 1988 Local Government Act (see Chapter Five for details), and also to tackle other inequalities related to sexuality (Porter, 2007).

In contrast, the political right asserted the primacy of the self-reliant individual, pursuit of individual interest, personal gratification and the release of the enterprise of individuals by freeing them from collective controls. From this point of view, although the constraints of racial and sexual discrimination were seen as intolerable, equally unacceptable was to reward collective interests or recognise collective rights (Hall, 1983). In pursuing equality for individuals, the market was seen as the best guarantor of fairness. Enoch Powell claimed that 'the market economy ... is the most effective enemy of discrimination between individuals, classes and races' (Foot, 1969: 129). At the same time, on the right, there was a renewed emphasis on British nationalism, building on Powell's philosophy of the 1960s by attempting to draw and define the boundaries of the nation and 'Britishness'. There was a heightened emphasis on the idea of a unified and unitary British national culture. As part of this ideology, the 1981 Nationality Act (see Chapter Five) was used to redefine British citizenship and in the process excluded large numbers of people in Commonwealth countries.

At the same time, there were accusations that minority ethnic people were 'swamping' Britain with 'alien cultures'. In 1986, a Conservative Education Minister, in a speech to Her Majesty's Inspectors of Schools, declared:

> I believe that ... there is a genuine and not dishonourable fear that British values and traditions – the very stuff of school education – are likely to be put at risk if too much allowance is made for cultural backgrounds and attitudes of ethnic minorities. (Tomlinson, 1990: 27)

Norman Tebbit, a Conservative minister, came up with his infamous 'cricket test' to gauge a person's 'Britishness'. If any Asian or African Caribbean gave their support to India, Pakistan or the West Indies cricket teams while they were playing England, they had failed.

One of the major policy thrusts of the government was to reduce public expenditure through cuts in state welfare services, such as nurseries and elderly day care. This had a disproportionate effect on women as the major carers in society. The predominant political climate during the 1980s meant that there was no likelihood that the government would strengthen or develop the EO&D legislation. In 1991, the Commission for Racial Equality (CRE), the body set up by the government of the day in 1976 to oversee, monitor and make recommendations for the improvement in race legislation, noted that it had yet to receive a formal government response to its 1985 proposals for reform of the Race Relations Act (CRE, 1991). In fact, the necessity of organisations such as the CRE and Equal Opportunities Commission (EOC) (which were simultaneously campaigning for changes to the 1975 Sex Discrimination Act) was questioned by the political right. The government was also resisting 'equal value' amendments to the 1970 Equal Pay Act, which were emanating from the European Union (EU). Given this climate, the vociferous campaigns by disabled people's organisations for anti-discrimination legislation were ignored, and attempts to introduce an anti-discrimination Private Member's

Bill for disabled people were actively blocked by the government. As Dickens (2007) argued:

> Underpinned by European law, the equality provisions stood as an island in the sea of deregulation measures of the 1980s (many of which – such as the removal of minimum wage provisions – disproportionately affected women and BME workers). (Dickens, 2007: 467)

The public relations and professional era: acceptance of EO&D and hopes for disability

Increasingly in the 1990s, a business case was argued for EO&D (see Chapter Three). This essentially rested on two premises: first, that both private and public sectors of the economy were under-utilising the full range of skills and talents in the population because of continuing unequal opportunities for some groups in society; and second, that it should be possible for organisations to increase their efficiency and effectiveness by projecting a more pluralistic self-image and thereby widening their pool of potential customers. Joanna Foster, the then chair of the EOC, stated that 'equal opportunities in the 90s is about economic efficiency and social justice' (Ross and Schneider, 1992: xxi). Virginia Bottomley, the then Conservative Minister of State for Health, when launching a nationwide EO&D programme for minority ethnic staff in the National Health Service (NHS), stated:

> I want to stress that taking action to promote equality in employment is not just a matter of moral justice, or of fairness to people from minority ethnic groups, it is good, sound common sense, and it makes business sense, too. Otherwise the NHS will lose the benefit of their skills. (*Indian Mail*, 1993: 12)

As part of this change in outlook, a **managing diversity** approach was advocated, which claimed to harness EO&D strategies to business competitiveness (Kandola et al, 1995) (see Chapter Six for a full discussion of this approach). It was argued that diversity and difference between people can be managed in such a way as to add value to the organisation. The primary aims were said to be the improvement of all the skills of all staff through personal development, and the creation of a workforce that was representative of the organisation's customer or client base. But however innovative this approach was, it must be tempered by organisations' acknowledgement that 'although the breadth of focus is quite different' it did have 'many initiatives in common with old approaches to equal opportunities' (Kandola et al, 1995: 34).

Dickens (1999) argued that the business case for EO&D was not sufficient justification on its own, because private and public sector employers had different views on economic realities and organisational objectives. The CRE acknowledged this by distinguishing a 'business case' for EO&D in the private sector and a 'quality case' in the public sector. However, EO&D policies could be viewed as a chance for organisations to portray themselves as good and fair for customers or clients. In the 1980s, this was already beginning to become a priority even for organisations in the public sector such as local authorities that were major service providers:

> The centrepiece of the GLC's anti-racist strategy was the declaration of London as an 'anti-racist zone' and the announcement that 1984 was to be an anti-racist year in which the struggle against racism would be a continual and primary focus of the council's work. These commitments took the council into the realm of popular politics, and relied on public awareness campaigning marshalled through billboards and press advertisements. (Gilroy, 1987: 138)

EO&D become buzz words and an integral part of the jargon of professional, white-collar workers, especially those with responsibility for personnel and human resource matters in organisations. It thus enhanced the careers of certain professionals:

> The successful promotion of an equal opportunities policy may well be seen as a means of increasing the role of personnel at the expense of line management. Resistance to the policy on the part of line management may then be a manifestation of a disagreement over policy but it may equally be motivated by considerations of power unrelated to the policy in question. (Mason, 1990: 58)

It has been argued that this managerial adoption of EO&D contributed to its depoliticisation. The concept of EO&D, in its adopted form of equal treatment, came to represent administrative procedures rather than ideological and political issues.

> Equal opportunity policy development seems plausibly linked to bureaucratisation, and possibly appeals to bureaucratic organisations or branches of organisations because of its

> formalising qualities.... The promotion of equality of outcome,
> by contrast, requires the suspension or sidelining of bureaucratic
> norms and procedures within an organisation and (at least
> temporarily) the elevation of politics to a position of command.
> (Gibbon, 1993: 248; see also Chapter Six)

Through this system of sanatisation and incorporation into bureaucratic procedures, the true and original objectives of EO&D became diverted and subverted. Young (1990: 32-3) argued that policies that emphasised procedural routines and operations are 'regulatory rather than redistributive. They give prominence to those who will play a role in achieving greater systematisation of procedures: personnel managers and "race" relations staff.... The criteria for the success of such a policy are generally implicit and the activity seen as self-justifying'. In the area of race, Law (1996: x) identified this process as 'a move from the politics of "race" to the management of "race"'. He argued that 'liberal equal opportunities management has flowered and become entwined with the "new managerialism" to form a dominant policy ideology which may be termed, ethnic managerialism'.

While equality and group justice was the concern of the political left in the 1980s, the emphasis was predominantly on quality. Citizens' and customers' charters were advocated by the government in many service delivery areas, and local government was using phrases such as 'total quality management' and asking departments and voluntary organisations that received funding to come up with measurable 'quality standards' (Bagilhole, 1996a, 1996b). As Gilroy (1993: ix) pointed out: 'The "e" has been dropped and there is now a new buzz word: "quality"'. However, she argued that the emphasis on quality should result in equality becoming the underlying focus of services that must be delivered to, and meet the needs of, the whole community, including women, minority ethnic people and disabled people.

We can see a possible change of heart during the 1990s. Although the conventional thinking of the 'new right' Conservatives was to celebrate inequality (Forbes, 1991), both Valerie Amos and Herman Ouseley, the then heads of the EOC and CRE respectively, argued that the 1990s were 'characterised as the decade of equal opportunities in Britain' (Amos and Ouseley, 1994: xi). Michael Howard, the then Conservative Minister of Employment, vigorously endorsed the principles and practice of EO&D policy in a speech to a national conference jointly hosted by the EOC and CRE in 1991 where he launched the Employment Department's 'Ten Point Plan for Equal Opportunities'. The plan included specific recommendations that had previously been regarded as controversial, and were certainly beyond the legally required minimum action, including systematic ethnic monitoring of employees and the setting of equality targets. Also in 1991, the Prime Minister, John Major, made a supportive speech at the launch of Opportunity 2000, a business-led campaign to increase the quantity and quality of women's participation in the workforce (EOR, 1992). It would seem that in the 1990s, some EO&D policies in the areas of gender and race were not only compatible with political thinking on the right, but were also encouraged. We can see from this that EO&D as equal treatment can coexist with the idea of individualistic competition: 'equal opportunity is not rejected, just redefined into a vision of a perfectly competitive society' (Forbes, 1991: 27).

However, it is important to note that during this era few and diminishing resources were allocated to EO&D policy development. EU proposals for women were resisted, the EU Social Chapter was blocked, and structural changes in the public sector as a result of compulsory competitive tendering disproportionately and detrimentally affected women's work in the context of inadequate childcare provision. The labour market was increasingly casualised and fragmented and maintained a high level of unemployment within some minority ethnic communities. There was no strengthening of EO&D legislation on gender or race or extension of help to individuals taking tribunal cases (despite calls from both the CRE and the EOC), and, although codes of practice were accepted, they were not mandatory. Moreover, proposals were designed to restrict the entry into Britain of refugees and those wishing to claim asylum, including the restriction of their right to social security benefits.

In the area of homosexuality, discriminatory laws still existed, despite other EU countries introducing the same age of consent for opposite and same-sex relationships. To stay within the law (despite the lowering of the age of consent from 21), gay men had to be over 18 and confine their sexual relationships to the private sphere (by contrast, lesbians and their relationships remain virtually invisible in the law). Section 28 of the 1988 Local Government Act forbade local authorities from 'promoting' homosexuality as an acceptable family relationship, and despite growing concern over the difficulties and discrimination faced by older workers in the job market, the Conservative government refused to introduce legislation in this area.

Despite all these negative trends, campaigning groups were active in the area of EO&D. Calling for Muslims to be recognised for their religion not their race, the AN-Nisa Society, was set up in 1985 by Muslim women. It campaigned for improvement in the provision of Muslim-sensitive services and argued in 1992 that 'the Act (RRA) has been the one major cause for the deprivation, alienation and marginalisation of Britain's Muslim community' (Filby, 2007:84).The UK Action Committee on Islamic Affairs, formed in 1988, sent a submission to the review of the Race Relations Act in 1992, calling for incitement to religious hatred legislation along the lines of that operating in Northern Ireland (see Chapter Five for more details), and the outlawing of discrimination against religious groups. In 1994, at a meeting of Muslim organisations and institutions, there was a call for an 'Islamic consensus on national affairs' and in 1997 the Muslim Council of Britain (MCB), an umbrella body for Islam in Britain, was inaugurated. The MCB opposed such labels as 'minority ethnic', with members describing themselves as 'British citizens with an Islamic heritage'. This coincided with the election of Mohammad Sarwar as the first Muslim MP for the former parliamentary constituency of Glasgow Govan in 1997.

Increasingly, other faith groups that felt excluded formed national organisations to fight for equality. The Hindu Council was formed in 1994, and Sikhs in England in 2000. These organisations worked to provide services and support for their communities, to speak on behalf of their religious group and to develop a better understanding of their faith in the media and among other religions. They played an important role in bringing the inequalities experienced by their members to public notice (Kimber, 2007).

In 1988, the Campaign Against Age Discrimination in Employment was formed and in 1992 the Scottish Pensioners Forum was established, initiated by the Scottish TUC with support from Help the Aged, Age Concern and the Scottish Old Age People's Association (OAPA), 'to allow pensioners to speak on behalf of pensioners'. Also in 1988, the Third Age Employment Network was set up with support from Help the Aged to advise older people on opportunities for work and training and to lobby to extend their opportunities (Thane, 2007).

Increasingly confident organisation within and across minority ethnic groups occurred. For example, in 1990 a trust grew out of the minority ethnic communities and lobby groups to coordinate campaigning on local and national issues and on behalf of individuals who suffered discrimination. In 1996, the Trust established Operation Black Vote and continues to be active in seeking to build political participation and a political voice among minority ethnic groups, urging people to register and use their vote, to campaign on issues of inequality and to promote cultural diversity (Kimber, 2007).

The Conservative government finally submitted to pressure to introduce a Disability Discrimination Act in 1995. This was after growing militancy, including direct action and civil disobedience, by disabled people and an increase in public support (Millar, 2007). Disabled people took to the streets to demonstrate against inaccessible transport and inadequate benefits.

Plentiful media images of demonstrators in wheelchairs effectively shamed the government.

This was a long-fought battle. Since 1979, opposition parties had attempted to introduce over a dozen Private Members' Bills on this issue. However, despite the important recognition the Act gave to the operation of discrimination against disabled people, it was much weaker in many respects than the equivalent Acts in the areas of race and sex discrimination (see Chapter Five). It did not meet the demands of disabled people's organisations.

Amos and Ouseley (1994: xi) argued that 'in many ways there has been a failure at national level to keep equality as a central feature of public policy debate and development' and that what was needed was 'a strategic approach at different levels of society'. Perhaps this was too gentle an assertion and what in fact was happening during this era was that obstacles and barriers to equality were not only being maintained but also increased – a continued 'backlash' against EO&D. One subtle form that this took was an emphasis on the increasing stresses and strains that women faced in maintaining paid work alongside their continuing responsibility for most of the unpaid work in the home, and then to blame these on feminism. Faludi (1991: 5) exposed this as 'the big lie, it stands the truth boldly on its head and proclaims that the very steps that have elevated women's position have actually led to their downfall'. She showed that, according to surveys in the US, 75% to 95% of women thought that feminism had improved their lives. As Baird (1992: 6) argued, the problem for women was 'hardly the product of too much equality: rather the universal outcome of universal inequality'. Faludi (1991) maintained that the backlash was strategic by occurring well in advance of women achieving equality. In Britain, the backlash occurred in the form of accusations of 'political correctness' against EO&D initiatives. This was often seen as sufficient criticism to ensure that policies and practices were viewed as a product of the 'loony left': illiberal, repressive, extreme and based on totally fallacious premises. This mirrored the increasing opposition to 'affirmative action' led by the Republican Party in the US in the areas of race and gender, which produced some important court cases that overturned previous affirmative practices such as quotas in EO&D.

Despite a confused picture during the 1990s, we can identify some changes in approach to EO&D, which involved less overt opposition from the Conservative government. Several reasons have been proposed for this phenomenon: a search for electoral advantage, through women's, minority ethnic and disabled people's votes; fears of further urban disorders, particularly in the light of the increasingly vocal and effective organisation on the part of sections of the Islamic community; and concern about the 'demographic time bomb' of fewer numbers of young people and anticipated labour shortages that would mean jobs being replaced by women and people from minority ethnic groups. Although this threat was mitigated by continuing high levels of unemployment, there was still concern over skill shortages. Industrial sectors keen to maximise the range of talents and abilities available to them from the whole of society, and to retain skilled and trained staff, recognised EO&D policies as cost-effective. As one Halifax Building Society manager put it:

> Having the right people with the right skills in the right job justifies any expense of an equal opportunities policy. When you get the wrong people it is very expensive. If equal opportunities are inherent then it saves you a lot of money. (*Independent*, 1992: 12)

The last suggestion to add to this list came from Jewson and Mason (1993). They argued that the demise of local authorities' power and therefore their advocacy of 'radical' EO&D reduced antagonism and thereby encouraged 'liberal approaches' by private firms.

The fairness tempered with economic efficiency era: positive action for race, disability and gender, broadening the EO&D project

The influence of EU legislation, as well as a political receptiveness by the politicians in power and a greater preparedness to re-regulate (Dickens, 2006), was considerable throughout the 2000s. The 1997 incoming 'New Labour' government reversed the UK opt-out from the EU Social Chapter, which immediately resulted in significant development of EO&D legislation. The subsequent influence of the EU is also obvious in the development of 'family-friendly' rights and in the widening and broadening of the substantive scope of British anti-discrimination law. This followed the EU Treaty of Amsterdam (1997) and the subsequent Racial Equality Directive (2000/43) and Employment Equality Directive (2000/78), although in some areas (race and disability) the UK was in advance of the other EU member states (Bagilhole, 2005).

Three areas of EO&D developed substantially under New Labour. First, the many family-friendly directives advocated by the EU and previously blocked or begrudgingly passed by Conservative governments were either enacted or extended. Patricia Hewitt, the then Trade and Industry Secretary, announced to the 2002 Labour Conference the intention that 'family-friendly working will be the business of every business in Britain'. Gordon Brown, the then Chancellor of the Exchequer, argued in the Pre

Budget Report 2004 that 'the successful economies and societies of the next twenty years will also invest in the potential of all children and transform the way parents are enabled to balance work and family life' (Bagilhole, 2004). These directives covered part-time workers' rights, the extension of maternity leave, the introduction of paternity and parental leave, working time restrictions, and the right to request flexible working (see Chapter Five for a full discussion of these).

These policies had a major positive effect on increasing the ability for parents to accommodate their family responsibilities with paid work. However, it must be pointed out that they were directed mainly at women and have not contributed very much to their equality in employment. As Fagan et al (2006) noted:

> Work-life conflict reconciliation measures, which are driven by a concern with increasing women's employment rate and not employment equality, have led to policies which still assume women will be primary carers and that their participation can and should be promoted on a different basis from that of men. (Fagan et al, 2006: 575)

As this suggests, although numerical or time-flexible working arrangements may be valued as an aid to combining domestic responsibilities and paid work or as a 'bridge' into paid employment, the quality and take-up of such 'non-standard' work is critical. Equality is unlikely to be served where such work is ghettoised into low-grade or stereotypically women's jobs or detached from an organisation's internal career and reward system.

Despite the introduction of family-friendly policies representing an important qualitative shift in EO&D thinking by bringing the domestic sphere into view and recognising the importance of the link between unpaid domestic and caring labour and paid employment, they cannot be seen as unequivocally positive for gender equality (see Bagilhole, 2006 for a fuller discussion of how these policies may work against women within organisational settings). These policies can be a double-edged sword for gender equality in that they reinforce the idea that women are primary caregivers, with a consequently intermittent and 'less committed' attachment to the workforce than men who are not seen as carers. As Fredman (2005) argued, there is a risk that women get cast as the 'problem holders', leaving men and the gendered distribution of domestic labour unchallenged.

Alternatively, measures aimed at men, such as paid paternity leave, may offer more in terms of gender equality. For example, paternity leave may help foster a greater sharing of social and occupational responsibilities and help challenge the male norm in the organisation of paid work. The current legislation makes a start here, but, unlike maternity leave, the right to take paternity leave is subject to service qualifications and the level of payment is not earning-related and its low level is a deterrent to take-up (Dickens and Hall, 2006). The period of leave allowed is also very short. Where family-friendly leave involves economic or career penalties for those taking it, and where male take-up is low, its potential equality impact is lessened.

The influence of EU legislation has also helped the New Labour government to broaden its EO&D project. Article 13 of the 1997 Amsterdam Treaty forbade discrimination on the grounds of sex, racial or ethnic origin, sexual orientation, religion or belief, age and disability. This was seen as far-reaching legislation and various social movements had lobbied intensively to ensure that their groups were covered by the Treaty. The increased number and effectiveness of organisations representing the interests of older people, for example, led to their inclusion (Thane, 2007). The response from New Labour was to pass the Employment Equality (Sexual Orientation) Regulations in 2003, the Employment Equality (Religion or Belief) Regulations in 2003, and the Employment Equality (Age) Regulations in 2006 (see Chapter Five).

Another important move by New Labour was to take the development of EO&D forward through positive action by placing a positive duty on the public sector to promote EO&D in the areas of race, disability and gender (see Chapter Five). This was driven initially by a sustained community campaign led by the family of the murdered black teenager Stephen Lawrence. The Report of the Macpherson Inquiry (The Stephen Lawrence Inquiry, 1999) into the poor police handling of the investigation into this murder brought the concept of 'institutional racism' into the public domain. To combat such racism, Macpherson proposed a duty on the public sector to promote racial equality. Positive duties were extended to disability in 2006, and gender in 2007. This was a significant development in the legislative approach. As the Equalities Review (2007: 20) claimed, 'the gradual trend towards focusing less on individual acts of prejudice and more on the way in which systems and organisations routinely disadvantaged entire categories of people reached its most radical, and controversial, stage'.

This enactment of positive duties to actively promote EO&D represented a very important development in the British legislative package. Dickens (2007: 473) argued that it was a 'shift away from legislative reliance on a retrospective, individualized, victim-centred complaints approach towards pro-active, pre-emptive action by power-holders'. This conceptual shift was important but its practical implementation may be less effective. As Godwin (2006) showed, four years on from the race duty being passed not all public authorities had met their statutory equality duties. The then CRE intervened in a number of organizations, but no compliance notices were served. Hepple (2006: 109) argued that the duty proved ineffective because in practice 'too much emphasis is placed ... on procedures and bureaucratic process rather than measurable outcomes'. The disability and gender duties made some progress towards addressing the weaknesses identified in the race duty, although public sector organisations are still only called on to 'pay due regard to' the need to eliminate unlawful discrimination and promote EO&D rather than to take progressive action towards specified goals (Fredman and Spencer, 2006: 156).

Alongside all these positive and sometimes radical moves in the development of EO&D was the continuing strong underpinning of an economic case as its justification. As Dickens and Hall (2006) argued:

Fairness at work has been promoted by the post-1997 New Labour government, but it shares with its Conservative predecessors a concern not to 'overburden' employers. There is a concern with fairness – but only up to a point. (Dickens and Hall, 2006: 340)

EO&D arguments are not privileged over those of economic efficiency. Rather, economic efficiency ends that are seen to be furthered by EO&D measures can help encourage and justify legislative intervention. The 2002 Employment Act, for example, groups 'family-friendly rights' under 'participation, retention and development of skills'. In 2004, the Prime Minister, Tony Blair, argued that:

> Equality and human rights underpin our vision of a modern, fairer and more prosperous Britain.... Delivering prosperity for all means harnessing the skills and potential of every member of society, whatever their background. (Blair, 2004: 1)

The government's policy statement, *Success at Work* (DTI, 2006: 9), described discrimination as 'economic drag' and stressed the 'economic imperative for more diverse workplaces' and the waste of talent caused by discrimination.

Certainly, all the new challenges identified in the *2004 White Paper on equality and human rights: A new equality framework for Britain* (DTI and DCA, 2004) were primarily and predominantly based on economic arguments. Although such an instrumental, economic approach can drive change and increase the likelihood of the acceptance of EO&D, it may in practice be problematic if it is the only driver (Bagilhole, 2002a; Lombardi and Meier, 2006). It can leave necessary action dependent on voluntary initiative or consensus. This can be seen in the government's preference for so-called 'soft law' approaches, an example of which was the largely ineffective code of practice on age discrimination (DfEE, 2000) rather than legislation before the latter was required by the EU Directive. It was seen also in the government's rejection of calls for mandatory gender pay audits, preferring to rely instead on voluntary employer approaches despite evidence of their failure to make significant change (Adams et al, 2005). This caution could also be witnessed in the weak 'right of carers to request' flexible working, rather than a right to flexible working per se and a duty on employers to fulfil that right. It was evident also in not including the private sector in the enacted positive equality duties despite survey data evidence suggesting that this may be where they are needed most (Dickens, 2006). Another example is the various exceptions for age discrimination under the 2006 Employment Equality (Age) Regulations (Sargeant, 2006). Dickens (2007: 470) went as far as arguing that: 'The British legislation itself provides for business arguments to be posited against the equality principle to justify what otherwise would amount to discriminatory practice or requirements'.

Conclusion

The ideological and historical background to EO&D can be traced through five different eras, which can be distinguished by differing driving forces and catalysts leading to differing legislative and organisational approaches to EO&D. These forces include moral, political, economic and professional interests, both national and international. Social movements have played an important part in the recognition of EO&D and the different eras demonstrate its radical underpinning. These include the civil rights movement, the women's movement, anti-racist movements, the disability rights movement, gay rights activism, campaigns for the rights and recognition of religious belief, and activism around issues of age. We can see that there is often a combination of forces acting on the developments of EO&D in the different eras identified. However, major distinctive forces tend to predominate and change through time.

In terms of developments, the first era was hardly an EO&D era at all. Nevertheless, early thinking on EO&D during the 1940s and 1950s was based on morality, and ideas of social equality and justice, and this era produced the first protective legislation in the area of disability. During the second, 'liberal legislative', era of the 1960s and the 1970s, social movements marked the beginning of a concerted period of action towards EO&D, in which policies began to be understood in terms of anti-discrimination and equality instead of protection. A wave of legislation attempted to fill the gaps in discrimination law and to widen its scope and the major legislation that exists to outlaw 'race' and sex discrimination was laid down.

The third era, the 1980s, brought a major change in political outlooks, policy objectives and economic organisation, with a shift to an emphasis on markets and individuals, and a sharp division between the political left and right. The Conservative government during this era demonstrated its hostility to EO&D by blocking EU legislation, attempting to deregulate business and focusing on the idea of defining Britishness. However, the fourth era, the 1990s, saw a partial acceptance by the Conservative establishment of bureaucratic EO&D, encouraged by the professional interests of those working in the field and an acknowledgement of the economic case. The pressure from the growing militancy of disabled people's groups for their own anti-discrimination legislation eventually succeeded during this era.

Finally, in the 2000s, came New Labour and with it a more politically accepting approach to EO&D, a willingness to re-regulate and an enthusiastic compliance with EU EO&D policies that have encouraged family-friendly policies and broadened the EO&D project beyond gender, race and disability to include sexual orientation, religion or belief and age. New Labour importantly made a move towards positive action and away from merely outlawing discrimination. Underpinning all this is, nevertheless, a continuation of the strong underpinning EO&D by the economic case and the desire not to over-burden businesses in the private sector. This may be seen as an opportunity lost in the EO&D field by otherwise politically positive governments.

Summary

- The radical heritage of EO&D should not be forgotten, EO&D legislation and policies came about because people campaigned and struggled for them.
- The major driving forces and catalysts for EO&D in the different decades have changed in dominance over time, and can be categorised respectively as morality, liberal legislation, political opposition, economic and professional interests, and finally a combination of supranational, political will and economic drivers.

Questions for discussion

- Which has been the most effective era for EO&D?
- Would EO&D policies have developed without social movements' campaigns?
- What will be the main drivers for change in EO&D in the future?
- Are we moving into a new 'era' for EO&D?

Further reading

Bagilhole, B. (1994) *Women, work and equal opportunities*, Aldershot: Avebury.

Bagilhole, B. (2005) 'From equal treatment to positive action: the influence of the European Union on equal opportunities in the UK', *Construction Information Quarterly, Journal of the Chartered Institute of Building, Special Issue*, vol 7, no 3, pp 79-83.

Filby, L. (2007) 'Religion and belief' in P. Thane, T. Evans, L. Filby, N. Kimber, H. McCarthy, S. Millar, M. Porter and B. Taylor (eds) *Equalities in Great Britain, 1946-2006*, Report commissioned by the Equalities Review, London: Centre for Contemporary British History, Institute of Historical Research, University of London.

Kimber, N. (2007) 'Race and equality', in P. Thane et alP. Thane et al *Equalities in Great Britain, 1946-2006*, Report commissioned by the Equalities Review, London: Centre for Contemporary British History, Institute of Historical Research, University of London.

McCarthy, H. (2007) 'Gender equality', in P. Thane et al *Equalities in Great Britain, 1946-2006*, Report commissioned by the Equalities Review, London: Centre for Contemporary British History, Institute of Historical Research, University of London.

Millar, S. (2007) 'Disability', in P. Thane et al *Equalities in Great Britain, 1946-2006*, Report commissioned by the Equalities Review, London: Centre for Contemporary British History, Institute of Historical Research, University of London.

Oliver, M. (1990) *The Politics of Disablement*, London: Macmillan.

Porter, M. (2007) 'Gender identity and sexual orientation', in P. Thane et al *Equalities in Great Britain, 1946-2006*, Report commissioned by the Equalities Review, London: Centre for Contemporary British History, Institute of Historical Research, University of London.

Weeks, J. (1990) *Coming out: Homosexual politics in Britain from the nineteenth century to the present*, London: Quartet.

Equal opportunities and diversity: the legislation

Overview

This chapter:
- sets out and examines the most significant Acts in the areas of disability, gender, race, religion or belief, sexual orientation, and age in both Great Britain and Northern Ireland;
- includes directly relevant legislation, such as the major anti-discrimination Acts and duties in the devolved legislatures of Northern Ireland, Scotland and Wales, as well as legislation that has had an indirect but very important impact, such as family-friendly policies, the 1998 Human Rights Act and immigration and asylum legislation;
- compares and contrasts the approaches of 'equal treatment', 'positive action', and 'positive discrimination';
- interrogates the 'same treatment' versus 'different treatment' approach.

Key concepts

Anti-discrimination; family-friendly policies; human rights; immigration; asylum; equal treatment; positive action; positive discrimination

Equal opportunities and diversity legislation

The carrot or the stick?

The idea of legislation regulating human behaviour is fundamental to UK law. Equal opportunities and diversity (EO&D) legislation is no exception. Many people mistakenly believe that such legislation is aimed at their personal attitudes and that it attempts to govern how they think or feel about certain aspects of their life. This is far from the truth, although the Members of Parliament who drafted the original Bills probably expected them to change society eventually. Some people believe that eliminating discrimination requires the use of strong enforcement powers: the 'stick' approach. Others believe that over time education, persuasion and voluntary measures will be sufficient and that 'you catch more flies with jam than with vinegar': the 'carrot' approach. Whichever route is taken, the law has an essential part to play in the provision of EO&D and the elimination of discrimination by underpinning society's fundamental belief in fairness and justice. However, it must be borne in mind that legislation, by eliminating overt discrimination, may encourage covert and more subtle forms of discrimination that are harder to uncover and eliminate. In this area, we must always be vigilant. Moreover, the complexity and bluntness of some of the EO&D legislation has come in for some strong criticism. As the Equalities Review (2007: 10) argued:

> The tools available are not fit for the purpose of achieving equality in today's Britain. There are limitations in the law – which is complex, inconsistent in the way it treats different groups, and poorly understood. In some cases the law actually restricts action on inequality, and in others the action possible has been interpreted too narrowly – as for example with public procurement. There has also been a tendency to focus legal requirements, and the action that follows, on process rather than the outcomes sought. And problems with the form of the law have been made worse by unclear guidance and insufficient support, and by a blunt and inflexible enforcement regime.

This led to an increase in the political will to reform the EO&D legislation, as indicated in the 2008 Equality Bill.

The politics of EO&D in the UK have in the past enforced the public assertion that the interests of different social groups are inherently non-conflicting. EO&D was largely framed in terms of formal anti-discrimination legislation for most of the six strands of EO&D: gender, race, disability, religion or belief, sexual orientation and age. It has been a hard and long-fought struggle for all groups to gain this legislation (see Chapter Four for a full discussion). Positive action strategies were largely rejected until the 2000s, and then only put in place in the areas of race, disability and gender in the form of positive duties placed on public sector organisations but not the private sector. The major legislative focus remained consonant with a liberal egalitarian approach. As Howard and Tibballs (2003) showed, this would appear to coincide with the general population's views on equality: people tend to feel more comfortable with the language of 'fairness', 'tolerance' and 'having the same chances in life', and are uncomfortable with positive action and reluctant to think of themselves as experiencing inequality:

> Women have less well paid jobs, or do much more domestic work, but people see this as a result of an individual's choice and natural gender differences, rather than bias in society as a whole. (Howard and Tibballs, 2003: 8)

Devolution

Constitutional reform took place in the form of devolution in 1999. Prior to this, the UK (England, Scotland, Wales and Northern Ireland) was a centralised state with power concentrated in the Westminster Parliament. Now there is some degree of power geographically devolved to the Northern Ireland Assembly, Scottish Parliament and Welsh Assembly. The power to enact and change anti-discrimination legislation is reserved to the Westminster Parliament, except in Northern Ireland, which can enact its own EO&D legislation. The policy framework for the promotion of EO&D is a complex one, in which both UK and devolved governments interact. The Belfast Agreement in 1998 incorporated statutory obligations on Northern Ireland public bodies to promote equality of opportunity and good relations on nine grounds: religion and political opinion, gender, race and ethnicity, disability, age, sexual orientation, marital status, and those with dependents. It also amalgamated the existing anti-discrimination bodies in Northern Ireland into the new single equality commission.

In both Scotland and Wales, there were concerted campaigns to include the EO&D agenda in the devolution of power. In Scotland, a range of women's organisations, trade unions, gender experts and grassroots activists campaigned for women's representation in the Scottish Parliament (see Mackay et al, 2003; Breitenbach and Galligan, 2006; Mackay, 2006). Consequently, the 1998 Scotland Act imposed a duty on the Scottish

Parliament to encourage EO&D, but this was to be done without 'prohibition or regulation'. EO&D was defined in the Act as 'the prevention, elimination or regulation of discrimination between persons on grounds of sex or marital status, on racial grounds, or on grounds of disability, age, sexual orientation, language or social origin, or of other personal attributes, including beliefs or opinions, such as religious beliefs or political opinions' (Office of Public Sector Information; 1998).

In Wales, equality campaigners sought to redress the poor historical record on EO&D and successfully lobbied for the inclusion of an equality clause in the 1998 Government of Wales Act. This legal duty went beyond the statutory requirements placed on other UK legislatures, for it effectively required the Welsh Assembly to be proactive and 'make appropriate arrangements with a view to securing that its functions are exercised with due regard to the principle that there should be equality of opportunity for all people' (Office of Public Sector Information;1998). The Welsh duty was unique because of its non-prescriptive phrasing and all-embracing scope. The Assembly's equality imperative applied to all devolved functions of government in Wales including education, economic development, health, local government, social services, planning, transport, housing and industry.

A UK government report summarised these developments as follows:

> Devolution has provided a new political settlement in Scotland and Wales, creating new contexts within which work on equality and human rights must operate. The different political, social and cultural environments and the provisions for promoting equality of opportunity within the Scotland Act and the Government of Wales Act will have important implications for these nations. (DTI, 2004: 16)

In contrast to the situation in Westminster, the new legislatures in Northern Ireland, Scotland and Wales were placed under equality laws that required a proactive stance from government and the general promotion of EO&D. Initial analysis following devolution saw this as a positive development and Mackay and Bilton (2000: 109) concluded that 'constitutional change and the government's modernisation agenda are seen as an important enabling context within which equalities work can develop'. Subsequent work in Scotland asserted that 'the political climate for equalities has undoubtedly improved and new structural spaces have opened up' (Breitenbach et al, 2002: 11). Chaney (2004: 74) even more positively argued for Wales that 'constitutional reform has provided an enabling context for the promotion of equality of opportunity by government, led to the pursuit of different priorities, and underpinned the development of a distinctive agenda'.

The most significant EO&D Acts

This chapter does not attempt to provide comprehensive coverage or detailed description of the EO&D legal provisions or jurisprudence (this is available elsewhere; see Fredman, 2002a; McColgan, 2005; Sargeant, 2006). Rather, it compares and contrasts, highlights strengths and weaknesses, and critically examines enforcement approaches and mechanisms in both Great Britain (England, Scotland and Wales) and Northern Ireland. *Table 5.1* sets out the most significant Acts in chronological order, demonstrating the extent of EO&D legislation.

Table 5.1: Most significant legislation in the areas of disability, gender, race, sexual orientation, religion or belief, and age

1940s and 1950s	1944 and 1958 Disabled Persons (Employment) Acts 1948 British Nationality Act
1960s and 1970s	1962 Commonwealth Immigration Act 1965 Race Relations Act 1966 Local Government Act 1967 Sexual Offences Act 1968 Race Relations Act 1968 Commonwealth Immigration Act 1970 Chronically Sick and Disabled Persons Act 1970 Equal Pay Act (amended 1983) 1971 Immigration Act (amended 1986) 1975 Sex Discrimination Act 1976 Race Relations Act
1980s and 1990s under Conservative governments	1981 British Nationality Act 1983 Equal Pay Act (amended) 1985 Companies Act 1986 Sex Discrimination Act (amended) 1986 Public Order Act 1988 Local Government Act 1989 Fair Employment Protection (Northern Ireland) Act 1994 Sexual Offences Act (amended) 1995 Disability Discrimination Act 1996 Asylum and Immigration Act 1996 Employment Rights Act

Table 5.1: continued

1990s and 2000s under New Labour governments	1998 Human Rights Act
	1998 Belfast Agreement
	1998 Scotland Act
	1998 Government of Wales Act
	1998 Crime and Disorder Act
	1999 Immigration and Asylum Act
	2000 Sexual Offences Act (amended)
	2000 Local Government Act
	2000 Race Relations (Amendment) Act
	2001 Sex Discrimination Act (amended)
	2002 Nationality, Immigration and Asylum Act
	2002 Employment Act
	2002 Adoption and Children Act
	2003 Employment Equality (Sexual Orientation) Regulations
	2003 Employment Equality (Religion or Belief) Regulations
	2003 Sexual Offences Act
	2004 Asylum and Immigration Act
	2004 Civil Partnership Act
	2005 Disability Equality Duty
	2006 Equality Act
	2006 Employment Equality (Age) Regulations
	2006 Racial and Religious Hatred Act
	2006 Work and Families Act
	2006 Government of Wales Act
	2007 Gender Equality Duty
	2008 Equality Bill

We now examine the legislation in more detail, first as it relates to disability, then to race and religion, gender, sexual orientation, age and human rights. Finally, we consider the 2008 Equality Bill.

Disability legislation

1944 and 1958 Disabled Persons (Employment) Acts

Until 1995, these two Acts were the key pieces of legislation governing the employment of disabled people. Provoked by returning disabled soldiers from the Second World War, the 1944 Disabled Persons (Employment) Act, as amended by the 1958 Act, concentrated on the individual disabled person rather than on their physical and social environment. The 1944 Act defined a disabled person as 'a person who, on account of injury, disease, or congenital deformity, is substantially handicapped in obtaining or keeping employment'. It was based on the belief that disabled people could not be expected to compete for work with non-disabled people because of their medical condition. Therefore, they were perceived to need compensation for their misfortune and access to low-status occupations often in segregated settings.

These Acts led to the establishment of a disabled persons' register. Registration was voluntary and open to both employed and unemployed disabled people who fitted certain criteria. The legislation placed certain duties on employers with 20 or more employees in relation to the employment of registered disabled people. The 1944 Act established the **quota system** under which an employer of more than 20 workers had a duty to employ a three per cent quota of disabled workers who were registered under the Act. It was not an offence to be below the quota, but in this situation an employer had a duty to employ suitable registered disabled people, if any were available when vacancies arose, until the quota was reached. They could not engage or offer to engage anyone other than a registered disabled person without first obtaining a permit from the Disablement Resettlement Officer (DRO) to do so, and they could not discharge a disabled worker without reasonable cause. Two occupations were designated under the Act as especially suitable for disabled people: passenger electric lift attendant and car park attendant. An employer was not allowed to engage or transfer into these occupations anyone other than a registered disabled person unless a permit to do so had been obtained from the DRO, and these employees were not included in the quota. Importantly, employers could apply for overall exemption from the quota each year, if there were not enough suitable applicants. Therefore, despite the quota being set as low as three per cent it was not adhered to by the majority of employers, with exemption permits being allowed as a matter of course (Gooding, 1994). Employers were required to keep records relating to the employment of disabled people for two years from the time to which they relate, which had to be open to inspection.

1970 Chronically Sick and Disabled Persons Act

The 1970 Chronically Sick and Disabled Persons Act was recognised as a milestone in the establishment of the right of access to services for disabled people, which made significant improvements to the level and type of benefits and services available (Birkett and Worman, 1988). The Act placed a new obligation on local authorities to know how many disabled people were in their catchment area and to make arrangements to meet their needs. This led to social services departments in local authorities keeping registers of disabled people and Birkett and Worman (1988) argued that their access to services improved. The Act was wide-ranging and included:

- provisions for welfare and housing (for example, home helps, aids and adaptations);
- access to and facilities at public premises and educational establishments;
- the setting up of advisory committees; and
- co-options to local authority committees.

The Act also introduced the Orange Badge Scheme, whereby badges were issued by local authorities for motor vehicles driven by or used for the carriage of disabled people. This increased access by allowing more lenient parking rules for disabled people.

It must be remembered, however, that the funding for the majority of these services and provisions in the Act came out of hard-pressed local authority budgets and therefore 'tended to be uneven', leaving many 'vulnerable to economic pressures' (Birkett and Worman, 1988: 33). In addition, there was confusion as to how far these rights could be enforced. The clause 'in so far as it is in the circumstances both practicable and reasonable', which appeared in various sections, could be used to cancel out the intentions of the Act.

1985 Companies Act

A section of the 1985 Companies Act required companies with on average more than 250 employees to state the policy they had operated for the recruitment of disabled people, arrangements made for the continuing employment of those workers who had become disabled, and details of the training, career development and promotion of disabled workers in the previous financial year. This statement had to be published in the company's annual report. These requirements related to all disabled workers, not just those who were registered disabled, as was the case with the 1944 and 1958 Acts.

1995 Disability Discrimination Act

The 1944 and 1958 Acts that included the three per cent quota proved to be a dismal failure. Schools and colleges, public places, transport systems and even health and welfare services continued to exclude and segregate disabled people, often forcing them into poverty and dependence. As a result, there was a concerted campaign for an anti-discrimination law for disabled people. Disabled people wanted self-determination not charity, and individual enforceable rights to set boundaries between acceptable and non-acceptable behaviour to encourage a change of attitude so that disabled people were seen as equal citizens not as objects of pity and charity. We can trace these politics to the US civil rights movement and the US disability lobby, which persuaded Congress to pass the Americans with Disabilities Act 1990. This and other US laws make detailed provision for individual rights in employment, public services, transport and housing. Parallels can be drawn with anti-racist and feminist politics, but disability takes many forms and can happen to anyone, and an extra dimension needs to be considered when equal rights legislation is designed for disabled people – the discriminatory effect of 'unequal burdens'. These are extra expenses directly related to a person's disability, for example, a special diet or transport costs.

Laws in the US placed an obligation on employers, education institutions, transport systems and services to take reasonable steps so that disabled people could live as equal citizens. For employers, this meant making the workplace accessible, restructuring jobs or modifying equipment. As a result of individual suits brought under the American law, the Washington Metro system was overhauled, lift buttons were marked with raised printing and Braille, lights on platforms warned deaf people of approaching trains, and discounted fares helped those who needed a travelling companion. By contrast, London's Underground at that time made no accommodation for disabled people. Wheelchair users had to ride in the guard's van of some British Rail trains, along with carrier pigeons and bicycles. It remained a common experience among blind people in Britain to be told by minicab drivers that they did not take dogs. In Australia, in comparison, it was a criminal offence for an employer to require a blind person to part company with a guide dog.

From 1982 to 1995, there were seven attempts to introduce anti-discrimination legislation for disabled people along the lines of the 1975 Sex Discrimination Act (SDA) and 1976 Race Relations Act (RRA) in the areas of gender and race (Barnes, 1991). Each attempt failed, sometimes as a result of the government 'talking out' the Bill so that no time remained for a vote in Parliament. The government based its major reason for opposition on the cost implications. To counter this, both moral and economic arguments were advanced: first, that all citizens had an equal right to participate in society; and second, that if disabled people were given the means to make use of their skills, this would save money that would otherwise be spent on social security and special programmes.

The Rights Now campaign heavily criticised and disputed the government's cost analysis. It argued that it did not take into account any gains that might accrue from savings in benefits and increased taxation gathered if disabled people were given jobs. In addition, it argued, the government had overestimated the costs, as many buildings had already been made at least partly accessible for disabled people (Gooding et al, 1994). Those who opposed the legislation also argued that the laws against sex and race discrimination had not worked well, so there was no point in having any more legislation of this kind. The counter-argument to this was that for all their shortcomings, the laws had had a positive impact on many individuals' lives, and had played a role in creating a climate favourable to change. Another very contentious argument advanced by some government ministers against the legislation was that disabled people would not be able to handle it. In this vein, Hugh Rossi, a Conservative MP from 1966-86, argued: 'I wonder whether we should be doing disabled people, who have enough to contend with in life, a wrong if we were to invite them into such seas of uncharted and uncertain litigation' (Bagilhole, 1997: 65). Nicholas Scott, when he was the minister responsible for disabled people in 1987, said progress was being made and that: 'Rather than legislating, the most constructive and productive way forward is through raising awareness in the community as a whole' (Bagilhole, 1997: 65).

The 1990 Americans with Disabilities Act was seen as an example to Britain, and each attempt to introduce legislation received more support. Finally, the government succumbed to pressure and Royal Assent was given to the Disability Discrimination Act (DDA) on 8 November 1995. The arguments that Barnes (1991) had consistently advocated were finally recognised: 'The denial of equal rights for disabled people cannot be morally justified when other disadvantaged groups have protection under the law, no matter how inadequate that protection may be' (p 35). William Hague, the Minister for Disabled People in 1995, stated in a press release that: 'Taken together, the measures will play an important role in changing attitudes towards people with disabilities' (Bagilhole, 1997: 66). But, perhaps ominously, he also stated that: 'They will also give disabled people greater opportunities without imposing undue burdens on business or employers' (Bagilhole, 1997: 66). In fact, the legislation was described as 'a minimalist stance in which potential rights are hedged about with qualifications, limitations, and "escape clauses" for employers and others, and in which exhortation replaces compulsion as the main tool of implementation' (Blakemore and Drake, 1996: 32). Indeed, it was a weaker Act than either the SDA or RRA. First, it excluded employers with fewer than 20 employees (subsequently lowered to 15); second, its formulation of discrimination was more limited than that in the SDA and RRA; and third, it was backed up by a commission, the National Disability Council (NDC), that lacked some of the key powers of its counterparts, the Commission for Racial Equality (CRE) and Equal Opportunities Commission (EOC).

In addition, the legislative framework differed in one important aspect: the imposition of a positive duty on employers to make 'reasonable' adjustments for disabled employees. While this was a significant move away from the non-disabled norm, the term 'reasonable' provided employers with a potential get-out clause.

The Act was considerably strengthened when the NDC became the fully-fledged Disability Rights Commission (DRC) in April 2000. Then in 2007, the DRC, along with the EOC and CRE, were subsumed through the 2006 Equality Act into the Equality and Human Rights Commission (EHRC) (this is discussed in Chapter Six). At the time, the DRC had an annual budget of twice that of the EOC, but only three-quarters that of the CRE. However, as with the SDA and RRA, the DDA had depended primarily on individual enforcement rather than proactive or preventative action, and had therefore had limited impact.

Despite this, disability was predicted as being one of the key EO&D issues in the late 1990s, and the DDA was heralded as 'the most important discrimination legislation in a generation' and as being 'in some respects the most radical of discrimination laws' (EOR, 1996: 31). The Act:

- deemed people to have a disability if they had 'a physical or mental impairment which has a substantial and long-term adverse effect on their ability to carry out normal day-to-day activities' (long-term is defined by the fact that the disability must last or be expected to last for 12 months);
- made it unlawful for employers to discriminate on the grounds of disability;
- placed a new duty on employers of 20 (subsequently lowered to 15) or more employees to reasonably accommodate the needs of a disabled person by at least considering making changes or additional provisions to enable them to work;
- contained a right of access to goods, facilities, services and premises; further and higher education; and public transport, including taxis, public service vehicles and railways;
- established a National Disability Council (which later became a fully fledged Commission) to advise the government on the elimination of discrimination against disabled people;
- gave disabled people the right to take complaints of discrimination to industrial tribunals with no upper limit placed on compensation awards;

- amended and repealed some provisions of the 1944 Disabled Persons (Employment) Act, including the quota system.

The 2001 Special Educational Needs and Disability Act extended the obligation of public authorities to assist independent living and to avoid all forms of discrimination to all educational institutions and the youth service. The 2002 Private Hire Vehicle Act extended anti-discrimination into this sphere, and in 2006 all forms of public transport were required to make adequate provision for disabled people.

2005 Disability Equality Duty

All public bodies in Great Britain are covered by the Disability Equality Duty (DED), which came into force in December 2006, and was an important positive action measure. There is a general duty, plus additional specific duties. The basic requirement for public bodies when carrying out their functions is to have 'due regard' to:

- promote equality of opportunity between disabled people and other people;
- eliminate discrimination that is unlawful under the DDA;
- eliminate harassment of disabled people that is related to their disability;
- promote positive attitudes towards disabled people;
- encourage participation by disabled people in public life;
- take steps to meet disabled people's needs, even if this requires more favourable treatment.

'Due regard' means that public bodies should give due weight to the need to promote disability equality in proportion to its relevance. The duty applies in England, Scotland and Wales. The duty that applies in England and Wales is in all key respects the same as that applied in Scotland, except in matters relating to education, where legislative differences exist. There is a Statutory Code of Practice for England and Wales and a separate one for Scotland.

The general duty applies to all public bodies (apart from a small handful that has specific exemptions). It includes government departments, executive agencies and ministers, local authorities, governing bodies of colleges and universities, governing bodies of schools, NHS trusts and boards, police and fire authorities, the Crown Prosecution Service and the Crown Office, inspection and audit bodies and certain publicly funded museums. It also includes any organisation that exercises some functions of a public nature, but a major restriction to its effectiveness is that it does not cover the private sector.

Race legislation

1966 Local Government Act

The 1966 Local Government Act contained the provision for government money to help subsidise local government posts named in Section XI of the Act that were set up by local authorities to deal with what was considered to be the 'problem' of 'disproportionate' numbers of immigrants from the New Commonwealth and Pakistan in their service delivery areas. This was seen very much as compensation for local authorities for having to deal with 'problems' such as non-English-speaking children in schools and immigrants with social difficulties. The posts funded were mostly in teaching and social work. 'Section XI' funding was always a contentious and contested issue. Criticism came from the minority ethnic communities that it was not used in the right way; either the posts were seen as irrelevant or the appointees to the posts were seen as inappropriate – for example, too many white people were recruited without suitable bilingual skills or sufficient cultural awareness. In addition, they were often insecure and dead-end specialist posts, with funding from government always under threat. They were never seen as permanent and in fact the level of subsidy to local authorities was gradually withdrawn despite protests.

1976 Race Relations Act

The first anti-discrimination legislation in this country was the 1965 Race Relations Act, which was followed by a subsequent Act in 1968. These were limited in scope. The 1965 Act outlawed direct discrimination in public places where previously 'whites only' admittance procedures were legal. This was an odd assortment of places: hotels, restaurants, public houses, theatres, sports grounds, swimming pools and public transport, but not shops or boarding houses. The 1968 Act included employment and housing, therefore eliminating overt signs such as 'No coloureds, Irish or dogs' outside accommodation for rent. However, the effectiveness of the Act was seriously undermined by the use of voluntary industrial disputes procedures as the primary means of enforcement in industries only covering a third of the workforce and by the absence of any rights for individuals. As Blakemore and Drake (1996: 121) pointed out, the 'deeper and more pervasive effects of racism continued to be felt'.

These extremely cautious Acts were replaced by the 1976 Race Relations Act (RRA), whose main provisions came into force on 13 June 1977. It remains the central legislative source of protection against discrimination on the grounds of race, colour, nationality and ethnic or national origins. It mirrored the Sex Discrimination Act passed the previous year, repealed previous race Acts, and established the CRE to oversee the Act for the government and to make recommendations to enhance its effectiveness.

The Act makes racial discrimination unlawful in employment, training and related matters, education, the provision of goods, facilities and services, and the disposal and management of premises. The conditions of the Act are expressed in terms of 'racial grounds' and 'racial groups'. These terms are defined as relating to 'colour, race, nationality (including citizenship) or other ethnic or national origins'. A group can be defined by reference to its ethnic origins if it constitutes a separate and distinct community. However, the Act only gave individuals a right of direct access to industrial tribunals. 'Class actions' could not be taken under the legislation.

The jurisdiction of the Act did not cover Northern Ireland and it did not cover religious discrimination. This later came to be covered by the 1989 Fair Employment (Northern Ireland) Act and the 2003 Employment Equality (Religion or Belief) Regulations in Great Britain which are discussed on pp 106-7. Despite CRE calls to extend the Act to outlaw religious discrimination, it was still possible until 2003 to discriminate on those grounds unless religious affiliation counted as membership of an ethnic group, such as the Jewish community. Indirect discrimination might have been deemed to have occurred if an employer did not recruit Muslims, because this would have disproportionately discriminated against people from Pakistani and Bangladeshi origins, many of whom are Muslims. However, this was a rather complicated and convoluted way of gaining redress under the Act. Incitement to racial hatred, included in the 1986 Public Order Act, and racially aggravated violence and harassment, included in the 1998 Crime and Disorder Act, are the only criminal offences where the courts have to take account of racial motivation as an aggravating factor when passing sentence. The use of the criminal law is outside the remit of this book, but suffice it to say that it has been beset with problems (see Leng et al, 1998; Holroyd, 1999).

The RRA recognised three kinds of discrimination:

- direct discrimination;
- indirect discrimination; and
- victimisation.

Direct discrimination arises where a person treats another person less favourably on racial grounds than they treat, or would treat, someone else. An example of direct discrimination would be not considering a job applicant from a particular racial group because it was felt that they might be unreliable. **Indirect discrimination** is an important aspect of EO&D law. It consists of treatment that can be described as equal in a formal sense between racial groups, but discriminatory in its effect on one particular racial group. To establish indirect discrimination it must be shown that:

- the requirement/condition was applied equally to persons of any racial group;
- a considerably smaller proportion of a particular racial group could comply with it;
- it was to the person's detriment because they suffered as a result;
- it cannot be shown to be justifiable for a particular employment.

Examples of indirect discrimination include recruiting by word of mouth from friends or relatives of employees if this excludes certain racial groups, or requiring women to wear skirts, as this would rule out some Asian women who wish to wear trousers for religious or cultural reasons. In practice, there was very little use made of the category of indirect discrimination. Finally, **victimisation** counts as discrimination under the Act when a person who has asserted their rights under the Act, either by bringing proceedings or giving evidence, is treated less favourably.

Discrimination is not unlawful where a person's race is a **genuine occupational qualification** (GOQ) for a job. GOQs apply for reasons of authenticity or where the job-holder provides individuals with personal services promoting their welfare or education or similar personal services, and those services can most effectively be provided by an individual of a particular race. The Act permits employers to take **positive action** to overcome the effects of past discrimination in a very limited way: where there is an imbalance in the numbers of particular racial groups doing particular work for an employer in the preceding 12 months, the employer may provide training for a particular racial group for that work and/or encourage members of the minority racial group to apply through advertising.

Positive action should not be confused with **positive discrimination**. Discrimination at the point of selection for work because of under-representation of a particular racial group is not permissible.

The CRE had both duties and powers. Its duties were to:

- work towards the elimination of discrimination;
- promote equality of opportunity and good race relations between people of different racial groups;
- keep the workings of the Act under review and propose amendments, (amendments were proposed from 1985 onwards, but no formal response was forthcoming from the then Conservative governments);
- make grants to organisations, promoting their aims, and allocate money to research and educational activities with the approval of the Home Secretary.

Its powers were to:

- carry out formal investigations, on its own initiative or as required by the Secretary of State, where there was suspicion of racial discrimination;
- serve non-discrimination notices where there were found to be discriminatory practices;
- help, advise and represent individuals taking cases under the legislation, (people who had this support were more successful than others, but support was limited by budget restraints);
- produce and publish a code of practice. This was not legally binding but was admissible in evidence to tribunals.

One of the major problems with the CRE was that it did not have recourse to sufficient sanctions to make reluctant employers change bad and discriminatory practices. In addition, as Blakemore and Drake (1996) pointed out, there was always confusion about its role – whether it advocated the 'carrot or the stick' approach. The question of 'how far it should be a regulatory agency as opposed to a public awareness body, has dogged its history and weakened its impact in the employment field' (Blakemore and Drake, 1996: 128).

Lord Lester (2007) frankly conceded that the CRE, the body he helped create, was flawed:

> There was no effective implementation of the fuller strategy to tackle racial disadvantage. Those appointed as chairs and commissioners ... did not regard strategic law enforcement as the main priority for the CRE, and the organization was not staffed with the degree of professional experience and skill required for that important role. The use of the CRE's investigatory and enforcement powers ... were eventually all but abandoned. Individual cases were supported even though they were weak or unlikely to have any value. While this does

not really do justice to the CRE's achievements it remains the case that the CRE ... did not carry out the mandate given to them 30 years ago. (Lester, 2007: 2)

However, despite being underfunded, underpowered and inadequately staffed from the beginning, the CRE could at least point to solid achievements. Its last strategic document, *A lot done, a lot to do* (CRE, 2007), before being subsumed into the EHRC, said more than anything else about the task the CRE was set and the way the challenges had constantly changed over 30 years. Minority ethnic communities themselves often split between those who supported the CRE, which tried to counter bias in British society no matter how flawed, and those who condemned it as a badly constructed sop designed to placate their anger. There was always an uneasy relationship between community-based activists, mainly black or Asian, and the mainly white lawyers and administrators of the London-based CRE. It also endured increasing hostility from the right and those who raised the spectre of the 'race police'. However, the CRE was essential to ensuring that the 1976 Act was not just ignored.

A lot done, a lot to do builds on the CRE's four priorities for change:

- developing and enforcing existing and new powerful legal tools to promote racial and religious equality;
- reducing racism and extremism;
- tackling racial inequalities in education, health, the criminal justice system, housing and employment;
- promoting interaction between people of all ages and backgrounds and increasing participation in local community work by people from all ethnic groups.

The document urges the EHRC to adopt in full its 10 recommendations for the future:

- focus on setting and meeting measurable targets, which help to close the gaps in life chances between people from different ethnic groups;
- focus on improving community cohesion and integration, recognising the ways in which these concepts are closely intertwined with equality;
- develop and promote good relations providing the necessary financial resources to build stronger, healthier communities;
- develop an ambitious and academically credible research programme;
- target economic inequality and relative poverty;
- maintain pressure on the government, police and the legal profession to eradicate institutional discrimination in the criminal justice system;

- develop strong partnerships with the voluntary sector, academia, policy makers and political parties to bring people from all areas of society together in building a society based on equality and human rights;
- work with the private sector to develop best practice, regardless of the current legislative requirements;
- be a rigorous, courageous and ambitious regulator of the public sector;
- where experience proves that it is necessary, lobby for enhanced legislation to make sure that the aims of our equality laws can be realised.

The CRE ventured, tentatively and then with increasing confidence, into more areas of national life than most realised. The first non-discrimination notice was served in 1978 on a Birmingham nightclub, Polyanna's, to counteract racist entry policies. Officers carried out investigations into the allocation of council housing in Hackney and Walsall and school places in Berkshire. Training for chartered accountants and medical students was scrutinised, as were the employment practices in hotels and recruitment in the Civil Service. An inquiry was held into racism in the Household Calvary following complaints from black soldiers. The prison service was also investigated. In its later years, the CRE put less emphasis on individual cases, but one case alone resulted in a record £1.4 million pay out.

2000 Race Relations (Amendment) Act

The case of Stephen Lawrence, a student who was the victim of racist assault and murder, led to a watershed inquiry after much campaigning by his family and community groups. Allegations were made of the failure of police to investigate the murder properly and successfully prosecute the perpetrators. The report of the inquiry publicly recognised that racism extended beyond individual acts of prejudice and identified **institutional racism** pervasive in police decision making in this case. Institutional racism was seen as existing within the culture and structures of organisations, and as the 'collective failure of an organisation to provide an appropriate and professional service to people because of their colour, culture or ethnic origin. It can be seen in or detected in processes, attitudes, and behaviour which amount to discrimination through unwitting prejudice, ignorance, thoughtlessness, and racist stereotyping which disadvantage minority ethnic people' (The Stephen Lawrence Inquiry, 1999: para 6.34). Following directly on from the Macpherson Inquiry into the Stephen Lawrence murder, the 2000 Race Relations (Amendment) Act placed new responsibilities on public authorities, but again not on the private sector, to promote equality.

Under this legislation, public authorities (including further education and higher education institutions) have a statutory general duty to promote race equality while carrying out their functions, meaning the full range of their duties and powers. When carrying out their functions, they must aim to:

- eliminate unlawful racial discrimination;
- promote equal opportunities; and
- promote good relations between people from different racial groups.

The general duty's aim is to make race equality a central part of the way public authorities work, by putting it at the centre of policy making, service delivery, regulation and enforcement, and employment practice. Public authorities can meet the duty in their own way, taking account of their functions, the areas they cover, and the size and variety of the communities they serve.

To help them meet the general duty to promote race equality, the Home Secretary made an order under the Act that provides specific duties in the areas of policy making, service delivery and employment. Under the order, organisations must take basic steps to meet the general duty. These include publishing a race equality scheme, which must:

- list the functions and policies (including proposed policies) that the organisation has assessed as being relevant to the general duty to promote race equality;
- set out arrangements to monitor its policies for any adverse impact;
- publish the results of its assessments, consultation, and monitoring;
- make sure that the public has access to information and services;
- train staff on the general duty and the specific duties;
- monitor staff in post and applicants for jobs, promotion and training, by their racial group.

If public bodies have more than 150 full-time staff, they must also monitor, by racial group, the number of staff who:

- receive training;
- benefit or suffer from performance appraisals;
- are involved in grievances;
- are subjected to disciplinary action; and
- end their service with the organisation (for whatever reason).

Under the Act, the then CRE (now EHRC) was given the power to enforce the specific duties and issue a 'compliance notice'. This is a legal document that orders organisations to meet the specific duties within a certain timescale, and show how they plan to meet the duties and observe the conditions of the notice. If they do not observe any part of the notice, application can be made to the courts for an enforcement order. If the court issues the order and the notice is still not observed, the organisation can face legal action for contempt of court.

There is evidence that the race equality duty influenced public authorities' practices positively (Audit Commission, 2004). However, despite recognising this first important step of the legislative shift into positive duty measures, the Equalities Review (2007) felt that this innovation in policy had not achieved much in practice. It argued that 'although it has value in forcing public authorities to confront some of their shortcomings, it is too bureaucratic and process-laden to provide a really effective vehicle for change' (Equalities Review, 2007: 37).

Immigration legislation and controls

The 1948 British Nationality Act confirmed the right of 800 million citizens of British colonies to enter the UK. Their acquired status of 'citizen of the United Kingdom and colonies' helped their active recruitment to meet the demand for labour in the UK. It was not expected that many would take up their rights, and as Kimber (2007: 28) pointed out: 'Even the relatively small number who arrived from the Caribbean on the SS Windrush in 1948 provoked some panic'.

Once this demand for labour was satisfied, the political climate and agenda changed and assertions began to be accepted that good 'race relations' were only possible by restricting the numbers of minority ethnic immigrants into Britain. Restrictive immigration controls of black minority ethnic people became the flipside of progressive anti-discrimination legislation. The most articulate expression of this 'two-pronged attack' approach of 'keep them out, treat them fair' came from Roy Hattersley, a former Labour MP: 'without integration, limitation is inexcusable; without limitation, integration is impossible' (Hattersley, 1965: 20).

Immigration therefore became synonymous with 'black minority ethnic migration', with its obvious racial overtones. The issue of the immigration of minority ethnic people centred on what Fredman (2002a) called the 'numbers game', and around questions such as:

- How many can Britain take?
- Will they take white people's jobs and houses?

- How many will it take to change British culture?

As Fredman (2002b: 40) pointed out: 'Beginning with the Commonwealth Immigration Act 1962, the resulting web of immigration controls, although ostensibly neutral, were widely perceived as primarily aimed at the restriction of entry of black and Asian people'.

Thus, successive governments blatantly attempted to regulate, control and eventually stop the immigration of black minority ethnic people to Britain. The first legislative measures controlling the immigration of citizens of the UK and the colonies were introduced in the 1962 Commonwealth Immigration Act, with its system of work vouchers that had to be obtained prior to entry. The 1968 Commonwealth Immigration Act was passed in Parliament in three days withdrawing African Asians' right to enter the country, which had been given as part of independence settlements. It introduced immigration control for Commonwealth citizens who were non-patrials (that is, those who did not have a parent or grandparent born in Britain) and put a limit on the number of work vouchers issued. This revealed the blatant racism underlying the law, as white immigrants from such places as Australia, America and South Africa were far more likely to be patrials.

The 1969 Immigration Appeals Act extended the deportation powers of the Home Office. However, the 1971 Immigration Act was the most significant piece of legislation up to that date. It extended deportation powers even further, but, even more importantly, it abolished the work voucher system and therefore effectively stopped primary black minority ethnic immigration. From this time, the major form of immigration was restricted to secondary immigration, that is, to the wives and dependants of earlier immigrants. Added to this, the promise that men who entered Britain before the enactment date of 1 January 1973 were to be given the automatic right to be joined by their dependants was revoked by the 1988 Immigration Act.

There followed a rather crude call to nationalism, with an insidious view being voiced about the 'fear of swamping' the national culture. Typical of this approach is the following extract from a speech by Margaret Thatcher:

> The British character has done so much for democracy, for law, and done so much throughout the world, that if there is any fear that it might be swamped, people are going to react and be rather hostile to those coming in. So if you want good race relations, you've got to allay people's fears on numbers. (Gilroy, 1993: 20)

The next significant piece of legislation came in the 1981 British Nationality Act. This stated that citizenship could only be acquired by birth, descent or naturalisation. Eligibility for citizenship was largely confined to people born of British parents or parents settled here. Many British citizens, for example those with dual nationality of Britain and an African Caribbean country, had to register their desire to become a citizen under the new rules to retain their citizenship, which they had previously thought was theirs as of right.

Immigration controls have also always discriminated on the grounds of gender, seeing men as workers and women as dependants. As Brah (1992) argued, the arranged marriage system in some Asian communities was seen as a license for immigration that might override rules no matter how tightly drawn. Therefore, immigration controls determining the entry of foreign husbands and fiancés were tightened up for minority ethnic immigrants five times from 1969 to 1983. In 1985, the European Commission of Human Rights pronounced that British immigration controls discriminated against women. The government's response was to equalise the issue by making it as difficult for black minority ethnic men as it was for women to bring their husband or fiancé into the country. Where a partner was brought into the country, admission was subject to the 'primary purpose rule'. The immigrant had to prove that the prime reason for entering was to marry rather than any other social or economic reason. They had to prove that their marriage was 'genuine'. There have been cases in the past of Asian women having to endure the humiliation of 'virginity tests' to gain entry. Due to these numerous immigration controls, many Asian families remain separated, and some women and children who had been settled sometimes for many years in Britain became liable for deportation due to divorce or the death of their husband.

The most recent pieces of legislation in the long history of the tightening and restriction of immigration of black minority ethnic people to the UK focus on political asylum seekers. Many people fleeing from oppression, violence and poverty in their home countries have sought asylum in the UK. As Fredman (2002b: 42) stated: 'This has created a great deal of fluster and alarm in official circles, a reaction which conceals but also permits the often inhuman treatment of many of the people who arrive uninvited but desperate'. A whole new legislative and administrative structure has been created to deal with the 'problem'.

The then Conservative government introduced the 1996 Asylum and Immigration Act. This included a so-called 'white list' of countries that were considered safe and asylum seekers from these countries were automatically viewed as 'economic migrants' and were refused entry. It also restricted the rights of refugees and asylum seekers who were allowed to enter, specifically their rights to employment, housing and entitlement to benefits (Child Benefit was withdrawn altogether). However, the most significant change for asylum seekers was the withdrawal of mainstream social security benefit entitlements to 'in-country' asylum applicants, that is, those who had passed through British ports and airports before applying for asylum. This led the Joint Council for the Welfare of Immigrants (JCWI) to challenge the law in the Court of Appeal. This challenge was successful. The judge stated:

> [The 1996 Regulations] necessarily contemplate for some a life so destitute that, to my mind, no civilised nation can tolerate it. So basic are the human rights here at issue that it cannot be necessary to resort to the [European] Convention for the Protection of Human Rights and Fundamental Freedoms to take note of their violation. (Cholewinski, 1998: 462)

The Act also made it an offence for an employer knowingly to employ a person who is not permitted to work under the immigration rules. Employers must check a worker's documents to ensure that they have permission. The New Labour government elected in 1997 did not repeal this Act, despite the fear of potential discrimination against employing black and Asian people generally as a consequence.

The period following the High Court ruling was characterised by a growth in media debate around the issue of asylum seekers and society's responsibilities to them. This produced stories of how our nation was being 'swamped' by 'bogus asylum seekers'. Some of the media, particularly the tabloids, used an emotive language and tone to create a false impression of the situation in the UK, and indeed the circumstances of these vulnerable people. The media misrepresentation of asylum seekers drew on xenophobic and racist arguments from the past, including that of the swamping of 'British' values (Sivanandan, 2001). As Fekete (2001: 23) argued:

> A whole new anti-refugee discourse emerged in popular culture. Those seeking asylum are demonised as bogus, as illegal immigrants and economic migrants.

According to both Fekete (2001) and Sivanandan (2001), this popular discourse heralded the emergence of a new racism, which cannot be colour-coded: 'xeno-racism'. This racism is based on the fear of and hostility to impoverished strangers and foreigners even if they are white. Fekete (2001: 24) argued that the New Labour government incorporated 'xeno-racism' into its domestic asylum policy by 'making "deterrence" (of "economic migrants"), not human rights (the protection of refugees), the guiding principle'.

This increased public concern, which, coupled with the disastrous effects of the 1996 Asylum and Immigration Act, fuelled the public's desire for New Labour to be seen to be doing something about the issue of asylum. Furthermore, the government's response would need to withstand court challenges, and thus be more thorough than the 1996 Act, and promote a notion that the government was 'tough' on home affairs. Thus, in the 1998 White Paper (Home Office, 1998a), the Home Office argued that it was essential to introduce new legislation to 'minimise the attraction of the UK to economic migrants' by removing access to social benefits and making cash payments as small as possible. Jack Straw, as Home Secretary, made it clear that he viewed the introduction of vouchers as essential, as 'cash benefits in the social security system are a major pull factor that encourage fraudulent claims' (Bamber, 2001: 10). This was analysed by Sivanandan (2001: 2) as: 'The rhetoric of demonisation, in other words, as racist, but the politics of exclusion is economic. Demonisation is a prelude to exclusion'.

The provisions of the 1999 Immigration and Asylum Act affected 'genuine refugees' and 'bogus asylum seekers' alike. It could be argued, therefore, that the government's stated intention to protect genuine refugees was compromised, when such measures as food vouchers and forced geographical dispersal were indiscriminately enforced on all asylum seekers. Fekete (2001) argued that the government's approach to the welfare of asylum seekers had not been seen before in modern times. She equated it to the Poor Law of 1834, which was designed to make workhouses so uncomfortable, punitive and stigmatised as to deter all but the most 'needy' poor. Asylum seekers were thus labelled the new 'undeserving' poor by the government. As Sivanandan (2001) argued, although the government was prepared to go along with the recommendations of The Stephen Lawrence Inquiry (1999) and attempt to dismantle institutional racism in the public sector, it reinforced a new form of racism in the Immigration and Asylum Act. By so doing, it had 'stoked the fires of popular racism' (Sivanandan, 2001: 3).

The 2004 Asylum and Immigration Act set out the third phase of reforms to the asylum and immigration system, building on the action taken in the 1999 Immigration and Asylum Act and the 2002 Nationality, Immigration and Asylum Act. It also responded to the alleged continuing and increasingly sophisticated abuse of the system. The Act:

• unified the immigration and asylum appeals system into a single tier of appeal with limited onward review or appeal;

- dealt with undocumented arrivals and those who failed to comply with steps to cooperate with the re-documentation process;
- enabled failed asylum seekers to participate in community activities;
- created a system of integration loans for refugees; and
- tackled so-called 'sham' marriages.

An Institute for Public Policy Research (Kyambi, 2005) report entitled *Beyond black and white* argued that policy and perception would have to adjust to the fact that the majority of migrants now came from outside the traditional source regions of the Commonwealth. Commentators pointed to highly relevant changes in migration policy and the public debate, including positive economic arguments for a 'points system'. Certainly, the advocacy of the 'points system' had ushered in a climate that was more expansive toward immigration; the government decides on the requirements of the economy for particular skills and allocates points to individuals accordingly. Those with sufficient points may then enter the UK for work. Politicians and the media now argue that this economic immigration can be beneficial. However, Beynon (2006) stated:

> It would be precipitate to argue that race is out of the picture on immigration, either at the level of policy formation or public debate. In fact it is fair to say that we can continue to expect some negative association between the two. (Beynon, 2006: 5)

While the points system holds out the promise of greater objectivity, workers from the European Union (EU) member states have unlimited entry to the UK. Thus economic migrants subjected to the points system will be those seeking to enter from outside the EU, a situation that runs the risk of criminalising visible minority communities as a whole. Members of these communities are already disproportionately subjected to 'stop and search' procedures by the police. The advent of a system of immigration control based on surveillance within the UK, rather than simply at port of entry could easily lead to stereotyping. Where there is workplace enforcement against irregular working, officials are more likely to target people from visible minorities for checks.

While it is right to be more optimistic about the more positive tone of the recent debate on economic migration, it is difficult to argue that the link between race and immigration has been broken. What may be truer is that the relationship between race and immigration is simply being remade in different and less overt ways.

Legislation relating to religion

1989 Fair Employment (Northern Ireland) Act

In the UK, the first legislation against religious discrimination was restricted to Northern Ireland. The 1989 Fair Employment (Northern Ireland) Act took a firm, proactive and innovative approach to improve equality between the Catholic and Protestant communities in terms of employment.

- It outlawed direct and indirect discrimination on religious grounds.
- It required private sector employers with more than 10 employees and all public sector employers to register with the Fair Employment Commission (FEC) (similar to the then EOC and the CRE, but with stronger powers over employers), and to monitor the religious composition of their workforces.

The FEC could also enforce compulsory monitoring of recruitment and selection by employers with more than 250 employees. In addition, all employers had to review their employment practices every three years to make sure that they complied with the law. Failure to do so was a criminal offence. If the review revealed a problem, employers were required to take appropriate affirmative action, and provide targets with a timetable. Both government contracts and grants could be removed if employers refused to comply with the legislation.

However, there were limitations to this legislation, as Sheehan (1995) identified. Because of the stipulation of the size of firms that were covered by the law, 30% of employers were excluded from monitoring. These small firms were those in which women tended to be disproportionately represented. In addition, the undefined concept of 'fair participation' in employment underpinned the legislation and powers of the FEC rather than anti-discrimination as in the SDA and RRA. As Sheehan (1995: 75) explained, 'the Act has no remit to ensure equal treatment and just outcomes'.

2003 Employment Equality (Religion or Belief) Regulations

The EU gained the right to act in a widening EO&D capacity from the Amsterdam Treaty, which expanded its competence beyond gender and race. This led to several directives on the issue of employment equality in various areas of social policy, one of which was religion or belief. This in turn led to pressure on the UK government, which introduced the Employment Equality (Religion or Belief) Regulations in 2003. Similar to the earlier anti-discrimination acts for gender and race, these outlawed discrimination in employment that was classified as:

- direct discrimination;
- indirect discrimination; or
- victimisation.

Protection against discrimination in employment on the grounds of religion or belief was subsequently extended in 2006 to the provision of goods, facilities and services or public functions.

2006 Racial and Religious Hatred Act

This Act was the New Labour government's third, and finally successful, attempt to create an offence of inciting or 'stirring up' hatred against a person on the grounds of their religion. It contained wording to amend the 1986 Public Order Act:

- 'Religious hatred' means hatred against a group of persons defined by reference to religious belief or lack of religious belief.
- A person who uses threatening words or behaviour, or displays any written material which is threatening, is guilty of an offence if he intends thereby to stir up religious hatred.

Critics of the Bill claimed that the Act would make major religious works such as the Bible and the Qur'an illegal in their current form in the UK. While sympathising with those who promoted the legislation, comedians also feared prosecution for making religious references in their work. Supporters responded that all UK legislation had to be interpreted in the light of the 1998 Human Rights Act, which guarantees freedom of religion and expression, and so denied that an Act of Parliament is capable of making any religious text illegal. The House of Lords passed amendments to the Act that had the effect of limiting the legislation to 'a person who uses threatening words or behaviour, or displays any written material which is threatening ... if he intends thereby to stir up religious hatred'. This removed the abusive and insulting concept, and required the intention, and not just the possibility, of stirring up religious hatred.

Gender legislation

1970 Equal Pay Act (amended 1983)

There has been pressure for equal pay between men and women for a very long time. The Trades Union Congress passed a resolution in favour of this principle as far back as 1888, but it was not until 1970 that the first legislation in this area was passed in Britain. The legislation did not become operational until December 1975. The 1970 Equal Pay Act (EPA) allowed women to claim equal pay with men if they were engaged in equal work on an individual case basis. The EPA applied to both women and men, but the likelihood of a man making a claim for equal pay with a woman was, of course, less likely than vice versa, given the disparity in women's wages. This is in fact an indictment of the Act itself, in that it has not significantly narrowed the gap between the average earnings of men and women.

In July 1982, the European Court of Justice ruled that the EPA did not fully comply with the EU's 1975 Equal Pay Directive. The British law was considered deficient because a woman could only obtain equal pay in respect of work that had an equal value to that of her male counterpart if a job evaluation scheme or study had been implemented. Although disagreeing with the judgement, the government finally changed the law in 1983. Therefore, as the Employment Department (1995) guide explained, even two different jobs can have 'equal value' if they place equal demands on workers in terms of effort, skill and decision making. It is important, too, under the Act, that traditional male abilities such as physical strength are not given greater weighting than skills that are considered to be typically female, such as manual dexterity.

One of the most famous equal value claims began with five domestic assistants working at Belfast's Royal Victoria Hospital. In 1985, they claimed equal pay for work of equal value with male porters and groundsmen at the same hospital. Ten years after the claim was first lodged, the number of domestic assistants claiming equal pay had risen to 900 and the Health Board eventually agreed a settlement in 1995. According to Patricia McKeown of Unison:

> The case showed that it was unacceptable for public sector employers like the NHS to claim to be equal pay employers. However, it took from 1995 to early 2000 to really introduce equal pay into the Royal Victoria Hospital. As a result of two and a half years of negotiation and partnership domestics, porters, security staff, caterers and gardeners were awarded

£5.03 per hour – the highest rate for support workers in the UK. (*Guardian*, 2000).

1975 Sex Discrimination Act (amended 1986)

The main provisions of the Sex Discrimination Act (SDA) came into force in 1975. It was amended in 1986 to bring it into line with the EU's Equal Treatment Directive. The employment provisions of the Act were extended to include private households, firms with five or fewer employees and collective agreements relating to pay. The Act made discrimination on the grounds of sex or marital status unlawful in employment, training and related matters, education, the provision of goods, facilities and services, and the disposal and management of premises. Although the Act was drafted in terms of women being the object of discrimination, men can, and have, successfully brought claims under its provisions. For example, men have gained cheaper admission to swimming pools for retired people on an equal age basis to women by bringing a case to an industrial tribunal on the grounds of indirect discrimination. This was because although the conditions for cheaper entry applied equally to women and men – that is, they had to be retired – disproportionately fewer men could comply with the condition because of their later retirement age. The Act gave individuals a right of direct access to industrial tribunals.

There were, however, exceptions to the SDA where discrimination between the sexes was not unlawful, for example:

- in situations where discrimination was necessary in order to comply with a statute or regulation in force before the passing of the Act, as in the provisions of the 1961 Factories Act in relation to the employment of women;
- in situations where female employees were given special treatment in connection with pregnancy or childbirth; and
- in respect of provisions relating to death or retirement.

EU law may have implications for the last general exception contained in the Act, and may limit its broad scope. There has been controversy over pension rights, with a successful case being taken to the European Court of Justice where an employer was found to be discriminating against a woman by making her retire at 62 while her male colleagues could continue working until 65. The government has now decided to phase in equal retirement ages for men and women at 65.

Lawful discrimination in the form of GOQs was allowed in the same way as for the RRA. However, in respect of sex discrimination only, certain extra GOQs apply where:

- for reasons of decency or privacy it is desirable to employ men only or women only for a particular job (for example, because the job-holder works with people who are in a state of undress or where physical contact is necessary);
- a job makes it necessary for the job-holder to live on the premises and the only available building provides sleeping and sanitary facilities for one sex (in these cases the employer may continue to employ people of one sex, providing that it is not reasonably practicable to alter accommodation or provide other premises);
- the job is in a single-sex establishment for persons requiring special care; and where the job was a joint appointment to be held by a married couple.

The SDA led to the establishment of the EOC, which had similar duties and powers as the CRE, but in the area of gender. The SDA also advocated similar positive action provisions, with similar conditions attached, in the areas of training and advertising. The Act also recognised the same three categories of discrimination:

- direct discrimination
- indirect discrimination; and
- victimisation.

An example of direct discrimination would be failing to interview or appoint a woman on the grounds that, because of her sex, she would not fit into a predominantly male organisation. Examples of indirect discrimination include insisting on an unnecessary height requirement or requiring a person to work in the evenings when this is not operationally necessary, and refusing training or promotion to part-timers, if most part-time jobs are held by women and most full-time ones by men. Indirect discrimination against a married person is similar in concept to indirect sex and race discrimination and may arise where a condition or requirement is applied equally to married and unmarried people of the same sex but which is discriminatory in its effect on married people. A requirement to be mobile for a job, for example, might be detrimental to more married than single people.

A fuller example of the way in which the courts decide whether indirect sex discrimination has taken place is illustrated by the following successful case of *The Home Office versus Holmes* involving a woman employee returning to work following maternity leave. On her return, she asked to work on a part-time basis. The Home Office refused. Ms Holmes then took her case to an industrial tribunal on the grounds of indirect discrimination. The tribunal decided that the requirement to work full-time:

- disproportionately affected women. Proof of this was accepted by statistics that showed that there were fewer women of childbearing age in employment because of domestic responsibilities, which put a greater burden on women;
- was unjustifiable as it was convenient for management to impose a requirement of full-time working, but it was not strictly necessary.

However, the tribunal added that if, as a result of its decision, a greater demand for part-time work arose so as to substantially affect the organisation's efficiency, it would be open to the Home Office to re-impose the condition of full-time working. It is important to note that this was an individual case and every case is heard on its own merits (Bagilhole, 1997).

2001 Sex Discrimination Act (amended)

By the late 1950s, there was growing public awareness of, and access to, surgery and developments in the field of hormone research for transsexuals. However, surgery did not remove obstacles to equality for transsexuals, who did not acquire the legal rights of their reassigned sex, could not marry and often experienced discrimination in society and dismissal from work (Hall, 2001). In 1996, a seminal case was taken to the European Court of Justice. The Court upheld that discrimination against transsexuals was a species of sex discrimination. As a result, the SDA was amended to outlaw discrimination against transsexuals and people undergoing gender reassignment.

Gender Equality Duty

In April 2007, the biggest change to sex equality legislation since the SDA came into force. As with positive duties in the areas of race and disability, the Gender Equality Duty (GED) requires public sector organisations to take steps to:

- eliminate unlawful sex discrimination and harassment; and
- promote equality of opportunity between women and men.

For example, the GED means that the NHS has to ensure that the design, development and delivery of health services takes into account the different needs of women and men, including transsexual people.

Family-friendly arrangements

Although not specifically introduced under the EO&D banner, 'family-friendly' arrangements are often viewed as being part of the legislative EO&D package. Maternity leave and pay provisions introduced in the 1975 Employment Protection Act were improved in the 1996 Employment Rights Act. This Act applies to all employees but is of particular interest in EO&D terms for women in relation to maternity provisions. These provide that a woman may claim maternity leave, maternity pay and the right to return to work, provided that she complies with certain conditions of employment and notifies her intentions to exercise her rights under the Act. The Act also provides that a woman cannot unreasonably be refused time off for antenatal care and has the right to be paid for the time off.

From 1999, under the New Labour government and the influence of the EU, other family-friendly measures were introduced. Paternity leave (initially unpaid and then paid), parental leave and emergency family leave were introduced, and from 2002 the Employment Act gave the right for parents and carers of young and disabled children to have their request for flexibility in working arrangements taken seriously by employers. Childcare and tax credits were introduced (Child Tax Credit to cover some of the costs of childcare) and money provided to families on low incomes through the Working Tax Credit. Further improvements to this 'string of piecemeal offerings' (James, 2006: 272) were enacted in the 2006 Work and Families Act, with the right to request flexibility extended to those caring for elderly or sick adults (see **Table 5.2** for a list of the family-friendly arrangements).

These family-friendly policies continue to be extended and improved. Levels of take-up are high, and they are clearly making an impact. For example, the proportion of mothers changing their employer following maternity leave halved from 41% in 2002 to 20% in 2005 (Smeaton and Marsh, 2006).

Legislation relating to sexual orientation

Fredman (2002b: 54) argued that 'discrimination on the grounds of sexual orientation is a particularly vicious denial of dignity and quality, since it strikes out against the sexual intimacy at the very core of an individual's

Table 5.2: *Family-friendly arrangements*

Parental leave	Grants all employees the basic right to unpaid leave following the birth or adoption of a child, and the right to time off work for urgent family reasons.
Paid and unpaid maternity leave	Grants mothers the right to paid leave for a certain number of weeks following the birth of a child, and further unpaid leave thereafter.
Paternity leave	Grants fathers the right to paid leave following the birth of a child.
National Childcare Strategy	Ensures free education for all four-year-olds, and additional funding for pre-school and out-of-school clubs.
Child Tax Credit	Meets a percentage of eligible childcare costs up to a maximum figure depending on the number of children.
Working Tax Credit	Guarantees a minimum income for families on low earnings.
Working Time Regulations	Protects workers from working more than a set maximum hours a week unless they agree to do so.
Flexible working	Grants mothers and fathers, and those caring for elderly or sick adults, the right to apply to work flexibly; confers on employers the duty to consider such requests seriously.

identity and well-being'. It involves not just equal rights, but also human rights in the form of rights to privacy and family life.

Until the 2000s, discrimination on the grounds of sexual orientation manifested itself in three ways:

- greater restrictions were placed on same-sex sexual activity than on heterosexual sex;
- there was less respect for the family life of same-sex partners than for heterosexuals;
- protection against discrimination and harassment in the workplace and other parts of society was non-existent.

Same-sex sexual activity between men remained a criminal offence until 1967. Interestingly, there has never been any outlawing of lesbian sexual activity between women. The Wolfenden Committee on Prostitution and Homosexual Offences was set up in 1954, and reported its findings in 1957. It fulfilled the intention of clamping down on offences in public, and its recommendation to allow homosexual acts in private was not implemented for 10 years, but it has nevertheless been described as 'a crucial moment in the evolution of liberal and moral attitudes' (Weeks, 1990: 164).

Eventually, the 1967 Sexual Offences Act made some progress towards equality by decriminalising sexual activity between two consenting men aged 21 and over, in private. Although controversial at the time (see Chapter Four), the legislation has been widely criticised as having established the basis for long-standing legal inequalities between homosexual and heterosexual behaviour. It established an unequal age of consent and made strict impositions of 'privacy' that left male homosexual acts still open to prosecution. It also tightened the restrictions on public offences, resulting in a doubling of reported incidents of indecency from 1967-76, a trebling of prosecutions and a quadrupling of convictions (Weeks, 1981).

In 1988, the then Conservative government expressed its hostility to homosexuality by including the insidious 'Section 28' in the 1988 Local Government Act, which concerned general duties for local government. Section 28 prohibited local authorities from intentionally 'promoting' homosexuality or 'promoting' the teaching of the 'acceptability of homosexuality as a pretended family relationship'. This had a grave impact of self-policing in libraries, where books were removed, and in schools and colleges, where teachers were fearful of discussing homosexuality.

In this climate of hostility and prejudice, it took 18 years (until 1994) for the age of consent for homosexual men to be reduced to 18, which is still unequal compared with that for heterosexuals (which is 16).

Further impetus for change came in 1997 when a British gay man took a case to the European Commission of Human Rights. He claimed that the higher age of consent violated his right to respect for his private life and was discriminatory. Attempts by the New Labour government in 1997 to repeal Section 28 still met with vociferous opposition from the Conservative Party and the House of Lords. It was not until 2000 that the law was repealed in Scotland. In England and Wales, a caveat was inserted in 2003, stating that the prohibition on the promotion of homosexuality did not prevent schools from taking steps to prevent any form of bullying. Only in Scotland has the provision been removed. Further evidence of deep-seated hostility and prejudice occurred when the House of Lords twice threw out a Bill to equalise the age of consent. Eventually, the 2000 Sexual Offences Amendment Act 2000 was passed, equalising the age of consent for sexual activity. However, inequalities were still maintained, with homosexual behaviour restricted to a maximum of two men in private and contraventions punishable by up to two years' imprisonment. Heterosexual sex in public is only an offence if it 'outrages public decency', and the penalty is usually a small fine.

The 2003 Sexual Offences Act replaced older sexual offences laws with more specific and explicit wording, in effect finally decriminalising homosexual behaviour. It also created several new offences, such as sex tourism. People who travel abroad with the intent to commit sexual offences can have their passports revoked or travel restricted. The Act also widened the definition and interpretation of the concept of lack of consent in rape.

The 1973 Matrimonial Causes Act specified that marriage partners must be of opposite sexes. This prohibition on 'gay marriage' meant that same-sex partners, unlike spouses, had no rights to pensions or employment-related benefits, no rights to make decisions or even be informed about a partner's ill health or death, no inheritance rights without a will and no immigration rights. Similarly, it was difficult for a gay parent to retain custody of a child of a heterosexual marriage, and virtually impossible for same-sex couples to adopt or become parents through artificial insemination or surrogacy arrangements.

The adoption issue was tackled in 2002 in the Adoption and Children Act. This allowed single people or couples to apply to adopt a child. The previous condition that the couple be married was dropped, thus allowing same-sex couples to apply. The House of Lords initially rejected the Bill, but it was argued that rather than being a 'gay rights' issue, it was one that was concerned with taking as many children as possible out of care and providing them with a family environment.

In 2004, a momentous achievement in sexual orientation equality came about as a result of the Civil Partnership Act, which enabled same-sex couples to register as civil partners and have their relationships legally recognised. The Equalities Review (2007: 30) described this piece of legislation as 'spectacular'. From then on, anyone who registered a civil partnership had the same rights as a married couple. In addition, same-sex marriages and civil unions made in other countries were recognised as civil partnerships in the UK, which previously had not been the case. Civil partners were given equal treatment in a wide range of legal matters such as:

- tax, including inheritance tax;
- employment benefits;
- most state and occupational pension benefits;
- income-related benefits, tax credits and child support;
- duty to provide reasonable maintenance for a civil partner and any children of the family;
- ability to apply for parental responsibility for a civil partner's child;
- inheritance of a tenancy agreement;

- recognition under intestacy rules;
- access to fatal accidents compensation;
- protection from domestic violence; and
- recognition for immigration and nationality purposes.

Two people may register a civil partnership provided:

- they are of the same sex;
- they are not already in a civil partnership or lawfully married;
- they are not within prohibited degrees of relationship (for example, closely related);
- they are both aged 16 or over (or, if either of them is under 16, the consent of the appropriate person has been obtained either parent or guardian).

As far as discrimination at work was concerned, the first area to be tackled was the military. This was because it had an overt policy of exclusion of gay men and lesbians. This was more extreme than the somewhat covert discrimination experienced in other sectors of the economy, which often prevented homosexuals from being open about their sexuality and 'coming out'. Gay men and lesbians in the military were openly dismissed, and those suspected of homosexuality were the target of intrusive investigations and interrogations. Many attempts to end this policy failed until some high-profile cases to the European Court of Human Rights in 1999 showed this policy to be a breach of right to privacy and respect for private life. The policy was lifted by the 2000 Local Government Act.

2003 Employment Equality (Sexual Orientation) Regulations

New powers given to the EU under the Treaty of Amsterdam led to a directive in 2000 that required member states to legislate to prohibit discrimination on the grounds of sexual orientation in all employment situations. This led to the passing of the 2003 Employment Equality (Sexual Orientation) Regulations, which as in the areas of gender, race and disability outlawed the following types of discrimination:

- direct discrimination;
- indirect discrimination; and
- victimisation.

The Act was the result of much campaigning to extend anti-discrimination legislation to the provision of goods, facilities and services. In addition, a provision of the 2003 Criminal Justice Act stated that hostility based on sexual orientation must be treated as an aggravating feature for sentencing offenders.

Under the post-1997 New Labour governments, the pace of legislation in the area of sexual orientation increased dramatically, equalising the age of consent; extending rights to immigration, adoption and fostering; providing protection against discrimination; and sanctioning civil partnerships. These reforms have been described as 'a remarkable modernisation of the law, historically unprecedented and one of the most important batches of reforms introduced by the Blair government' (Weeks, 2007).

Age legislation

Another major area of disadvantage that stands out historically as being not addressed by anti-discrimination legislation is age. McEwen (1990) argued that age was 'the unrecognised discrimination'. It was certainly an area in which successive governments refused to consider legislation until prompted, yet again, by an EU directive emanating from the Amsterdam Treaty, this time on age discrimination. Until then, age discrimination was legal in Britain, provided it did not contravene the SDA whereby women were less likely than men to be able to comply with lower age restrictions on posts because of taking time out of careers for childbearing and rearing. Despite this, an Age Concern survey of job advertisements showed that over a quarter stated an age preference and two-thirds asked for applicants aged under 35 (Laczko and Phillipson: 1990: 88).

It could be argued age discrimination is the most difficult of all types of discrimination to tackle. Its effects are felt by everyone, albeit differently at different life stages, and there is no clearly demarcated boundary between the group subject to discrimination and others. Moreover, there may be clear conflicts of interest, for example between younger and older workers. Ageism is sometimes justified by saying that older workers should in fairness make way for younger workers. In this case, discrimination towards older people is considered legitimate, as protection is provided through the social security system of pensions and other benefits, while for younger workers, there is some positive discrimination in terms of employment protection. However, young workers also experience negative discrimination. For example, the 1998 National Minimum Wage Act sets a lower rate for younger workers, broadly those under 26. Moreover, the experiences of the two groups are different: while young people grow out of this group and are more transient, older people increasingly grow into stigma and stereotyping, material disadvantage and social exclusion.

There has, however, been a change in the political and economic agenda. Older workers are experiencing high levels of unemployment, while there has also been an increasing trend towards early retirement. Moreover, the recent demographic trend towards an ageing population is costly in terms of older people's economic dependency. As Dickens (2007: 62) argues, the 'new emphasis on combating age discrimination is not, therefore, a result of the sudden appreciation of the need for fairness, but gains its chief impetus from business and macro economic imperatives'.

Traditionally, anti-discrimination law has not been seen as the way forward in tackling age-related issues. New Labour government policy has focused instead on providing training, individual advice and help with job seeking differentiated by age categories, as evidenced by the New Deal for Young Workers (18-24), the New Deal 25 plus and the New Deal 50 plus. However, the new political and economic agenda, as well as prompting from the EU through the Amsterdam Treaty, means that attitudes are changing.

2006 Employment Equality (Age) Regulations

The Employment Equality (Age) Regulations, outlawing direct and indirect discrimination in employment – including recruitment, promotion, vocational training, terms and conditions of employment, pay and dismissal – in both the public and the private sectors were passed in 2006. Social security payments are not included, but compulsory retirement ages were prohibited unless they could be objectively justified.

Universal human rights

1998 Human Rights Act

Parekh (2006: 8) argued that contemporary multicultural societies, such as the UK, are integrally bound up with world opinion that 'demands subscription to the body of universal values embodied in the various statements on human rights and imposes some degree of moral homogeneity'. In line with this, the UK government incorporated the provisions of the European Declaration on Human Rights into British law in the 1998 Human Rights Act. Importantly, this complemented existing EO&D legislation. It requires compliance from all public bodies unless an Act of Parliament makes that impossible. It also requires all UK legislation, including Scottish, Northern Ireland and Welsh legislation enacted under their devolved powers, to be interpreted in a way that fits with the rights it endows, wherever possible. The Act covers the following:

- right to life;
- prohibition of torture or inhuman or degrading treatment or punishment;
- prohibition of slavery and forced labour;
- liberty and security of person;
- right to a fair trial;
- prohibition of retrospective criminal laws;
- respect for private and family life, home and correspondence;
- freedom of thought, conscience and religion;
- freedom of expression;
- freedom of peaceful assembly and freedom of association, including the right to join a trade union;
- right to marry and found a family;
- protection of property;
- right to education;
- right to free elections; and
- non-discrimination in the enjoyment of these rights and freedoms.

However, there is a caveat to the idea of fundamental universal human rights enhancing EO&D. As Parekh (2006) argued, these values have some defects. For instance, they retain a liberal bias or, in EO&D terms, an 'equal treatment approach'. Moreover, they impose a view that sees the state and its institutional structures as responsible for human rights alone and as these structures 'cannot take root and function effectively unless they suit a society's traditions and moral and political culture, they necessarily vary from society to society' (Parekh, 2006: 134). The danger, Parekh argues, is that, in order to ensure consensus, we end up with a body of universal values that are 'too thin and few to cover all important areas of life' (Parekh, 2006: 266). For example, in the UK, how do we handle respect for others as a shared value when racists, anti-Semites and others do not agree with this value.

'Same treatment' versus 'different treatment'

The build-up of EO&D legislation in the UK started with an equal treatment approach. However, as starkly pointed out by the Runnymede Trust Commission (2000: ix):

> Citizens have differing needs, equal treatment requires full account to be taken of their differences. When equality ignores relevant differences and insists on uniformity of treatment, it

leads to injustice and inequality; when differences ignore the demands of equality, they result in discrimination.

This has been recognised in the development of the legislation and leads us to the 'sameness versus difference' debate that feminists have grappled with over the decades.

In law, there are two ways in which you can discriminate: you can treat those who are the same as if they were different; and you can treat those who are different as if they were the same. To treat alikes as unalike, treating sameness differently, is the basis for most discrimination cases. You cannot treat people who are the same as if they were different, for example, equally qualified women and men competing for jobs. However, it is also true in the discourse of EO&D that you cannot treat unalikes as alike, or treat different people the same. Discrimination can lie in treating things that are different as though they were exactly alike. Recognised and unavoidable difference can be treated differently through positive action in the name of EO&D, for example making provisions for the fact that women get pregnant and give birth. Discrimination is ignoring sameness when it is salient and ignoring difference when it is salient.

Unequal treatment in the name of EO&D is increasingly allowed in British legislation. This acknowledges the need for different treatment and condones different treatment to counteract past discrimination and disadvantages experienced by groups. Legal positive action can be distinguished quite clearly from illegal positive or reverse discrimination:

> Although positive action focuses on group outcomes (for instance, representative proportions of men and women), the emphasis is still upon individual merit or capabilities. (Blakemore and Drake, 1996, 11)

Positive action is about bringing individuals up to a point, for example through training or the acquisition of qualifications, where they can compete equally with other individuals. Despite popular myth, it does not constitute preferential treatment, which, for example, gives people jobs purely because they are minority ethnic people, women or disabled people. In fact, the UK EO&D legislation legitimises positive action for particular groups on the basis that they are disproportionately under-represented in certain positions or levels within an organisation, and the positive equality duty in the public sector for race, gender and disability expects the active promotion of equality.

Despite these positive developments, until 2008 the EO&D legislation in the UK continued with an additive approach, listing newly discovered categories of disadvantage and dealing with them separately and differently, without acknowledging multiple disadvantage or seeing intersections between them.

See *Table 5.3* for the 'hierarchy of protection' afforded by the anti-discrimination legislation.

This compartmentalised way of thinking could be enriched by an intersectionality approach as a way of moving EO&D legislation forward. An intersectional approach could take EO&D out of separate boxes, and could offer different and imaginative options for marginalised groups. This new approach may be possible with the single EHRC (see Chapter Six) and the proposed 2008 Equality Bill.

2008 Equality Bill

After a long review process and the move to amalgamate the previous separate equality bodies into one commission, the EHRC, a unique attempt has been made to strengthen and simplify the EO&D legislation across the six strands of gender, race, disability, sexual orientation, religion or belief, and age. This is a significant move away from all previous EO&D legislation, which has concentrated on one strand at a time and has been built up in a piecemeal fashion.

On 26 June 2008, Harriet Harman, Minister for Women and Equality, announced a new single Equality Bill, *Framework for a fairer future*. Its main proposals are to:

- introduce a new equality duty on the public sector, bringing together the three existing duties and extending them to gender reassignment, age, sexual orientation and religion or belief;
- outlaw unjustifiable age discrimination by those providing goods, facilities and services (to allow businesses and public authorities to prepare, there will be further consultation on the design of the legislation and a transition period before it is implemented);
- require transparency from public bodies, which are to report on gender pay, minority ethnic and disability employment, and equal opportunities measures in contracts purchased from other bodies. The private sector will have a voluntary scheme with a 'kite-mark' for good practice.
- extend the scope of positive action so that employers can take into account, when selecting two equally qualified candidates, under-representation of disadvantaged groups, for example, women and minority ethnic groups;

Table 5.3: Anti-discrimination legislation by date, 'protected group', grounds covered and positive duty requirement

	Legislation	Protected group	Grounds covered	Positive duty to promote equality of opportunity
Gender	1975 Sex Discrimination Act (amended 1986, 2001)	Both sexes	Employment, provision of goods, facilities and services	Yes (public sector)
		Married people	Employment only	No
		Transsexual and gender-reassigned people	Employment, provision of goods, facilities and services	No
	1970 Equal Pay Act (amended 1986)	Both sexes	Pay and other terms and conditions of people doing equal work	No
Race	1976 Race Relations Act (amended 2000)	All racial groups	Employment, provision of goods, facilities and services	Yes (public sector)
Disability	Disability Discrimination Act 1995 (amended 2005)	Disabled people	Employment, provision of goods, facilities and services, and, to a limited extent, public transport	Yes (public sector)
Sexual orientation	2003 Employment Equality (Sexual Orientation) Regulations	All sexual orientations	Employment, provision of goods, facilities and services	No
Religion or belief	2003 Employment Equality (Religion or Belief) Regulations	All religions or beliefs, and none	Employment, provision of goods, facilities and services	No
Age	2006 Employment Equality (Age) Regulations	All ages	Employment	No

- strengthen enforcement and allow tribunals to make wider recommendations in discrimination cases, which go beyond benefiting individuals taking cases to the rest of the employer's workforce;
- explore further how to allow discrimination claims on combined multiple grounds, for example, a claim made by a black woman;
- consider how to take forward representative actions to allow trade unions, the EHRC and other bodies to take group discrimination cases to court.

Some of these provisions are particularly worthy of comment. Importantly, the Bill proposes to bring together the three separate duties on the public sector for race, disability and gender, which were introduced at different times and with different requirements, and extend this duty to the other strands of EO&D. It will also extend the coverage of the age regulations beyond employment, in line with the other strands. Positive action is to be enhanced by allowing the selection of equally qualified candidates taking account of under-representation of particular groups. Important moves away from the very individualistic consequences of single cases are contained in the proposed changes to the powers of tribunals and in the consideration of how to take forward representative or class actions. Finally, there are the beginnings of an acknowledgement of an intersectional approach by considering ways forward for claims on multiple grounds of discrimination.

These are in some ways radical moves, but many are hedged around with caveats and the need for further consideration. Moreover, compulsion for compliance has still not been extended beyond the public sector to the private sector. When the Bill went out to consultation, the EHRC's response centered on the issue of non-compulsion on the private sector. Some 80% of the British workforce is employed by the private sector and the Equalities Review (2007) has revealed stark inequalities within this labour market. The EHRC argued that:

> The reliance on voluntary measures will not lead to the necessary change of culture and practice, thus allowing inequalities which affect large sections of British society to continue. Therefore, the Commission recommends that there should be limited compulsory obligations on the private sector to review employment practices annually; monitor the composition of the workforce, pay and benefits; produce a tri-annual plan to show how they propose to comply with equality law and improve representation where appropriate; and to publish the results of monitoring data. (EHRC, 2008)

The government has announced that the earliest the Bill will be implemented is some time during the Parliamentary session of 2010/11. This simplification and strengthening of the EO&D legislation is long overdue. The consequences of the previous incremental approach to legal arrangements for EO&D remains bewildering for employers and the public, and therefore dysfunctional for the EO&D project.

Conclusion

EO&D legislation covers both employment and access to services in the areas of disability, race, religion or belief, gender, sexual orientation and age. The relevant Acts are numerous and have been enacted over a period of many decades. Legislation in some decades concentrated on anti-discrimination, focusing on single strands of disadvantage. In other decades, governments implemented what could be seen as negative action in the fields of immigration and sexual orientation. Finally, since the election of New Labour in 1997, more positive action has been part of the agenda, in the form of positive duties on the public sector and the duties placed on the three devolved legislatures, and the widening of the groups covered by the legislation. In the process, EO&D legislation has became incrementally more complex, fragmented and often inconsistent, both within and between the different strands.

For the EHRC, the single equality commission created in 2007, applying different and unequal protection across the six strands of EO&D would be a contradiction. Therefore, the formulation of the 2008 Equality Bill is crucial. It could, through a simpler and strengthened framework, provide the opportunity to create coherence between the different strands of inequality in terms of protection for discrimination and in terms of positive duties on the public sector, with a focus on outcomes rather than processes. This could, and, some would argue, should be extended to cover the private sector. The Bill could strengthen the enforcement of the legislation and move away from the idea of individualistic compensation on the grounds of a single discriminatory factor, such as being a woman or a member of a minority ethnic community. The move towards representative class actions and cases on the grounds of multiple discrimination, for example as a black woman, is a very positive way forward for the EO&D project.

Summary

- The law has an essential part to play in the provision of EO&D and the elimination of discrimination by underpinning society's fundamental belief in fairness and justice.
- The policy framework for the promotion of EO&D is a complex one, in which both UK and the devolved governments of Northern Ireland, Scotland and Wales interact.
- The complexity and bluntness of some of the EO&D legislation has come in for some strong criticism, which led to an increase in the political will to reform the EO&D legislation, as indicated in the 2008 Equality Bill.
- The politics of EO&D in the UK have in the past enforced the public assertion that the interests of different social groups are inherently non-conflicting. EO&D was largely framed in terms of formal anti-discrimination legislation for most of the six strands of EO&D: gender, race, disability, religion or belief, sexual orientation and age.
- The build-up of EO&D legislation in the UK started with an equal treatment approach, which leads us to the need to examine the 'sameness versus difference' debate that feminists have grappled with over the decades. This acknowledges the need for different treatment and condones different treatment to counteract past discrimination and disadvantages experienced by groups.
- However, positive action strategies were largely rejected until the 2000s, and then only put in place in the areas of race, disability and gender in the form of positive duties placed on public sector organisations but not the private sector.
- An intersectional approach could take EO&D out of separate boxes, and could offer different and imaginative options for marginalised groups. This new approach may be possible with the single EHRC and the proposed 2008 Equality Bill.

Questions for discussion

- Who should be the targets of EO&D legislation and why?
- Who else could be the targets of EO&D legislation and why?
- Legislation, by eliminating overt discrimination, may encourage covert and more subtle forms of discrimination that are harder to uncover and eliminate. How can this be avoided?
- How could EO&D legislation take into account multiple discrimination and an intersectional approach?

Further reading

Dickens, L. (2007) 'The road is long: thirty years of equality legislation in Britain', *British Journal of industrial Relations*, vol 45, no 3, pp 463-94.

Fredman, S. (2002b) *Discrimination law*, Oxford: Oxford University Press.

James, G. (2006) 'The Work and Families Act 2006: legislation to improve choice and flexibility?', *Industrial Law Journal*, vol 35, pp 272-8.

Kyambi, S. (2005) *Beyond black and white: Mapping new immigrant communities*, London: Institute for Public Policy Research.

Parekh, B. (2006) *Rethinking multiculturalism. Cultural diversity and political theory* (2nd edn), Basingstoke: Palgrave MacMillan.

Sivanandan, A. (2001) 'Poverty is the new black', *Race and Class*, vol 43, no 2, pp 1-5.

Weeks, J. (1990) *Coming out: Homosexual politics in Britain from the nineteenth century to the present*, London: Quartet.

six

Equal opportunities and diversity: the policy process

Overview

This chapter is structured in two parts. The first part:
- examines the enforcement agencies in the UK at national level and in Northern Ireland at devolved level, focusing in particular on some of the 'institutional architecture' to equal opportunities and diversity (EO&D) policies and legislation;
- analyses the establishment of the national single equality body, the Equality and Human Rights Commission (EHRC) in 2007, and its implications both from and potentially for the EO&D project;
- examines the potential for the Northern Ireland approach to 'equality and diversity mainstreaming' as a model to be used in Britain combined with an intersectional approach to policy making.

The second part of the chapter:
- examines different approaches to EO&D policies and practices at the organisational and institutional level;
- details two case studies that illustrate different approaches to EO&D policy;
- discusses some of the key concepts in EO&D that are emerging from the implementation of policies in organisations, including 'critical mass', 'glass ceiling', 'sticky floor', 'trapdoor' and 'glass cliff'.

Part One: enforcement agencies

Dickens (2007) identified what she called a 'two-pronged approach' to the enforcement of EO&D legislation. The first was the provision for administrative agency enforcement through the former separate UK commissions: the Equal Opportunities Commission (EOC), the Commission for Racial Equality (CRE) and the Disability Rights Commission (DRC) (see Chapter Five for a discussion of their rights and duties). These have now been subsumed into the Equality and Human Rights Commission (EHRC), which has similar formal investigative powers to the previous commissions, including the ability to issue enforceable non-discrimination notices, and is responsible for overseeing the 1998 Human Rights Act.

The second was the right of individuals to take discrimination cases to Employment Tribunals (ETs) under the anti-discrimination legislation. This illustrates the tradition of the individualised law model of the EO&D legislation (see Chapter Five). The EOC, CRE and DRC initially supported individuals taking cases to ETs. However, demand for their help always outstripped their resources, both in financial and human resources terms. In 2000, the three equality commissions supported a combined total of around 300 cases, compared with over 20,000 discrimination cases being taken to ETs (DTI, 2004). In fact, the vast majority of individual discrimination cases are withdrawn, and the few cases that are not abandoned have a very low success rate. Compensation levels in the 1980s were described as 'derisory' (Hepple, 1983: 73). Even successful applicants were seen as securing 'Pyrrhic victories' (Leonard, 1987) because, despite winning, they received little financial compensation, had often already lost their jobs or felt that there was no longer a place for them with their employer as a result of having brought a claim against them. The level of awards did increase following a European Court of Justice decision to remove a statutory maximum in the early 1990s and guidance from the Court of Appeal in 2003 to allow for 'injury to feelings'. There were a few large, high-profile awards, but most were low. In 2005/06, in sex, race and disability cases the average award was between £5,500 and £9,000 (Dickens, 2007). Unlike in Northern Ireland, where a separate division of Fair ETs was created under the 1989 Fair Employment (Northern Ireland) Act 1989, no specialist discrimination tribunals have been established in Britain despite repeated calls for them from the then CRE and EOC.

Significantly, individual cases brought to tribunal, even if successful, can only bring financial compensation to that individual; they cannot bring about the structural changes that are often required to remove the discriminatory issues in the organisation involved (see Chapter Five for proposals to remedy this through the 2008 Equality Bill). Therefore the 'first prong' of agency enforcement is crucial to tackling structural discrimination and performing an educative role. As Dickens (2007: 475) argued:

> Agency enforcement also highlights the importance accorded by the state to the elimination of discrimination, emphasizing the elimination of discrimination in the public interest rather than punishment of, or redress for, individuals.

However, she also pointed out that, in fact, the weight of enforcement has fallen on the 'second prong' – the individual 'victim-complaints' route of ETs. It would be useful to examine the remit and vision of the EHRC to see if it has potential to change this.

The formal investigatory powers granted to the original commissions were intended to play a significant enforcement role. The CRE was particularly active, beginning 24 investigations in employment between 1977 and 1982, focusing on sectors deemed most important – particularly labour markets in which minority ethnic workers were strongly represented – and targeting some 'household name' companies (McCrudden, 1987). The EOC was less willing to utilise its powers, although a small number of employment-related investigations were started. In the mid-1980s, however, concern for the rights of employers under investigation grew, and the courts imposed procedural requirements that acted to constrain the ability to mount investigations (see Chapter Four for the approach to EO&D during this era). Many early investigations had to be abandoned and later attempts by the CRE were bogged down in legal challenges.

Around this time, the then Conservative government, which was convinced of the need for a free market and pledged to reduce public spending, was abolishing some public bodies and severely cutting the budgets of others. Under this political agenda, the CRE's emphasis moved much more towards a persuasion rather than enforcement approach, the 'carrot' not the 'stick' approach (see Chapter Three). However, as Hepple (2006) argued, it was important that the possibility of enforcement action remained. Since the late 1990s, the CRE had used formal investigations only as a last resort when attempts to persuade employers and organisations to change potentially discriminatory practices had been exhausted. This produced results in organisations such as the Ministry of Defence (Household Cavalry), HM Prison Service and Ford Motor Company (Hepple, 2006). The EOC also used this approach but much more sparingly (for example, in relation to sexual harassment in the Royal Mail, where it started its first formal investigation for a decade).

The DRC, the last of the three single issue commissions to be established, was given an additional power that built on the practice of the other two: a provision for 'agreements in lieu of enforcement action' in return for named persons undertaking not to commit any unlawful acts and to take positive action as specified in the agreement. If the agreement was breached, the DRC could apply for a court order to enforce it. The DRC made some use of this provision, securing a few binding agreements with employers in lieu of enforcement action. It also had the power to require action plans for the purpose of avoiding repetition or continuation of the unlawful act.

The EHRC has enforcement powers modelled on those of the DRC, effectively extending these powers to the areas of gender, race, sexual orientation, religion or belief, and age. It took over the role of monitoring and enforcing compliance with the new positive equality duties in the areas of race, disability and gender. It also took over the CRE's and EOC's power to litigate in respect of discriminatory practices aimed at entrenched unintended discrimination unlikely to give rise to individual complaint, and the power to take action against discriminatory advertisements, instructions and pressure to discriminate. These powers had been unused by the previous commissions (McColgan, 2005).

Development of the EHRC

In 2002, the government launched the Equality Institutions Review, which produced a report entitled *Equality and diversity: Making it happen* (2002). This was proclaimed by the government as the 'most significant review of equality in over a quarter of a century' (Blair, 2004). The government subsequently announced its intention to establish the EHRC. This was partly due to pressure from campaigning groups and partly in response to a raft of legislation coming from the European Union (EU) in the form of directives on sexual orientation, religion or belief, and age. As Barbara Roche, the Minister for Women (2001-02), argued: 'We cannot have six separate commissions dealing with six separate strands' (DTI, 2003: 1). Patricia Hewitt (Trade and Industry Secretary and Minister for Women) claimed that the new EHRC would 'give greater support and more joined-up advice to individuals, businesses and communities to crackdown on discrimination, and promote equality and diversity. Tackling discrimination in the 21st century requires a joined-up approach that puts equality in the mainstream of concerns' (DTI, 2003: 1).

The reactions were varied. The CRE and EOC tentatively supported the idea of one equality body, and Stonewall, the campaigning organisation for lesbians, gay men and bisexuals, was in favour of it. There were concerns from the DRC that unless a single Equality Act was introduced in advance of the EHRC, the voice of disabled people would be drowned out. The

Women's National Commission also argued that a single Act should underpin the EHRC. The Commission on the Future of Multi-Ethnic Britain (Runnymede Trust Commission, 2000) was in support of a single Act and single commission for the following reasons:

- to give the principle of equality a higher profile;
- to ensure more consistent advice across a range of specific issues;
- to be able to tackle cases of multiple discrimination more readily;
- to better mirror equality units in most public bodies and private sector companies.

The creation of the EHRC enforcing body could make things easier for both employers and employees by providing a 'one-stop shop' for advice and assistance and could make EO&D policy less confusing for both employers and employees. Some also believed that under its guidance the various pieces of EO&D legislation could be amalgamated and more closely aligned (see Chapter Five for discussion of the 2008 Equality Bill).

However, there were genuine and deeply felt fears about the consequences of the creation of the single commission. It was feared that:

- specialist knowledge might be dissipated;
- rivalries between groups within the Commission might surface;
- differences between various kinds of discrimination might be neglected or marginalised;
- the turbulence of organisational restructuring might be detrimental (Choudhury, 2006).

We will now examine the functions, intended role and duties of the EHRC to see whether it has been set up to take a persuasive or enforcement approach – the 'carrot' or the 'stick'.

The EHRC has certain core duties and additional responsibilities, outlined in *Box 6.1*.

Box 6.1: Functions of the EHRC

Core functions
- Encouraging awareness and good practice on equality and diversity;
- promoting awareness and understanding of human rights;
- promoting equality of opportunity between people in the different groups protected by discrimination law;
- working towards the elimination of unlawful discrimination and harassment;

- promoting good relations among different communities and between these communities and wider society.

Additional responsibilities
- Keeping relevant legislation under review (except for the 1998 Human Rights Act, responsibility for which remained with the Joint Committee on Human Rights);
- acting as a centre of expertise on equality and human rights.

The wording of these core functions and additional responsibilities seems to lean towards a persuasive approach. This is reinforced by statements on the intentions behind the EHRC's role and duties laid down in the government's White Paper (Blair, 2004) (see ***Box 6.2***), and reflects the fact that New Labour governments were sensitive to the accusation of imposing regulations on the private sector, which constantly complains of being overburdened by state intervention.

Box 6.2: Role and duties of the EHRC

- It is intended that the EHRC will be balanced in its approach as a regulator and promoter. It will need to be sensitive to the needs of those who have a responsibility to comply with the law (employers and service providers in the private, public and voluntary sectors), while also championing the rights of individuals and communities who experience prejudice and discrimination.
- EHRC will focus on the public sector with only a 'lighter touch' to be applied to the private sector. Private companies will not experience compulsion but instead be encouraged to follow new codes of good practice. (DTI, 2004: 22)

However, it was also argued that: 'More of the same will not be enough to respond to these challenges and deliver the changes we seek at the pace necessary' (DTI, 2004: 12). This resulted in proposals for additional duties on the EHRC that had not been the responsibility of the previous equality commissions:

- a new duty to consult stakeholders on its strategic plans;
- regional arrangements to promote tailored delivery of its work;
- powers to promote human rights, including powers to undertake general inquiries;
- powers to promote good practice and enforce the law in the new areas of discrimination legislation covering sexual orientation, religion or belief,

and age (but no enforcement powers over the 1998 Human Rights Act, responsibility for which remained with the Joint Committee for Human Rights).

Underpinning conceptualisation of the EO&D approach under the EHRC

Identity approach

The *White Paper on Equality and Human Rights: A new framework for Britain* (DTI and DCA, 2004) emphasised that there was a need to 'deliver for everyone, whatever their identity' (DTI, 2004: 12). It did not emphasise a structural definition of discrimination or 'institutional discrimination' as the Macpherson Inquiry (1999) had done (see Chapter Five), but instead introduced a different language of 'protected groups'. It sought to promote the message that equality and human rights matter to everyone, not just to 'traditional equality communities of interest' (DTI, 2004: 24), which, it was claimed, had been the more divisive approach of the past.

Protected groups were defined in the White Paper as groups of people protected by discrimination legislation in respect of less favourable treatment based on particular characteristics or personal circumstances: men and women; people of different racial groups; people who have or have had a disability; people of different sexual orientations; people of different religions or beliefs (including those who do not have a religion or belief); people of different ages; and people who intend to undergo, are undergoing, or have undergone gender reassignment – in sum, everyone.

The business/economic case

The new challenges identified in the White Paper primarily and predominantly continued to be based on economic arguments. Tony Blair, the then Prime Minister, argued:

> Equality and human rights underpin our vision of a modern, fairer and more prosperous Britain…. Delivering prosperity for all means harnessing the skills and potential of every member of society, whatever their background. (Blair, 2004: 1).

He continued:

> A step change is now necessary in how we promote, enforce and deliver equality and human rights if we are to achieve the prosperous and cohesive society we seek. (Blair, 2004: 12)

Britishness, core values, cohesiveness and social inclusion arguments

There was a drive to redefine and promote British pride. The Home Office (2004) launched a consultation paper entitled *Strength in diversity*. It hoped to promote a debate on the changing nature of Britishness as part of a drive to overcome the problems of racially segregated communities and political and religious extremism. There was a new emphasis on building a more integrated Britain following the riots in Oldham and other northern English towns three years earlier and the growing profile of the British National Party, with its racist, anti-immigration agenda. This reflected arguments by ministers that it was time to 'move beyond multiculturalism' to stress the common values of being British as well as valuing different cultural backgrounds. Trevor Phillips, the then Chair of the CRE, declared that the concept of multiculturalism was out of date and no longer useful. Fiona MacTaggart, a Home Office minister, stated:

> Integration is not about assimilation into a single homogeneous culture. It means ensuring that ethnic, religious or cultural differences do not define people's life chances and that people with different backgrounds work together to build a shared future. (Travis, 2004: 2)

This was all reflected in the White Paper introducing the EHRC:

> Greater diversity in our society poses a significant challenge to how we shape and promote the shared values that underpin citizenship. While respecting and celebrating our differences, citizenship will need to promote wider ownership of these values and a shared sense of belonging. Human rights, establishing basic values for all of us, will play an increasingly important role in this, providing a language we can all share. (DTI, 2004: 15)

Human rights versus EO&D

The promotion of human rights was viewed in the White Paper as having much in common with the promotion of EO&D:

> Human rights are based on an idea of fairness for all, establishing basic principles of dignity, respect and protection for everyone, regardless of our differences. Human rights are not just for those who experience discrimination. They are inclusive and affect

everyone. Human rights will give the work of the EHRC a real impact at ground level. The promotion of a wider culture of respect for human rights will also be important in developing strategies to promote good relations between different groups of people, building and encouraging cohesive communities. (DTI, 2004: 15).

However, the White Paper also acknowledged that there were differences between EO&D and human rights (see Chapter Five for critique of a human rights approach):

> Unjustifiable discrimination needs to be tackled by detailed measures, which may not always be appropriate to the promotion and protection of wider human rights. (DTI, 2004: 20)

It was felt that the approach required of the EHRC in Britain was one that avoided any inequalities being left out or any rivalry or competition between different interests. Otherwise, there would be a danger of stronger and more vociferous interests rising above others. As diversity and difference are socially constructed and variable, issues can become more or less significant according to geopolitical and cultural space. Thus, differences through discursive practices can be privileged at certain times and marginalised at others. For example, Fagan et al (2006) have argued that in the EU the visibility of gender issues has faded. Here, issues of migration, immigration, race and religious belief began to dominate the agenda as a result of events such as the riots in the minority ethnic areas of Paris, and the murders of the politician Pim Fortuyn and film maker Theo Van Gogh in the Netherlands. Gender mainstreaming has been a useful strategy advocated by the EU and has continuing potential. However, the danger of this approach is that gender equality may lose out to the milieu of diversity.

Equality Commission for Northern Ireland: a model to follow?

Devolution of power to Northern Ireland, Scotland and Wales enabled positive EO&D duties to be placed on their respective legislatures. This has proved to be very beneficial for the EO&D project (see Chapter Five for an analysis). A raft of devolved public sector inspectorates in Scotland and Wales now affect the promotion of EO&D, including Her Majesty's Inspectorate of Education Scotland, the Scottish Social Work Inspection Agency, the Wales Audit Office and the Health Service Ombudsman for Wales. The power to enact and change anti-discrimination legislation in

England and Wales is, however, the reserve of the Westminster Parliament. By contrast, Northern Ireland can enact its own EO&D legislation. Its single Equality Commission – the first of its kind in the UK – is a useful benchmark for assessing the efficacy of the EO&D mainstreaming approach and its potential for the development of the EHRC for Great Britain (England, Scotland and Wales).

Given its history of conflict, developing the equality agenda has been a major preoccupation of policy intervention in Northern Ireland. Legislation was initially based on radical intervention in the area of discrimination on the grounds of religious belief. The 1976 Fair Employment (Northern Ireland) Act, aimed to tackle religious discrimination between Protestants and Catholics in employment and followed the EO&D legislation of this era in the rest of the UK outlawing discrimination on the grounds of sex and race in many respects (see Chapter Five). However, the Northern Ireland implementation agency – the Fair Employment Agency (FEA) – had an important advantage over the EO&D implementation agencies in the rest of the UK: the FEA was able to undertake investigations of organisations without having to demonstrate that discrimination was being practised. It undertook a large number of such investigations, most notably in its Civil Service, and exposed the failure of that organisation to implement good practice in personnel procedures as well as finding imbalances in the workforce, especially in senior posts, in favour of Protestants. The Civil Service implemented religion monitoring as a result and 'piggy-backed' gender and disability monitoring in the process, thus becoming a catalyst for improvements in the public sector generally (McCrudden, 1996).

The 1989 Fair Employment (Northern Ireland) Act introduced the key concept of **'fair participation'**, which was based on a comparison between an employer's profile and the availability of labour in its relevant catchment area. Fair participation took legislation beyond the 'equal treatment' approach of most EO&D policies in the UK at this time – one of removing barriers to different groups – towards a focus on specified results or outcomes – the 'equality of outcome' approach discussed in the second part of this chapter. Employers' workforces were required to reflect the proportion of Catholics present in their potential, relevant labour catchment area. The legislation was successful in its specific intention to improve the position of Catholics in the labour market. In fact, this happened to such an extent that some public sector employers had to take affirmative action activities to boost the proportion of Protestants in their organisations, an example of the solution to one EO&D problem leading to another, or the unintended consequences of policy implementation.

During the 1990s, attempts were made to introduce gender mainstreaming in policy making throughout the UK. However, in a more radical move, the

Northern Ireland Office launched the Policy Appraisal and Fair Treatment (PAFT) Guidelines across a more comprehensive range of EO&D issues: religion and political opinion, gender, race and ethnicity, disability, age, sexual orientation, marital status and those with dependants. The guidelines stated that in the public sector all new policies and service changes were to be assessed for their impact on these equality strands. In the event of any 'adverse impact' being identified, policy makers and service delivery agencies were required to consider altering the policy in order to offset or ameliorate the impact. There was no requirement for policy to be changed if other policy imperatives existed but policy makers were required to set out their reasons for inaction. In 1998, the Belfast Agreement imposed a statutory obligation on public bodies to promote equality of opportunity and good relations on the same nine grounds as in the PAFT initiative. It also amalgamated the existing anti-discrimination bodies in Northern Ireland into a new single Equality Commission.

Such mainstreaming in the context of diversity is extremely complex and represented a significant challenge. As Prasad and Mills (1997: 5) acknowledged: 'Managing diversity at the workplace presents as many dilemmas as triumphs, and is constantly fraught with innumerable tensions, conflicts and contradictions'. For this very reason, the decision was made to exclude class and socioeconomic status from the mainstreaming process. It was argued that their inclusion had the potential to become a general constraint on EO&D policy making by becoming totally dominant and drawing the focus away from the nine identified disadvantaged groups.

Despite this, a number of key problems were identified with the policy process in Northern Ireland (Osborne, 2003). These included the definition of 'adverse impact', how it was to be measured, and what scale of adverse impact was sufficient to trigger policy response. The main way of measuring 'adverse impact' was statistical, but in some areas statistics are hard to generate, an extreme example being sexual orientation, where only qualitative data is available. However, the major problem identified by Osborne in the context of diversity lay in reconciling adverse impacts in cases of conflict of interest between different strands of the EO&D dimension.

Intersectionality

This brings us to the need to address the potential value of intersectionality to further policy planning and development. It has been argued that the Northern Ireland model underpinned by the concept of intersectionality could offer a way forward for the EHRC (Bagilhole, 2008, forthcoming).

Gender mainstreaming as an equality instrument has been seriously encouraged by the EU. However, it has become increasingly common to talk about diversity and multiple discrimination in the EU. The legal basis for this development is found in the Lisbon Treaty, which identifies six key EO&D strands as requiring measures to combat discrimination: sex, racial and ethnic origin, disability, age, religion or belief, and sexual orientation (see Chapter Seven). Gender mainstreaming is now seen as a potential way forward for equality and diversity mainstreaming (E&DM), which incorporates these other strands of social differentiation.

The concept of intersectionality stresses the importance of the intersecting nature of various prohibited grounds of discrimination. In this way, EU policies on diversity and feminist theories of intersectionality could be seen to be pointing in the same direction. Intersectionality as a theory and methodology for research could be a springboard for the operationalisation of a social justice agenda based on E&DM. The concept of intersectionality could offer a theoretical base for the potential of trans-issue mobilisation, as it usefully illuminates the multiple, intersecting, interlacing nature of complex social relations both between and within socially disadvantaged groups in society. This can be useful for the development of EO&D policy as it raises important points concerning the fact that subject positions are multiple and questions complacent assumptions about the homogeneous nature of disadvantaged groups (see Chapter Two). However, its very complexity must in some way be contained to allow its utility for the reality and practicality of EO&D policy making.

Utilising the concept of intersectionality as used in McCall's (2005) second ('intracategorical') and third ('intercategorical') approaches may be a way forward for this process of recognition of multiple and intersecting disadvantage and the strategic reconstruction of the recognition of group social disadvantage that can underpin policies (see Chapter Three). Social divisions in society can be seen to be socially constructed and to manifest themselves in individuals in different ways, with a different impact at different times and in different circumstances. The relationships between gender, race, disability, sexual orientation, religion or belief, and age are dynamic and interactive, and often complex, but can and do form particular subjects and groupings that can be addressed through EO&D policy.

Brah (1992) used the intracategorical approach in her intensive, in-depth study of Asian women, revealing the complex nature of the daily, lived experiences of a previously invisible group. In this way, intersectionality accepts traditional categories, albeit critically, and uses them to identify and study finer points of intersections. McCall (2001) used the intercategorical approach in her research. She also referred to it as the 'categorical' approach, which gives us an obvious clue as to how it differs from the intracategorical approach – it strategically uses existing categories. It 'begins with the observation that there are relationships of inequality among already constituted social groups, as imperfect and ever changing as they are, and takes these relationships as the center of analysis' (McCall, 2001: 525). Unlike the qualitative, case study approach of Brah that analysed intersectionality within a single group, this approach analyses intersectionality between categories. For example, such an approach would not look simply at the effect of race on income, but at how that effect differs for men and women, and for women of higher and lower class, and men of higher and lower class. Thus, it is a comparative approach that lends itself to a quantitative methodology:

> It is not the intersection of race, class, and gender in a single social group that is of interest but the relationships among the social groups defined by the entire set of groups constituting each category. (McCall, 2005: 1787)

These two approaches to intersectionality offer a useful way into the political and policy making EO&D arena, allowing for the complexity and diversity of group differences and inequalities. The issue of violence against women provides an example of how these approaches might compliment each other in analysis for policy making. An intercategorical analysis by race, ethnicity, class, disability, sexual orientation, religious belief and age could be used to identify any categories that potentially need further and specialist interrogation. Intracategorical analysis of those particular groups identified could then be undertaken to see how the issue actually works in practice and is made visible through the day-to-day experiences of women who suffer violence. This could then be used to produce specialised positive action measures to tackle the problem.

An intersectional perspective can be the anchor for more complex, trans-issue analysis and a way forward for EO&D policy making. The concepts and theories of intersectionality can make a contribution towards dealing with some of the difficulties thrown up by the Northern Ireland model and adequately consider policy issues that transcend different interest groups.

Conclusion to Part One

In practice, the enforcement burden of EO&D legislation in Britain has predominantly rested on individuals bringing cases before Employment Tribunals, rather than agency enforcement. This could be adjusted back to the original intention of a strategic enforcement approach by a powerful and proactive EHRC.

The Northern Ireland model outlined in this chapter may point a way forward for the EHRC that would avoid some of the potential pitfalls identified by those critical of the amalgamation of the original single equality commissions. It is an exemplary example of EO&D equality and diversity mainstreaming with potential for duplication in other countries. This would be most useful if the issue of the complexity of diversity, and even the problem of conflicts of interest across and within disadvantaged groups, identified in the NI model, were approached from an intersectional perspective.

It would seem that the intersectional approaches that McCall (2005) identified as intracategorical and intercategorical could be a very fruitful way forward for the development of EO&D policy based on research evidence, building on and countering some of the problems of the Northern Ireland model in NI. These approaches acknowledge and illuminate those cases where disadvantages interplay and coincide, or conflict between and within groups where new policy approaches need to be considered. Thus intersectionality alerts us to the need to fine-tune policy in a more sophisticated manner than in the past.

Part Two: organisational approaches to EO&D policies

Research suggests that the debates around what EO&D really means at an organisational level raise many questions. Fundamental examples include:

- Do we mean 'equality of opportunity' or 'equality of outcome'? (Jewson and Mason, 1986)
- How much inequality or reward differential should there be in total in an organisation? (Cockburn, 1991)

The resulting confusion points to the need for a rounded, educational approach to EO&D, rather than a narrow 'implementation of procedures' approach. In other words, these issues need to be discussed and be part of awareness-training programmes within organisations to help the effective implementation of formal policies and procedures by changing organisational culture.

Because of this complexity, EO&D needs a 'long' agenda rather than a 'short' one (Cockburn, 1991). Several reasons account for this imperative. As some EO&D issues are dealt with, others arise; there are often no easy solutions and in some cases no 'right' answers; and one standard set of policies cannot suit the needs of all organisations. In addition, organisations need to commit resources to ensure the acceptance and implementation of their EO&S policies. For example, they may need to:

- provide awareness training;
- alter buildings to make them accessible and user-friendly for disabled people;
- provide nurseries and personal leave schemes for staff at all levels; and
- ensure workloads that recognise that staff may have caring responsibilities.

EO&D is not just about conforming to procedures, but also about how organisations function on a formal and informal level and the outcomes of this for employment and service delivery. We can take EO&D just to mean avoiding unjust discrimination and prejudice, or in other words rationally and impartially treating everyone the same. However, this is a very simple and rather superficial conceptualisation, which does not expose the complexity of the social, political and economic issues that are contained in the concept (see Chapter Three). Marshall (1994) takes us further in the attempt to unpick the concept of EO&D at an organisational level. He recognised three main types of approach, which may help us in our search for a fuller understanding by enabling a more penetrating examination of the complex concept of EO&D. The definitions get deeper and more radical as they progress.

First, there is **'equality of opportunity'**, which is the provision of equality of access to institutions and social positions among social groups. An example of this is the absence of formal rules that prohibit women's entry to a university education in a physical science, engineering or technology discipline. However, despite this, women enter these disciplines in relatively small numbers.

Second, Marshall (1994) offers us the concept of **'equality of condition'**, that is, equality not only of access but also in the circumstances of life for different social groups. It is possible to maximise 'equality of opportunity' without attending to 'equality of condition', as we have seen in the example of university education; merely allowing equal access does not resolve unequal chances of achievement. Proponents of 'equality of opportunity' who relish the differential benefits obtained by persons with different resources ignore the basis of the material and cultural advantages that some groups in society possess and others lack. Inequalities of 'condition' can be said to obstruct real 'equality of opportunity' because all those who are competing do not start from the same point.

Finally, there is **'equality of outcome'**. This offers a radical approach to EO&D: the application of different policies or processes to different social groups in order to transform inequalities of condition at the beginning into equalities at the end. An example here is positive action in favour of women in offering them access courses to disciplines where they are severely under-represented, such as physical sciences, engineering and technology. This could compensate for inequalities of 'condition', such as the lack of relevant qualifications due to inappropriate choices at lower levels of education, which, it can be argued, restrict their 'equality of opportunity'. Jencks (1988) described this approach as the favourable treatment of those who have been disadvantaged by previous and historical discrimination and disadvantage, which leads us to the important and challenging idea that 'past disadvantages require us to treat people unequally' (Jencks, 1988: 48).

Parekh (1992) is one writer who has advocated the idea of **'preferential treatment'** for disadvantaged groups, because 'in spite of its limitations it is one of the few policy tools capable of breaking through the self-perpetuating cycle of deeply entrenched inequalities' (Parekh, 1992: 278). On the other hand, Cunningham (1992) argued against this position. He took the fundamental view that, because the source of many inequalities of 'condition' start early in life and are personal, it 'would require considerable intrusion on individual liberty and the family, and this is both unrealistic and impossible to enforce' (Cunningham, 1992: 178).

As we see again EO&D remains a contested concept often determined by one's political commitments and general fundamental outlook on society and life.

EO&D in practice

The various different views and theories of EO&D make it a complex concept. Although it is important to look at the ideas behind it to further our understanding, if we get too bogged down in the theory we may lose sight of the practicalities and demands of application to different groups in different societies at different times. It is therefore useful to measure the relative merits of these different approaches on a more practical and applied level. The justifications for these approaches must be set in a social, political, economic and even organisational context. This may lead to the disentanglement of what appear to be contradictions and philosophical flaws. As Blakemore and Drake (1996: 75) pointed out, 'although there are important philosophical arguments to consider in relation to different concepts of equal opportunity, they cannot be applied as absolute principle'. EO&D is a matter of social policy, and as such is affected by political, economic and practical considerations. It is open to debate, different priority setting and ultimately decisions on the desirability of outcomes. The next section will consider theories around the more practical application of EO&D at an organisational level.

It is a reality that in employment some groups in our society are severely disadvantaged because of their race, gender, disability, sexual orientation, religion or belief, age or other factors, or a combination of these. Such people are disadvantaged in a variety of ways. For example:

- they may be less likely to get high-paid or high-status jobs in the first place;
- when they are employed they may be confined to particular types of jobs, such jobs generally being the most menial, the worst paid, and the least likely to carry promotion prospects;
- they may be subjected to harassment on the grounds of their sex, race, disability, sexual orientation, religion or belief, or age;
- they may suffer from institutional practices that indirectly discriminate against them.

Employers cannot be expected to tackle all of these causes of inequality, many of which are deeply embedded in the institutions and attitudes of society. However, they can carry out EO&D policies that seek to alleviate some of their worst effects.

Theory of EO&D in organisations

Cheung-Judge and Henley (1994: 4) argue that, at the organisational level, the 'equality of treatment' approach to EO&D means 'policies and practices [that] do not result in any individual or group receiving less favourable treatment on grounds that are not material'. They offer a detailed list of immaterial grounds: race, colour, ethnic or national origin, creed, gender, marital status, religious belief, class, disability and sexuality. Even so, other grounds can always be added, for example, the social division of age has grown in significance and recognition through legislation. Action on these issues usually takes the form of the introduction of regulations on procedures and practices that are designed to eradicate discriminatory practice and ensure equal treatment. While this is certainly an important aspect of reducing disadvantage, it could be argued that it is not sufficient, in that it does not recognise or acknowledge the ideas of different needs and the different capabilities of different people.

We can move on from this approach to differentiate institutional policies and practices based on outcomes and results – the **'equality of outcome'** approach. At the end of the 1980s, the CRE (1989) undertook research to assess the impact of its Code of Practice, which was designed to eliminate racial discrimination and promote EO&D in employment. The survey of 899 employers revealed a high level of awareness of the code, but only at a basic level. About two-thirds of employers had formal written policies. However, very few of these policies were comprehensive with effective monitoring in place. The CRE identified the differentiation between procedures and outcomes. Many employers mistakenly assumed that 'once the processes and procedures were put right the organisation would be an equal opportunity employer, irrespective of the end result' (CRE, 1989: 37).

This essential difference between procedures and outcomes was taken up by Jewson and Mason (1986) when they conceptualised EO&D into two basic approaches: the 'liberal' and 'radical' perspectives. They later extended these to identify three distinct positions on EO&D: the 'minimalist' position, 'liberal' perspective and 'radical' perspective (Jewson and Mason, 1993). The **minimalist** perspective, commonly encountered in private industry and among politicians of the right, assumed that market decisions will maximise fairness, and only individual irrationality and prejudice introduce distortions. The **liberal** perspective went a stage further, starting from the premise that EO&D exists when all individuals are enabled freely and equally to compete for social rewards and policy makers are required to ensure that the rules of competition are not discriminatory. It took on the 'equality of treatment' approach, assuming that a 'level playing field' will ensure EO&D, and recognising that institutional discrimination may exist in the form of unfair procedures and practices. The task of EO&D was seen as the elimination of barriers to free competition between individuals. It emphasised the development of fair, bureaucratic and formal procedures and rules for recruitment and selection, and training in these procedures: 'For liberals the aim of the policy is to ensure that procedural justice is done and seen to be done (Jewson et al, 1995: 51). This approach was favoured by private businesses that recognised that these policies produced insurance against potential future legal problems and difficulties, and preserved a reputation for good employment practice or paternalism, which was good for public relations and thus gave a commercial advantage.

The **radical** perspective took EO&D on to another plain by adopting the 'equality of outcome' approach. This was most often encountered in local authorities and on the political left. In contrast to the other two approaches, it 'seeks to intervene directly in workplace practices in order to achieve a fair distribution of rewards among employees ... [it is] primarily concerned with the outcome of the contest rather than the rules of the game' (Jewson et al, 1995: 7). It rejected individualistic conceptions of fairness and placed it at the level of the group. This was seen as a far more politicised approach and training programmes were directed at raising 'the consciousness of the oppressed and the oppressors' (Jewson et al, 1995: 8).

In practice, Jewson and Mason acknowledged that the approaches they identified were 'ideal types' not seen in a pure form in reality. They argued that in fact those engaged in forming EO&D policies were 'rarely theoretically or logically consistent' and 'practical political pressures as well as confused thinking often led to a mixing of the liberal and radical approaches' (Jewson et al, 1995: 24). Cockburn (1989) examined their conceptualisation and argued that their dichotomy of the 'liberal' and 'radical' approaches was not an adequate interpretation of what was really happening. She built on their theory by suggesting and adding the idea that organisations in pursuit of EO&D for women adopted either a **'short'** or a **'long agenda'**. The short agenda was broadly akin to the liberal approach, and introduced new measures to minimise bias in recruitment and promotion. The long agenda by contrast 'has to be recognised as a project of transformation for organisations ... it brings into view the nature and purpose of institutions and the processes by which the power of some groups over others in institutions is built and renewed' (p 35). So it favoured the radical approach, but went further because it 'looks for change in the nature of power, in the melting away of the white male monoculture' (Cockburn, 1989: 35).

Morris and Nott (1991) advocated the 'radical' approach of different treatment in the area of gender, which acknowledges previous and present inequality of condition. Their argument ran along the lines that:

> Eliminating discrimination and outlawing different treatment between men and women does not represent 'equality of opportunity' because it does not and cannot address the fundamental disadvantages that women experience throughout their lives. To aim simply to eliminate discrimination and ensure equal treatment, as opposed to 'equality of opportunity', is tantamount to asserting that the Ritz is open to all – the availability of a facility does not mean that everyone has the wherewithal to take advantage of it. Thus, an employer who espouses an 'equal opportunities' policy and advertises jobs accordingly is doubtless to be commended, but the policy is meaningless if no woman is in a position to apply because of the age limits imposed or the qualifications demanded or if the hours required rule out those with domestic commitments.
> (Morris and Nott (1991: 193)

As they acknowledged:

> Special treatment for women in the form of additional rights, positive action or positive discrimination might be said to advance the cause of equality of opportunity, but this is at the cost of equal treatment ... the argument that according special treatment to women implies discrimination against men ... has to be faced. (Morris and Nott, 1991: 194)

Cockburn's (1989) long agenda approach has not been widely recognised or adopted. Within organisations, the original push to get EO&D on the agenda was often a 'radical' one, but when accepted by management it can and often does become institutionalised as a matter of procedures. There is an emphasis now on considering EO&D as part of general organisational change theory. Opportunity Now (2001), the government-backed campaign to increase women's participation in management, both in terms of numbers and their position, was heavily based on this approach, stressing the rationale for EO&D as good business practice. So too is much of the research done on women in management, which often concentrates on the stresses placed on women in the workplace, but largely suggests methods of adaptation and assimilation, rather than suggesting that a cultural change within the organisation is appropriate (see Marshall, 1994).

Squires (1999) highlighted the contentious nature of approaches to EO&D for women in her analysis of the different feminisms that back them up (see Chapter Three of this volume). She sighted three feminist political strategies:

- **'Inclusion'** based on the principle of **equality**. This took the form of anti-discrimination policies, and aspired to impartiality and gender neutrality. It was supported by liberal feminism, and involved inserting women where women were not.
- **'Reversal'** based on the principle of **difference**. This approach was coherent with difference feminism. It sought recognition for a specific, different female-gendered identity. The problem was located in the dominance of a male norm. The solution was seen as transforming patriarchal norms, and recognition of women's identities and norms.
- **'Displacement'** based on the principle of **diversity**. This aimed at deconstructing, destabilising and displacing oppositions of male to female. It is illustrated in questions such as: Equality with whom? It sought to displace patriarchal gender hierarchies and deconstruct discursive regimes that engender the subject.

Squires (1999) argued that the strategy of inclusion is fundamentally an integrationist approach, and that only strategies of reversal and displacement might be transformative. In the UK, we could argue that we mainly have an inclusion strategy, and a little bit of reversal in family-friendly policies, but no radical displacement policies.

Kandola and Fullerton (1998) adopted and advocated a **'management of diversity'** approach. The reason for this was to try to avoid and circumvent the inertia, stigma and resistance that had grown up around EO&D policies based on disadvantaged categories and minorities. They attempted to pull it out of the political domain, arguing that 'diversity' recognised that there are visible and non-visible differences between people that will include factors such as sex, race and disability as well as background, and even personality and work style. They argued that harnessing all these differences should create a more productive environment, in which everyone felt valued, where their talents were fully utilised, and in which organisational goals were met. The 'managing diversity' approach was depicted as being distinct from EO&D in several ways, as shown in *Box 6.3*.

Box 6.3: EO&D versus the managing diversity approach

EO&D	Diversity management
Externally initiated	Internally driven
Legally driven	Business needs driven
Quantitative focus (numbers)	Qualitative focus (improving environment)
Problem focused	Opportunity focused
Assumes assimilation	Assumes pluralism
Reactive	Proactive
Race, gender and disability	All differences

Diversity management was supposed to lead to a creative mix in the workplace that led to economic growth. This was obviously linked to the business case (see Chapter Four). However, this approach was criticised primarily for being individualistic and therefore not addressing the issue of group inequality within an organisation.

Rees (1998) argued that **'gender mainstreaming'** (GM) was a systematic approach to integrating a gender perspective into analysis, procedures and policies. The goal was to take account of gender in all aspects and at all stages of policy making by focusing on the adverse effects of all policies on both women and men and addressing and rectifying persistent and emerging inequalities between them.

GM has been widely adopted by the EU and other international agencies. The United Nations (UNESCO, 1997) provided a definition:

> Mainstreaming a gender perspective is the process of assessing the implications for women and men of any planned action, including legislation, policies or programmes, in any area and at all levels. It is a strategy for making women's as well as men's concerns and experiences an integral dimension of the design, implementation, monitoring and evaluation of the policies and programmes in all political, economic, and societal spheres so that women and men benefit equally, and inequality is not perpetuated. The ultimate goal is to achieve gender equality.

GM concentrated on the reorganisation of every policy process so that gender equality was reflected in all planning and decision making. GM was said to move beyond previous EO&D methods that focused on equal treatment or even positive action, which used specific or targeted gender equality policies attending to women's different needs or perceived 'deficiencies'. It was said to move from an 'equality of treatment' approach to an 'equality of impact' approach. Therefore, GM often includes gender-sensitive as well as women-specific policies and programmes.

There was also an acknowledgement in the GM approach that gender did not work in isolation but in relation to other factors such as race, ethnicity, disability, sexual orientation, religion or belief, and age. As an illustration of this, the Center for Women's Global Leadership (2001) introduced an **intersectional analysis** of policy as part of gender mainstreaming. It argued that:

> These methodologies will not only underline the significance of the intersection of race, ethnicity, caste, citizenship status for marginalized women etc but serve to highlight the full diversity of women's experiences. (Center for Women's Global Leadership, 2001: 1)

The methodology they advocated at an organisational level had four distinct components:

- data collection – dependent on availability of desegregated data;
- contextual analysis – probing 'beneath the single identity to discover other identities that may be present and contribute to the situation of disadvantage' (Center for Women's Global Leadership, 2001: 5);

- intersectional review of policy initiatives and systems of implementation in terms of their efficacy in addressing problems faced by intersectional identities;
- implementation of intersectional policy initiatives based on above.

In this respect, intersectionality may be a way of moving E&OD policies forward, as was argued in Part One of this chapter. Verloo (2006) argued that policies addressing multiple inequalities should be developed as strategies at the organisational level. However, she argued that the fact that inequalities across the different strands recognised in legislation are dissimilar, and not independent but interacting, means that EO&D mainstreaming cannot be a simple adaptation of gender mainstreaming. Whether thinking of training, or impact assessment of policies, a clear conceptualisation of how intersectionality operates is needed. The method frequently used in organisations to deal with multiple inequalities is to ask for comments or advice from different groups representing specific inequalities in an additive way. This pays no attention to existing intersectional inequality.

Verloo (2006) offered two possible ways forward in using intersectionality in the policy-making process within organisations:

- Start where GM exists and take advantage of the existence of some infrastructures, routines, methods and tools, but encompass intersectional inequality.
- Develop other forms of mainstreaming (for example, race/ethnicity mainstreaming), start with similarities between groups while systematically exploring different inequalities.

Case studies

The following two case studies of different organisations' approaches to EO&D seek to bring to life the actual practical experience of attempting to create effective policies. Of course the approaches already examined are ideal types and the reality of EO&D approaches at organisational level is usually a mixture of approaches. However, often one approach tends to predominate.

Case study one (see Bagilhole, 2006 for the full discussion)

The first case study looks at a public sector organisation that took a predominantly proceduralist, liberal approach to EO&D. This was not an exclusively equal treatment approach, as it was tempered by some positive measures in terms of family-friendly policies. However, little attempt has been made at cultural change (Cockburn's 'long agenda'). This has negative consequences for the efficacy of the policies and created something of a backlash.

The large public sector organisation in question was one of the more active organisations in its sector in setting up and establishing relatively comprehensive EO&D structures, policies and practices. For example, codes of practice were issued on recruitment and selection, internal promotions, staff appraisal, harassment and bullying, disability, race and gender equality. An EO&D statement was included on all job advertisements and an action plan developed by all departments, which was annually monitored by the EO&D Committee. Family-friendly policies were introduced including maternity, adoption, paternity, compassionate and parental leave schemes, a workplace crèche/nursery, a school holiday play scheme, and formal schemes for flexible working hours and jobsharing. However, the organisation was large (over 2,500 staff) and diverse in terms of occupations, which suggested a challenge in terms of the effective communication of policies and their acceptance and use by all categories of staff.

Findings

Awareness of EO&D policies

The level of awareness of the institutional EO&D policies varied considerably:

- the vast majority of women and men across all occupational categories of staff were similarly aware of the general EO&D policy statement, and harassment and bullying policy;
- more women than men were aware of the work based crèche/nursery (75% women, 66% men) and compassionate leave scheme (70% women, 58% men);
- only around half of both women and men were aware of the maternity leave and flexible working schemes;
- other policies were even less well known, including the school holiday play scheme (42% women, 35% men), paternity leave scheme (38% both) and parental leave scheme (22% women, 21% men).

Use of EO&D policies

The use of EO&D policies was considerably lower than the awareness of them. Only 22% of the women and 9% of the men had used any of the policies. The vast majority of policies that had been used by the women were child or family related (11% compassionate leave, 2% crèche/nursery, 1% maternity leave and 1% parental leave). Only 4% of the women had used the harassment policy, and 2% EO training. Of the tiny minority of men who had used policies, most had used EO training (5%), only 2% had used the harassment policy, and 1% had used the paternity leave scheme.

Significantly, nearly two-thirds (64%) of the women and the vast majority (82%) of the men stated that they were not likely to use any EO&D policies in the future. For men, the reasons centred mostly on the fact that they perceived these policies as being for women only and certainly not for white, childless or heterosexual men:

> "I'm a white, heterosexual male without children so there aren't any for me!" (Male, 31–40 age group)

Even men with young children did not see the policies as relating to them, or they felt that it was not fully accepted that they could use them and therefore that they may be penalised for doing so.

> "The honest answer is that if you do there is the fear of being criticised and labelled a problem." (Male, 51–60 age group)

Benefits of EO&D policies

Overall just over two-thirds of women (69%) and just under two-thirds of men (61%) thought that EO&D policies were beneficial to mothers, but less than half thought they were beneficial to childless women (42% women and 48% men). While 42% of women thought they were beneficial to fathers, only 29% of men agreed. The group that were thought to benefit least by both women and men were childless men (31% and 21% respectively).

The comments from respondents to explain their views on who benefited from EO&D policies very much revolved around two axes; the axis of gender, and the axis of parenting, which in many cases overrode the axis of gender. First, the gender axis manifested itself in the view by mostly male respondents that they did not benefit from EO&D policies. The following comment illustrated this view:

> "I believe that many equal opportunities initiatives are in place for the benefit of women only." (Male, 51–60 age group, married, partner works part-time, children school age and over 18)

This leads on to the second axis, which revolved around the view that parents were the ones that benefited, as this was how EO&D policies were focused. It was felt that that having children, whatever your gender, was more of a factor than gender per se in whether or not you benefited from a policy. Some felt that EO&D policies were only geared towards those with family commitments.

> "Specific provision exists for men or women with children. There seems to be no comparable support mechanisms for single people." (Female, 31-40 age group, no children)

There was also the contrary view that women did not benefit, particularly those with children:

> "Women seem to be held back – either with or without children, but more so with children." (Female, 31-40 age group, no children)

Some women voiced negative experiences after using EO&D policies:

> "There is still the attitude that if women work then they should be treated as men, eg full time with no time off for the children. Even though the policies are there you feel awkward and guilty taking any time off for children." (Female, 41-50 age group, children of school age and over)

Some respondents, while agreeing that people with children benefited more from the policies, felt that fathers benefited less than mothers. The opinion that mothers benefited most was frequently expressed in a rather negative way, particularly by other women, who saw it as affecting their own workload and choice of time off. As most women work with other women, it would be interesting to know how much women are compensating for mothers who legitimately make use of EO&D policies, as insufficient support may be put into an institution to cover this potential problem.

> "From my long experience of work as a woman without children, I have had to 'carry' those who have had to have time off to care for their children. This has been in the form of extra work – always having to work earlier and later hours and always having last choice of holiday dates." (Female, 51-60 age group, married, no children)

Conclusion

The final picture in this case study organisation is a mixed one, but does tend to reinforce and reflect previous research in this field. There was a varied level of awareness of specific EO&D policies within the organisation. The take-up of policies was low, and differentiated by gender. The policies were perceived as differentially benefiting different groups categorised by gender and whether or not they had children. Mothers were seen to benefit most, then childless women and fathers, and childless men were seen to benefit least. A minority of respondents actually felt that the policies disadvantaged certain groups. Childless women were seen to be most disadvantaged, then mothers, followed by childless men and lastly fathers. So we again see a mixed picture and quite complex and sometimes contradictory reasons for these views.

While over two-thirds of the men agreed that concessions to allow fathers to spend more time with their families should be incorporated into EO&D policies, only an extremely small minority had used or intended to use these types of policy. The research reported here reflects previous work by Cockburn (1991) that highlights the underlying norms and beliefs that these policies are more appropriate for women, and that men are apprehensive about utilising them in terms of their careers.

The case study shows some implementation and commitment to EO&D policies, but nevertheless indicates ineffective communication, lack of strong support and encouragement within the organisation's hierarchy to make use of such policies, and, in some places, quite powerful resistance to them. EO&D policies were initiated and controlled by the human resources department, with the underlying assumption that the provision of detailed instructions on how to behave would result in improved practice. However, this type of bureaucratic approach was perceived as being imposed from above, without any apparent raising of awareness or ownership elsewhere in the organisation, creating perceived conflicts between different groups. This conflict manifested itself at times in resistance and hostility, and can be seen to revolve either around an axis of gender or one of having children or not. Interestingly, a perceived strong focus on family friendliness can mean that the 'child dimension' overrides the gender axis.

As Cockburn (1989) argued, EO&D policies must have a 'long agenda' that includes serious measures to change the culture of the organisation. However, there are arguments for going further and acknowledging and dealing with the disaffection of men generally, and the resentment of fathers and childless women and men towards these policies. Conventional EO&D measures focus on women as having problems rather than on changing organisational culture. As a result, women are seen as inadequate and men

– and even some women – become resentful of the 'special treatment' accorded to them. Changing perceptions cannot be achieved through conventional personnel-based bureaucratic approaches, which are invariably based on equal treatment with some additional measures to support under-represented groups. As Liff and Cameron (1997: 39) argued, this 'overall approach is formalistic and aims to achieve behavioural compliance rather than change understandings, values or attitudes'.

Case study two (*see Bagilhole, 1993 for a fuller discussion*)

The second case study examines another public sector organisation, a local government authority that moved from a mainly liberal approach to a more radical EO&D mainstreaming approach that made attempts at cultural change. Change came about in response to pressure from a variety of sources. There was political pressure from the black community, radical disabled people's organisations and women's groups, and a radical county branch of the Labour Party; and commitment from the leader of the council and his leadership team.

The local authority was innovative in its move to a more radical, mainstreaming approach. It set up centralised structures to implement corporate EO&D policies covering both employment and service delivery across all departments. It included radical council-wide changes in the areas of recruitment, selection and appointment procedures; training; monitoring; strategies for anti-racist, anti-sexist and anti-discriminatory policies across all service delivery departments; grievance and disciplinary procedures covering EO&D issues, including discriminatory behaviour and harassment; and relevant and purposeful forms and structures for consultation with the community. The councillors gave EO&D a pre-eminent place on the policy agenda. They introduced policy innovations that cut across all departments' responsibilities and involved fundamental changes in some areas. Strategies for policy development and implementation went to the very heart of the organisation, creating a centralised EO&D machinery.

EO&D implementation machinery

The implementation of the EO&D strategy comprised three stages:

- establishing an 'integrated' EO&D department;
- setting up a new committee structure;
- consulting with the community.

Integrated EO&D department

The local authority decided to adopt an 'integrated' approach to EO&D. This involved linking common EO&D issues surrounding race, gender and disability (the only areas covered by EO&D legislation at the time were race and gender) into coherent policies across both employment and service delivery areas.

A centralised 'integrated' EO&D department was set up as the principal mechanism for pursuing the corporate policy on EO&D and to act as a catalyst. This was a completely independent department funded from the council's mainstream budget and accountable to its own powerful sub-committee. It had 26 members of staff, including administrative back-up. The staff worked in four teams containing specialist officers in each of the three areas of race, gender and disability. The teams covered:

- employment;
- training;
- community and departmental liaison; and
- research.

Each team worked in two dimensions: as an integrated EO&D team and, when required, as a specialist. For example, the whole training team worked together on recruitment and selection training, but the women's training officer carried out women's assertiveness training.

The intention behind this integrated approach was to add impetus and strength to policies, to avoid competition and aid agreement between disadvantaged groups, and to eliminate the possibility of some issues involving multiple disadvantage or intersectional discrimination falling between two, or even three or more, stools. For example, the council's strategy to eliminate discrimination experienced by black women was introduced by the department, thus eliminating conflicts of interest that might have occurred between a separate race unit and a women's unit. Local authorities with separate units for race, women and disability were known to have suffered from this problem of 'possession' of various issues.

The EO&D department was set up to challenge and intervene in the decisions of all service-providing departments. It had high status in the organisation's hierarchy, with the ability to interact at every level, including chief officer and senior management level. The head of the department was a chief officer, ensuring that EO&D issues were kept on the agenda at weekly chief officer meetings where important corporate management decisions were made. EO&D could not be ignored, added on or at worst swept under the carpet through inaction at this crucial stage – an example of EO&D mainstreaming.

The EO&D officers had access to elected members through their own sub-committee and access to the organisation at strategic points. All service departments were required to consult with the EO&D department on policy decisions, and structures were set up to ensure that this happened. For example, a special section was established for detailing in all committee reports the full EO&D considerations for every issue and senior officers in the EO&D department were each given responsibility for a service committee. They acted as the liaison with their service department, participating in strategic meetings such as pre-agenda meetings, pre-committee meetings and committee meetings. They were therefore well placed to give advice and guidance at every stage of EO&D policy implementation and to monitor the policies once in place.

In the area of employment, the EO&D officers had the right to participate in all stages of staff recruitment within the authority, from the writing of job descriptions and personal specifications though to interviews. This was particularly important in the area of disability. Because discrimination on the grounds of disability was not prohibited by law at the time, the personnel policies of many organisations did not address the employment aspirations of disabled people. Disabled people had long been the poor relation of the EO&D family. However, in this case study, the 'integrated' approach ensured that disabled people's issues were on the agenda when recruitment procedures and practices were monitored. Accessibility of rooms was ensured, loop systems were provided as required, and special employment officers were available to give advice and guidance to the recruiting departments.

Linked to both employment and service delivery, training was considered to be an important mechanism in promoting EO&D policies within the local authority. Strategic initiatives included:

- compulsory training for all staff involved in recruitment and selection;
- training for members of the EO&D committee, including councillors;
- a requirement on chief officers of all departments to attend residential courses run by the EO&D department, leading to the production of an EO&D strategy and action plan for employment and service delivery across individual departments. These were then considered by the EO&D committee and relevant service committees to enable effective monitoring.

Committee structure

The EO&D department reported directly to an EO&D sub-committee, with strong channels of central influence. It was a sub-committee of the policy committee, the council's all-powerful parent committee, situated alongside the personnel and finance sub-committees. The chairs of all the council's service committees were members of the EO&D sub-committee. There was trade union representation on the sub-committee, and the chair and two vice-chairs of each of three community consultative forums (see below) also had full membership rights of the EO&D sub-committee, which included full voting rights until they were removed by the then Conservative government in the 1989 Local Government and Housing Act.

Community consultative structures

Meaningful EO&D policies have to be based on an understanding of the inequality experienced by disadvantaged groups as well as their aspirations. However, these groups do not normally have access to local authority decision-making structures. The case study local authority recognised the importance of women's, minority ethnic and disabled people's access to local decision making and their lack of it within their own organisation. Ways of enabling the opinions and needs of these communities to be heard and accepted by service department managers were perceived as essential to the success of EO&D policies. Therefore, after much consultation and negotiation, three community consultative forums were established:

- a women's forum;
- a disabled people's forum; and
- an ethnic minorities forum.

These forums met regularly every six weeks, fitting in with the committee cycle. They were serviced by officers and formal minutes were taken. Any resolutions passed at the forums were considered by the EO&D sub-committee and relevant service committees. Chief officers and senior managers were required to attend these forums on a regular basis to explain policies and answer any questions on them, and to report on any EO&D developments. They were then required to report back to the EO&D sub-committee and their respective service committees, a process that served as a way of monitoring their performance and making them accountable for both the policies and the consultation procedures. The forums offered normally disenfranchised groups the opportunity to experience the reality of local authority policies and procedures and potentially to influence them.

The authority encouraged its integrated approach to EO&D through the forums in two ways. First, full voting membership existed for minority ethnic and disabled women on the women's forum; women and disabled people on the ethnic minority forum; and minority ethnic people and women on the disabled people's forum. Second, there were some joint meetings of the forums where appropriate. The authority was aware of the differences between community co-option and consultation. Co-option was seen as the direct participation of representatives of outside groups, whereas consultation involved more distant and less continuous involvement. By implication co-option was more effective. This was the principle adopted by the authority when it gave the forums' representatives full membership of the EO&D sub-committee.

Conclusion

One suggested measure for the impact and effectiveness of EO&D policies is the coherence and comprehensiveness of the structures and processes set up to implement them. In this respect this local authority could be seen to have had some success in making radical changes within its organisation, which certainly mainstreamed the policies setting them centre stage and affected every department.

Discussion of emerging issues and concepts in EO&D policy implementation at organisational level

As EO&D policies are implemented in organisations, unintended consequences and unforeseen issues may emerge. We examine some of these below, including the concepts of 'critical mass', 'glass ceiling', 'sticky floor', 'glass cliff', 'trapdoor', and 'glass elevator or escalator'.

Critical mass

Kanter (1977) suggested that organisations with a better balance or **critical mass** (CM) of women would be more tolerant of difference and lead to the success of more women. CM theory investigates the question of 'How many people are needed to change an organisation culture?' (Morley, 1994: 195).

CM theory does have its dissenters. The magical statistic for the CM needed to change the culture of an organisation was defined by Kanter

(1977) as 15-20%, while Gale (1995) suggested 35%. Etkowitz et al (2000) were critical of the theory, arguing that the limited success of initiatives to increase numbers of women brings the theory into question. They pointed out that it matters what the proportion represented:

- if the women are homogeneous, they may self-isolate in different communities;
- if women are not free to associate, or work in different departments, the perpetuation of isolation may result.

CM has also been reported as having contradictory effects. As underlying conditions improve for the minority group, their situation may worsen as formerly repressed grievances come out. Rayman et al (1996) reported that as a CM of women appeared in medical schools, the rate of sexual harassment increased. One explanation for this is an increase in empowerment that leads to more complaints. Another explanation is an increase in perceived threat to the majority group, leading to more harassment. Bagilhole and White's (2008) study of women leaders in universities maintained that when women must be taken seriously because of proven ability, there is often a negative reaction from the dominant group. Powell et al (2006) found that younger women engineering students were often concerned that participating in activities for women would set them apart. This implied that the minority must gain power to overcome resistance as opposed to there being only a modest increase in numbers.

It would appear, then, that the issue is not simply one of the numerical representation of women but of women's ability to thrive as well as survive in organisations (Powell et al, 2006). Personal success for individual women does not equate with progress for women as a whole (Bagilhole, 2002b; Powell et al, 2006). Norris and Lovenduski's (2001) study of the representation of women in politics argued that CM theory depended on the existence of underlying differences in the values, attitudes and behaviour of the minority group. The result of assimilation and socialisation into a dominant male culture, attempts to 'fit in' that are counter to CM theory, reinforces rather than challenges the dominance of the majority group (Bagilhole, 2002b). This suggests that a CM of women is insufficient on its own and is unlikely to instigate organisational change.

Glass ceiling, sticky floor, glass cliff, trapdoor and glass elevator or escalator

The **glass ceiling** is still a reality for many women (Women and Work Commission, 2006). The term was first coined in the 1980s to describe an invisible barrier that women can see through but that prevents their rise to senior management and leadership positions (see Chapter Two for statistical evidence). The opposite of glass ceiling is **sticky floor** (Women and Work Commission, 2006). This is where women in low-skilled, low-paid jobs are denied access to higher-paid jobs because of a lack of training or promotion. They are not part of a career structure and therefore adhere to the bottom of their organisational hierarchy.

Although still under-represented in leadership roles, women's presence in management roles is greater than ever before (Davidson and Burke, 2000). Ryan and Haslam's (2005) research emphasised the context of women's appointments to leadership roles and demonstrated that women tend to get appointed under different circumstances than men, and are more likely to take over companies that have a consistently poor record of performance. They extended the glass ceiling metaphor to suggest that women were more likely than men to find themselves on a **glass cliff**. Women in such positions were likely to be exposed to unfair criticism and were in danger of being held responsible for negative events that were set in motion before their appointment.

Wilson-Kovacs et al (2006) argued that glass cliff positions, like glass ceilings, were not restricted to women, but affected other disadvantaged groups. Their research examined other factors circumscribing precarious appointments, such as lack of information and support from the immediate team and first-line superiors, lack of appropriate resources in dealing with everyday tasks, and ineffective networks of support in the organisations in which women operate. Wilson-Kovacs et al (2006: 683) argued for the presence of the 'pervasiveness of an invisible hegemonic culture that dominates professional fields and weakens organisational initiatives that seek to address women's unequal footing. As the present evidence suggests this informal culture fosters precariousness, which in turn can lead to lack of satisfaction at least and failure at most'. The consequences of dealing with new positions under these strains can be devastating for the individual (Bagilhole, 2002b). They are also costly for the organisation itself both in relation to EO&D initiatives set up to encourage wider participation in the first place, and in terms of performance and reputation with employees.

Crenshaw (1991) presented a graphic analysis of multiple disadvantage and how this affects who can make it through what she termed the **trapdoor** in the glass ceiling:

> Imagine a basement which contains all people who are disadvantaged on the basis of race, sex, class, sexual preference, age and/or physical ability. These people are stacked – feet standing on shoulders – with those on the bottom being

disadvantaged by the full array of factors, up to the very top, where the heads of all those disadvantaged by a single factor brush up against the ceiling.... A hatch is developed through which those placed immediately below can crawl. Yet this hatch is generally available only to those who – due to the singularity of their burden and their otherwise privileged position relative to those below – are in a position to crawl through. Those who are multiply-burdened are generally left below. (Crenshaw, 1991: 1265)

Williams and Villemez (1993) utilised the idea of a trapdoor in the opposite, downwards, direction. They pointed out that gender segregation in the workplace is reinforced by powerful social control mechanisms such as gender ideology, with men and women ascribed to separate spheres of employment. Childcare, for example, is commonly regarded as a 'natural' job for women, thus rendering it 'unnatural' for those men wanting to do it. They posited that men 'seem to enter female-dominated occupations ... through a "trapdoor" – most were not seeking entry' (Williams and Villemez, 1993: 66). The same metaphor is also deployed by Cameron et al (1999) and Bagilhole and Cross (2006) to explain how British men doing 'women's work' such as childcare appear to have fallen through an occupational trapdoor following a period of unemployment or redundancy. Here, the notion of a trapdoor could have a double meaning; it may serve as an escape route from unemployment as well as possibly a way of fulfilling a desire on their part to move into non-traditional work. Williams (1992) also looked at men in female-dominated workplaces and showed that they often pursued non-traditional employment, expecting to achieve senior positions in a relatively short time. She coined the phrase **glass escalator or elevator** to show how women could see these men's route to the top but could not join it.

Conclusion to Part Two

Organisational approaches to EO&D have varied considerably over time and continue to do so. Analysis and theories to explain these approaches have also changed. The approaches revolve around the difference between an emphasis on equal treatment and an emphasis on a more radical approach that allows different treatment according to different circumstances. In practice, as the two case studies in the chapter show, organisations tend to use a mixture of these 'ideal type' approaches. As EO&D policy making develops and changes, it throws up new phenomena, which call for analysis, explanation and conceptualisation. These include critical mass theory, and the concepts of the glass ceiling, sticky floor, trapdoor and glass elevator or escalator. A recent example of such change is the glass cliff: when women do succeed in breaking the glass ceiling and making it to the top of an organisation, they often find it difficult to succeed because they face a glass cliff – an uninitiated, precarious and unsupported position from which they are likely to fall. There is a need for continuing analysis of organisational practices and policies to tackle these issues as they arise.

Summary

Part One

- There is a 'two-pronged approach' to the enforcement of EO&D legislation; the provision for administrative agency enforcement through the former separate UK commissions has now been subsumed into the Equality and Human Rights Commission, and the right of individuals to take discrimination cases to Employment Tribunals.
- In practice, the enforcement burden of EO&D legislation in Britain has predominantly rested on individuals bringing cases before Employment Tribunals, rather than agency enforcement. This could be adjusted back to the original intention of a strategic enforcement approach by a powerful and proactive EHRC.
- The Northern Ireland model may point a way forward for the EHRC that would avoid some of the potential pitfalls identified by those critical of the amalgamation of the original single equality commissions.
- Research suggests that the debates around what EO&D really means at an organisational level raise many questions.

Part Two

- Research suggests that the debates around what EO&D really means at an organisational level raise many questions, and because of its complexity, EO&D needs a 'long' agenda rather than a 'short' one.
- There are various approaches to EO&D at organisational level, which are usually combined in different mixes within different organisations.
- As EO&D policy making develops and changes, it throws up new phenomena, which call for analysis, explanation and conceptualisation. These include critical mass theory, and the concepts of the glass ceiling, sticky floor, trapdoor, glass elevator or escalator, and glass cliff.

Questions for discussion

- What potential effect will the single EHRC have for EO&D development?
- Can we successfully take EO&D legislation out of its separate compartments?
- Can EO&D policies successfully take into account multiple discrimination?
- Can we expand gender mainstreaming to EO&D mainstreaming?
- Is it practical to have an intersectional framework for analysis of the EO&D policy process?

Further reading

Bagilhole, B. (1993) 'Managing to be fair: implementing equal opportunities in a local authority', *Local Government Studies*, vol 19, no 2, pp 163-75.

Bagilhole, B. (2006) 'Family-friendly policies and equal opportunities: a contradiction in terms?', *British Journal of Guidance and Counselling*, vol 34, no 3, pp 327-43.

Cockburn, C. (1991) *In the way of women: Men's resistance to sex equality in organizations*, London: Macmillan.

Dickens, L. (2007) 'The road is long: thirty years of equality Legislation in Britain', *British Journal of Industrial Relations*, vol 45, no 3, pp 463-94.

Hepple, B. (2006) 'The equality commissions and the future commission for equality and human rights', in L. Dickens and A. Neal (eds) *The changing institutional face of British employment relations*, Utrecht: Kluwer Law International, pp 101-14.

McCall, L. (2005) 'The complexity of intersectionality', *Signs: Journal of Women in Culture and Society*, vol 30, pp 1771-1800.

Parekh, B. (1992) 'A case for positive discrimination', in B. Hepple and E.M. Szyszak (eds) *Discrimination: The limits of law*, London: Mansell Publishing.

Powell, A., Bagilhole, B. and Dainty, A. (2006) 'The problem of women's assimilation into UK engineering cultures: can critical mass work?', *Equal Opportunities International, Special Issue, Gender Equality in Science, Engineering and Technology*, vol 25, no 8, pp 688-99.

Squires, J. (1999) *Gender in political theory*, Cambridge: Polity.

seven

The European Union: influence and effects on UK equal opportunities and diversity

Overview

This chapter:
- analyses the contribution of the European Union (EU) to equal opportunities and diversity (EO&D) policies in the UK;
- sets this analysis in the context of changes in national governments and their differing attitudes to the EU, from the 1970s to the present day;
- examines the 2007 European Year of Equal Opportunities for All.

Key concepts

Regulatory policy; soft law; equal pay; work of equal value; rights; representation; recognition; respect and tolerance

The UK joined the European Economic Community in 1973. This was renamed the European Union (EU) by the Maastricht Treaty in 1992. The term EU is used throughout this chapter even when European initiatives before 1992 are examined.

With the EU's increasing significance and influence on national legislation, it is important for any discussion of EO&D to look beyond national boundaries. Certainly in the area of equality between women and men, the EU has always been at the forefront of EO&D legislation and acted as a catalyst among member states. For example, the requirement for equal pay between women and men was included in the original EU Treaty of Rome in 1957. The preamble to the Treaty of Rome stated that its signatories were 'determined to lay the foundation of an ever closer union among the peoples of Europe' (Bagilhole, 1997: 78). Its objectives were the establishment of a common market, the approximation of member states' economic policies and the harmonious development of economic activities. To this end, it aimed to achieve the 'approximation of the laws of the member states to the extent required for the proper functioning of the common market' (Bagilhole, 1997: 78). Thus, the rationale behind equal pay for women and men was an economic one, with France arguing for its inclusion lest its own laws on equal pay put it at a disadvantage in the common market.

Gender equality policy is considered to be one of the EU's major success stories. However, the EU gender policy agenda has shifted from equal treatment to positive action; from 'hard' directives on equality to 'softer' legislation reconciling the competing demands of paid work and family life. This has affected policies in member states. In addition, since the late 1990s the EU has begun to accept and enforce its competency in other areas of EO&D, with the introduction of legislation on additional strands of equality including race, disability, religion or belief, sexual orientation and age.

The aims and principles of the EU dictate that its laws must be applied uniformly and have supremacy over conflicting national legislation. To enable EU Law to be enacted in the UK, it was necessary for Parliament to introduce the 1972 European Communities Act. This allowed EU laws to have effect in the UK without further UK legislation, but the Act is subject to the doctrine of parliamentary supremacy. In other words, it could, in principle, be repealed at any time. In 1992, there was further integration with the completion of the single European market, intended to give EU citizens the freedom to work, to establish businesses and to trade in other EU countries.

Legislation from the EU takes several different forms. Roelofs (1995) offers a useful distinction between two ways in which it is enacted, both of which have been used in the area of EO&D: 'regulatory policy' and 'soft law'. Regulatory policy takes the form of regulations and directives, both of which are binding on the member states. However, whereas regulations are immediately binding and rigidly applied in the form that has been mutually agreed, directives require member states to achieve a specific end result within a certain period of time through national legislation. Directives have been favoured in the past in the application of EO&D, particularly in the field of gender equality. They are only effective against the state, but the European Court of Justice (ECJ) has taken a broad view of what constitutes the state, including a variety of formerly autonomous bodies (see, for example, the UK case of *Foster v British Gas* in 1990). Soft law, on the other hand, takes the form of recommendations on policy goals. They attempt to influence member states, but have no sanctions attached to them. EO&D policy has tended to move more recently to this diluted form of regulation to attempt to ensure consensus.

Accession to the EU had a major impact on the UK's legal system, although the British government was firmly committed to the goal of ending sex discrimination, at least in the workplace, before becoming a member of the EU. The concept of equal pay, for example, was enshrined in law in the UK in 1970, before British accession to the EU in 1973, and although the 1975 Sex Discrimination Act (SDA) came after EU membership, it was inspired by domestic, political factors rather than any prompting from Europe. However, even previously established legislation, such as the Equal Pay Act (EPA) had to be amended to meet EU requirements (see Chapter Five). The EU can be seen to be fundamentally grounded in the issue of EO&D. Article 14 of the European Convention on Human Rights required that the other rights and freedoms secured under the convention 'shall be secured without discrimination on any ground such as sex, race, colour, religion, or political affiliation' (Bagilhole, 1997: 79).

In terms of policy outcomes, rather than just policy aims, the UK's political culture and policy delivery mechanisms have often placed it at variance with the EU approach. Successive British governments have adopted their own conception of what is meant by EO&D and their own methods of tackling the issue (see Chapter Four). As in many other policy areas, this often brought it into conflict with the EU. The UK has been characterised by a cautious, if not negative, approach to EU legislation. Between 1989 and 1997, successive Conservative governments showed a repeated reluctance to bring the UK into line with other member states.

Hard law

Gender policies

EO&D was originally seen by the EU largely in terms of gender (Spelling, 1995). Roelofs (1995) showed that, if we look at the EU's social policy framework in the 1980s and 1990s, there are only three areas in which it is clearly active. One is the equal treatment of women and men (the others being the coordination of social insurance schemes, and health and safety). Blakemore and Drake (1996: 42) argued that 'the teeth of European Community law are almost entirely felt in the area of equal opportunities for women'. As Meehan (1993a) demonstrated, gender equality was given 'pride of place' in EU legislation, while other areas, particularly race, were relatively ignored. Reasons suggested for this were twofold. First, as stated earlier, France insisted on equal treatment of women and men being included in the original Treaty, because it had already made policy moves in the area of equal pay for work of equal value and did not want unfair competition from other member states (Hantrais, 1993). Second, by concentrating on women's issues, the EU was reaching over 50% of its population, or, from a more cynical viewpoint, was convincing over 50% of its electorate that it was relevant and important (Roelofs, 1995).

As at European level, state involvement in EO&D began in the UK with substantial legislation. In the 1970s, a significant degree of congruence was achieved between British and EU objectives and methods, despite the UK's resistance to European jurisdiction. Each was concerned primarily with securing EO&D in the workplace, rather than with reconciling paid work and family life. Each turned to 'hard law', in the form of statute law in the UK (see Chapter Five) and directives at the European level.

The legal framework of EU law regarding equal treatment of women and men consisted of several directives, treaty terms and ECJ decisions as well as the general principle of the removal of sex discrimination as a fundamental right. It originated in Article 119 of the 1957 Treaty of Rome, which established the principle of equal treatment for women and men workers in terms of pay. It states:

> Each member state shall during the first stage ensure and subsequently maintain the principle that men and women should receive equal pay for equal work. For purposes of this article, 'pay' means the ordinary basic or minimum wage or salary and any other consideration whether in cash or in kind which the worker receives, directly or indirectly, in respect of his [sic] employment from his employer. Equal pay without discrimination based on sex means:
> a) that pay for the same work at piece rates shall be calculated on the basis of the same unit of measurement;
> b) that pay for the same work at time rates shall be the same for the same job. (Roelofs, 1995: 131)

This principle achieved very little until the 1970s, when there was a growth in the women's movement and a political climate that was more receptive to change. A series of five directives followed:

- a directive on equal pay, in 1975 (75/117/EEC, commonly known as the Equal Pay Directive);
- a directive on equal treatment, in 1976 (76/207/EEC, commonly known as the Equal Treatment Directive);
- a directive on equal treatment for men and women in matters of social security, in 1979 (79/7/EEC);
- a directive on equal treatment for men and women in occupational social security schemes, in 1986 (86/378/EEC);
- a directive on equal treatment for men and women in self-employment, in 1986 (86/613/EEC).

The Equal Pay Directive developed the principle of equal pay for work of equal value. In 1979, the EU found that the UK's 1970 Equal Pay Act (EPA) did not conform to this principle and subsequently forced its amendment (Maes, 1990: 55). The Equal Treatment Directive ruled out sex discrimination in access to employment, selection criteria, access to all jobs and all levels of the hierarchy, opportunities for training and vocational guidance, promotion procedures and other terms and conditions of employment. Exceptions were still possible where sex was a genuine occupational qualification for reasons of authenticity or the personal nature of the work, and for the protection of pregnant women and mothers (see Chapter Five for a discussion of how this corresponds to the UK SDA). The social security directive covered equal treatment in the area of statutory social security schemes for employed, self-employed, retired and invalided workers insured against sickness, redundancy, accidents at work, occupational diseases and non-contributory benefits. The directive on equal treatment in occupational social security schemes dealt with private occupational or non-statutory pension and insurance schemes, and the directive on equal treatment in self-employment covered self-employed people, especially in family businesses and in agriculture.

The principle of equal pay for work of equal value, developed in the Equal Pay Directive, seemed at first sight unproblematic for the UK, since it already had the EPA, which became fully operational in 1975. However, the ECJ judged that it should be strengthened because a woman could only obtain equal pay in respect of work that was exactly the same or of equal value to that of her male counterpart, but only if a job evaluation scheme or study had been implemented. The British government disagreed with the judgement, but pressure came from the EU in July 1982 for the UK to comply fully with its directive on equal pay. National legislation was finally changed on 1 January 1983. Now even two different jobs can be considered to have 'equal value' if they place equal demands on workers in terms of effort, skill and decision making. It is important, too, that traditional male abilities such as physical strength must not be given greater weight than what are considered to be typically female skills such as manual dexterity. Hence the following example:

> A female cook was held by an industrial tribunal to be employed on work of equal value with that of male painters, thermal insulation engineers and joiners working for the same employer. The jobs were assessed under five headings: physical demands; environmental demands; planning and decision making; skills and knowledge; and responsibility. The overall scores of the jobs were found to be equal. (Department of Employment, 1995: 4)

Similar problems arose with the UK's other major piece of EO&D gender legislation, the SDA. As with the EPA, pressure from the EU meant that the SDA had to be amended in 1986 to bring it into line with the Equal Treatment Directive. The employment provisions of the Act were extended to include private households, firms with five or fewer employees, and collective agreements relating to pay, which had previously been excluded.

The Equal Opportunities Commission (EOC) (see Chapter Five), set up as an independent body under the SDA, became an important EO&D actor at national and international level. European sex discrimination law was evoked on more occasions in the UK courts than in any other member state. The EU itself brought proceedings against the UK government to force its compliance, but the main protagonist was the EOC, invoking European law on behalf of individuals to win sex discrimination cases.

The Equal Treatment Directive has also been very influential in the area of pensions. Action programmes during the 1980s and later decisions by the ECJ made it unavoidable for the UK eventually to equalise retirement ages for women and men. Retirement age and subsequent pension entitlements for women and men had always been treated differently in the UK. Meehan (1993b) cites two examples of this:

- C–188/89 *Foster v British Gas plc* [1990], where the ECJ decided that female employees forced to retire at the age of 60, while men could continue until they were 65, must be entitled to compensation for loss of earnings.
- C–271/91 *Marshall v Southampton and South West Hampshire Area Health Authority* [1993]. Marshall complained that her compulsory retirement at 62 was less favourable treatment under the SDA. The complaint was rejected by the industrial tribunal on the grounds that the SDA excluded

retirement issues. Marshall then claimed that her forced retirement was contrary to the EU Equal Treatment Directive, and her case was upheld by the ECJ. The decision was based on the concept that compulsory early retirement constituted unfair dismissal rather than differences in pensionable age between men and women.

Another example of the influence of the EU's Equal Treatment Directive in UK law can be seen in the level of compensation given to women who were unlawfully dismissed from the armed forces because they became pregnant. The high compensation awards in these cases were allowed because the ECJ ruled in August 1993 that the £11,000 limit imposed by the UK government went against European law. In 1994, the first woman to have her case heard after the removal of the upper limit was awarded a record amount of £172,912 (EOR, 1994). However, European legislation in this area was criticised by some on the grounds that it was shaped on the principle of equal treatment for workers, which did little to break down 'stereotypes and to take account of the different, real experiences of men and women at work and in the family' (Meehan, 1993: 200).

The changes introduced by the UK government as a result of EU pressure appeared to have been carried out grudgingly, at the last possible moment, in the narrowest possible way and in a piecemeal fashion (Meehan, 1993b). Until the change in the voting system in 1986, with the introduction of qualified majority voting in the Single European Act, the UK blocked many of the proposed European EO&D directives, including those on parental leave, part-time work, the shifting of the burden of proof of discrimination from the complainant to the employer, and atypical work. Directive 92/85/EEC governing the protection of pregnant women at work came into force in 1992. However, the objections raised by the UK government meant that it was seriously neutralised and prescribed only the minimum norms. Over the years, the UK opposed the directive and attempted to water it down, and then finally implemented it in a minimalist way in the Trade Union Reform and Employment Rights Act of 1993 (Crawley and Slowey, 1995). The effect was that about 60% of women in the UK did not have automatic entitlement to maternity leave (Roelofs, 1995).

Soft law

Family reconciliation policies

From the mid-1980s onwards, while the EU concentrated its efforts on action programmes designed to allow for subsidiarity and exhorted member states to take their own initiatives to realise common goals, the policy environment in the UK was unusually hostile to calls for state or public intervention to secure EO&D (see Chapter Five). The New Right preached a creed of competition within a largely unregulated market as the only way forward in both pragmatic and idealistic terms. As Forbes (1991) argued, this led to the emergence of a conservative view of EO&D that celebrated inequality and claimed that the free market produced outcomes that cannot, technically, be found to be unjust.

The Conservative governments in power from 1979 to 1997 in the UK were opposed to any extension of EU control, especially in the field of social policy. As Roelofs (1995: 139) argued:

> EU law has given women more legal instruments with which to insist on an improvement in their position. But the restricted scope of the equal opportunities policy is largely a result of the decisive role which the member states themselves play in the Union's decision-making process.

Successive Conservative governments, determined to maintain a minimum level of regulation in the labour market, opted out of two notable developments of European legislation: the Community Charter of the Fundamental Social Rights of Workers (Social Chapter), approved by the EU in December 1989, and the Agreement on Social Policy, appended to the Maastricht Treaty in 1992. Their preference for non-state action, or soft law, remained intact (Bagilhole and Byrne, 2000). Even so, in 1994, the EU claimed that 'it is now widely recognised that the legal framework reflecting social policy at European Union level has been a catalyst for major social change in the Member States' (41) (Bagilhole and Byrne, 2000). Crawley and Slowey (1995: 8) also felt that EU influence had been a major benefit for women in the UK: 'Almost all the gains working women in the United Kingdom have made over the past decade can be traced to changes in legislation at the European level'.

In 1996, at the European Women's Summit hosted by the Italian Presidency of the EU, a 'Charter of Rome' was signed 'as a declaration of political will to promote the presence of women in decision-making' (Bagilhole and Byrne, 2000: 42). The member states that signed 'committed themselves to develop within their countries incentives, laws and regulatory measures to achieve a balanced participation of women and men in decision-making' (Bagilhole and Byrne, 2000: 42). There were only two member states that did not sign up to the charter: Spain, because it was in the process of forming a new government, and the UK, which refused to sign for political reasons. This obviously restricted the role that EU law could play in EO&D in the UK at the time. EU law was unquestionably moving towards equality as a fundamental right, but at this stage it was difficult to say exactly how this would affect UK law.

Using soft law, the EU made several recommendations in areas such as positive action (1984), education (1985) and vocational training (1987). A Recommendation on Childcare came into effect in 1992, intending to encourage more effective childcare, leave of absence arrangements for both parents from work, and a more equal distribution of responsibility between women and men for childrearing. The deterioration in the economic climate in Europe and political moves against regulatory policies from the EU led to the development, from the 1980s, of a series of EO&D action programmes for women rather than directives. These programmes concentrated on persuasion and carried no sanctions. The first, for 1982 to 1985, focused on consolidating and implementing existing legislation and attempting to promote positive action programmes. Despite many of these initiatives being limited and small in scale, the EU's assessment of them was positive and similar consolidating programmes were launched in later years. These covered technological change; the integration of women into the labour market; the improvement of the social position of women; 'gender mainstreaming' of EO&D through its integration into all policies measures and activities in the EU and its member states; support for projects aimed at identifying and transferring good practice; the conduct of studies and research; the implementation of any action to promote the exchange and dissemination of information on equal pay, equal treatment and equal opportunities; and the monitoring, analysis and assessment of action taken under the programmes (CEC, 1995).

The EU remained strongly committed to EO&D for women during this period, as the following statement demonstrates:

This adaptability and creativity of women is a strength that should be harnessed to the drive for growth and competitiveness in the EU. Lower activity rates of women in the EU (66%) compared to women in the USA, Japan and non-EU countries (72%) is a factor which militates against achieving greater competitiveness, especially given the current predominance of women in second- and third-level education in the EU and their generally higher educational attainments. (EC, 1994: 41)

Race policies

While the issue of gender has always been prominent at EU level, the same is not true for race. EU law was not as developed in the area of race discrimination as it was in sex discrimination; there were no comprehensive and effective measures to combat racial discrimination throughout the member states and in many states such measures were entirely absent

(Forbes and Mead, 1992). Sex discrimination, by contrast, had 'pride of place' in EU law (Meehan, 1993a). As Blakemore and Drake (1996: 41) put it: 'European legislation on gender and race equality could ... be seen as occupying the opposite ends of a spectrum from significant to minimal concern'. Given its proposals on EO&D for women, the EU demonstrated that it had the legal competence to tackle racial discrimination, and the lack of action on this issue represented a lack of political will and much less consensus among member states (Bagilhole and Byrne, 2000).

The European Parliament did call for the review and amendment of national legislation against political extremism, racism and racial discrimination, but fell short of community-wide legislation against racial discrimination. Increasingly well-developed community law existed against aspects of sex discrimination, so why not against racial discrimination? If the actual motivation for equal pay legislation was to ensure that no member states' employers were at a competitive disadvantage by providing equal pay, there was an equally forceful argument that no member states' employers should be at a competitive disadvantage by taking measures to eliminate racial discrimination. Despite this, anti-discrimination law on the grounds of race remained largely untouched by European law during the three decades of the 1970s, 1980s and 1990s. The European Court of Human Rights did condemn racial discrimination, but, as Forbes and Mead (1992: ii) argued:

- conventions are important only through the *pressure* they place on governments to introduce domestic legislation to prohibit discrimination in employment;
- access to the provisions of conventions is very poor;
- a prerequisite for effective protection from discrimination in employment is the *actual* introduction of such legislation.

In comparative terms, the UK had a better framework for protection against racial discrimination than the other member states of the EU (Forbes and Mead, 1992). According to the Commission for Racial Equality (CRE): 'Even as it stands, the Race Relations Act is in advance of specific race legislation elsewhere in the European Community' (CRE, 1991: 5). This meant that minority ethnic people coming to the UK from other EU member states came under the protection of its laws, whereas minority ethnic people going from the UK to other EU countries lost this protection. There was at this time a real danger that the process of harmonisation of laws might lead not to an improvement in protection from racial discrimination across the EU, but to a reduction in protection

– the lowest common denominator. That could have been done in the name of free trade.

Race issues did begin to move on to the EU agenda. There were reports to the European Parliament in 1985 and 1990 that documented disturbing facts on the rise in racism and xenophobia in Europe (Ford, 1992). They highlighted the facts that:

- extreme right-wing groups were on the rise in Europe;
- France and Germany had the largest numbers of extreme right-wing members of parliament among member states;
- the worst examples of racist attacks were to be found in Britain, Germany, France, Italy and Denmark; and
- racism was directed against Gypsies in Ireland.

Recommendations for the preparation of a draft directive on race discrimination were made following a declaration against racism and xenophobia adopted in 1986. However, a 1992 resolution adopted by the EU placed primary responsibility for action with the individual member states (Bourne and Whitmore, 1993). The EU still used language such as 'immigrants' and 'migrants' in this area, a discourse that was out of date and no longer relevant in the UK. However, in contrast to the UK where 'immigrants' had settled and were nationals, there were problems in Germany with the status of, for example, 'migrant' workers of Turkish origin who may have been born, educated, worked and paid taxes in Germany, but did not have German nationality.

During the 1990s, to facilitate freedom of movement within the EU, the emergent immigration policy developed into one of 'Fortress Europe', which, while providing 'freedom to move for those within the fortress' also provided 'insurmountable barriers excluding those who are not' (Hervey, 1995: 99). As part of this process, Brah (1992) described how the EU moved towards a common definition of European by a process of exclusion of what were labelled third country nationals (TCNs) whose 'otherness' was emphasised and became identified with race, ethnic origin and inevitably colour of skin. This led to the EU being labelled as a 'White Man's Club' (Dummett, 1991: 169). Sivanandan (1988), in his description of 'common market racism', showed how the 'negative list' of countries whose citizens needed visas to enter the EU disproportionately contained countries in Africa, the Caribbean, the Indian subcontinent and the Middle East. At the EU level, the same forums that discussed immigration issues dealt with drug trafficking and terrorism (Rex, 1992). Alongside this associated stigma, Hervey (1995) pointed out the language of racism in the EU's statements on immigration and asylum seeker policies, which used such phrases as 'migration pressure' and 'controlling migration flows' to solve a 'problem'. He argued that these policies to control and limit the immigration of TCNs had an impact on minority ethnic EU nationals (EUNs). Because the dominant image of the EU was white European, emphasised through the promotion of commonality of European cultural heritage, other cultures in the EU were 'marginalised or silenced'. Minority ethnic EUNs were also likely to be discriminated against by association with stereotyped 'problem' groups, such as TCNs and illegal immigrants (Paul, 1991). This led to reports of victimisation and harassment of minority ethnic EUNs by immigration officials and the police.

The European Council did propose a Consultative Commission in 1994 to encourage tolerance and understanding of foreigners. However, it resulted only in various forms of soft law, such as declarations on racism and xenophobia (fear of strangers), but nothing was backed up by regulatory policies, resulting in accusations that they remained at the level of rhetoric (Hervey, 1995).

Disability policies

The EU position on disability was originally similar to that on race. Despite recognition that there were 30 million disabled people in the EU – 10% of the population – there were no regulations or directives dealing specifically with discrimination against disabled people (EC, 1994). Instead, there were action programmes, recommendations and resolutions developed to promote the social and economic integration of disabled people. These included:

- Social Action Programme, 1974;
- Community Action Programme, 1983;
- a recommendation on employment, 1986;
- a programme on the integration of children in schools, 1987;
- Second Community Programme – Special Emphasis on Independent Living, 1988-91;
- Report on Equal Access to Vocational Training and Employment, 1989;
- Action Programme on Mobility and Provision of Transport, 1990;
- a resolution on the integration of children and young adults into education, 1990;
- Third Community Action Programme, 1992-96.

The 1986 recommendation did endorse the elimination of discrimination and positive action in the area of disabled people's employment. But, as in the field of race, this was only 'soft law' that was not followed up with binding directives (Oliver, 1996), even though the first official report on the progress of the Community Action Programme recognised that 'disabled people form one of the most disadvantaged groups in the population' (Daunt, 1991: 151). There was also recognition that there was a need for change: 'As a group, people with disabilities undoubtedly face a wide range of obstacles which prevent them from achieving full economic and social integration' (EC, 1994: 51). Despite this, the ECJ made an important judgement that was detrimental to disabled people's rights, deciding in the 1989 case of *Bettray v Staatssecretaris Van Justitie* that disabled people who were in rehabilitative sheltered employment did not constitute 'workers' and would therefore not be eligible to protection given to workers under EU law (de Burca, 1995).

Lunt and Thornton (1993) reported on the development of policies for the employment of disabled people in the EU member states. They found that generally there was an emphasis on the recruitment rather than retention or career development of disabled people, and mostly a commitment to compulsory employment measures stipulating targets for the open employment of disabled people. Lunt and Thornton (1993) identified a move away from compensatory measures towards facilitating the right to work and a shift to an ideology of independence and responsibility. This was in the context of the growing influence of disabled people's organisations and pressures for deinstitutionalisation.

Many member states developed proactive policies on employment opportunities for disabled people. The two examples of Germany and Italy, given below, were drawn from Lunt and Thornton's (1993) examination of employment policies for disabled people. Germany's legislative approach to the employment of disabled people was underpinned by rehabilitation rather than benefits and was rooted in traditions of compulsory employment. The former East Germany, when it was still a separate state, guaranteed all disabled people a job. Employers had to meet a 10% quota, but there were no sanctions. In unified Germany, a 6% quota of registered disabled employees was established for both public and private sector employers with at least 16 employees. Registration gave access to other benefits, including an extra week's holiday and travel concessions, and was not an obstacle to the success of the legislation. The Severely Disabled Persons Act introduced in 1974 and amended in 1986 was strictly enforced. If employers were below their quota, they paid a monthly fine that went towards the cost incurred by other companies in adapting their premises for disabled workers. This provided money from industry through the state to disabled people. On top of the compensation levy, employers were required to examine every vacant position for its potential for a severely disabled person, and provide special protection and representation of disabled workers in the workplace.

Another interesting example of an innovative project for the supported open employment for young people with severe learning difficulties came from Italy. Genoa had a completely integrated education system with no special schools. After compulsory schooling, the project 'intercepted' young people and prepared, matched, placed and gave continuous support for them in the workplace. The project relied on co-workers to teach job skills as opposed to professionals providing work skills, and the project was sustained by demonstrating success to employers. During the initial training period, the young person's salary was paid by the project and the employer provided the training and support of co-workers. After the training, the employer took on the full financial responsibility for the worker, but the project provided permanent support when needed.

New Labour approach to the EU: 1997 onwards

The New Labour government came to power in 1997 with a huge 179-seat majority in the legislature, and with women comprising around a quarter of all its Members of Parliament, which gave rise to some optimism that the UK would be more receptive to EU EO&D initiatives than in the past. Labour had a long tradition of endorsing social engineering, and talked openly of the need to reconcile work and family life as well as EO&D (Bagilhole and Byrne, 2000).

The new government reversed Britain's opt-outs from the Agreement on Social Policy as part of an explicit commitment to pursue a more 'constructive' relationship with the EU. Some steps were taken to bring the UK more into line with mainstream EU thinking on EO&D. It signed up to the parental leave directive, which it claimed would encourage family-friendly and flexible working patterns by giving all employees a basic right to three months' leave following the birth or adoption of a child, and the right to time off work for urgent family reasons. It also agreed to implement Directive 93/104/EC on the organisation of working time with the assumed norm of a maximum of 48 hours per week. The provisions of the directive were potentially costly, as working hours in the UK were longer than anywhere else in the EU: 10% of the British labour force worked a 'standard' 40-hour week, compared with 25% in Germany, and 45% in France and Italy (Bagilhole and Byrne, 2000). Labour confirmed its intention to implement the measure, but it also stressed that the directive included a range of flexibilities that would avoid imposing an undue burden on industry.

The EOC relaunched its Equality Agenda, which had been drawn up in 1991 and virtually ignored by previous governments. The agenda called for a national strategy for childcare, based on a partnership between government, employers and parents, and for a family policy that would address flexible working for women and men with young children. The relaunched version advocated a mainstreaming approach to EO&D in line with the new EU agenda, implying that responsibility for EO&D must be held by all parts of an organisation, and all policies, procedures and practices must be considered and appraised for EO&D implications, an approach that the New Labour government undertook to promote throughout its various departments.

Subsequently, the Labour government introduced the first ever National Childcare Strategy. Specific pledges were given to provide free education places for all four-year-olds, previously only available to those aged five and above, and additional funding was to be provided for preschool and out-of-school clubs. A new Childcare Tax Credit, later renamed Child Tax Credit, was proposed, the aim being to give low-income working families access to childcare by meeting 70% of eligible childcare costs up to a maximum figure depending on the number of children (Bagilhole and Byrne, 2000).

The most comprehensive statement of intent with regard to the reconciliation of paid work with family life was to be found in a Home Office consultation document 'Supporting Families' in 1998 (Home Office, 1998b). In it, the Home Secretary, as chair of the Ministerial Group on the Family, set out the government's commitment to 'sensible and pragmatic measures which will strengthen the family' (Home Office, 1998b: 5), but was careful to note that government was not 'interfering in family life', which remained the responsibility of parents, except if intervention was necessary to protect children (Bagilhole and Byrne, 2000). The government stated that it was contemplating acting to help families balance work and home in the interests of families, business, the economy and society. A family-friendly framework of employee rights and practices was to be promoted through flexible working arrangements. The government also confirmed its intention to implement the EU directives on working time, part-time work and parental leave, and improved maternity rights. It proposed to do so by setting a baseline of rights and opportunities, relying on voluntary cooperation between employees and management. The benefits to employers were to come through direct savings on training and recruitment costs by enhancing the retention of experienced staff, reducing absenteeism and encouraging employee loyalty. Parents stood to benefit through the greater choice given to both mothers and fathers to spend more time at home. The supply of well-qualified labour was expected to increase, women would gain greater financial independence, productivity would improve, and society would benefit from greater family stability.

Family-friendly policies continue to be high on the current British political agenda, along with other family-orientated debates.

Family leave arrangements

The UK signed up to the parental leave directive, which gives all employees a basic right to 13 weeks' unpaid leave following the birth or adoption of a child, and the right to time off work for urgent family reasons (extended to 18 weeks for parents of disabled children). The flat rate of Statutory Maternity Pay was increased and the period of paid and unpaid maternity leave extended. Paid leave was extended from 18 to 26 weeks, and unpaid leave to 26 weeks, enabling mothers to take up to a year off work. The government also has stated its intention of extending paid leave further to nine months and eventually to one year. The right to two weeks' paid paternity leave was introduced in the UK for the first time in 2003.

Tax credits

While work–family reconciliation policies are important, their influence is mediated by tax and benefit policies. Evidence suggests that while most countries of the Organisation for Economic Co-operation and Development have moved towards systems of separate taxation of earnings of couples, part of this change has been offset by tax relief and benefits granted to the family as a unit. This is particularly true for the UK, where the benefit system, in particular, is based on the family unit. Since 1997, financial support for families with children has been increased significantly. As a result, many of the UK government's tax and benefit policies have seen a shift in fiscal resources from childless families to families with dependent children (DEMOS, 2000). A new Childcare Tax Credit (renamed Child Tax Credit in 2003) was introduced, with the aim of giving access to childcare for low-income working families by meeting 70% of eligible childcare costs up to a maximum figure depending on the number of children.

Childcare makes it easier for women to take up full- or part-time employment, but the tax and benefit system combined to make low-paid work unattractive if, as was often the case, it resulted in loss of benefit. One of the main changes introduced was a Working Family Tax Credit in 1999 (renamed Working Tax Credit in 2003), intended to overcome this problem and guarantee a minimum income for families on low earnings. Families were able to choose whether the mother or father received the benefit, and if couples could not agree, the woman had the final choice.

This new approach was an important step towards greater integration of the tax and benefit system.

Working time arrangements

In 1998 the UK accepted the EU Directive 93/104/EC on the organisation of working time, which meant that no workers could be made to work over 48 hours a week unless they agreed to do so.

From April 2003, the 2002 Employment Act gave up to 3.2 million mothers and fathers of children aged six years and under, and working parents with disabled children under 18 years of age, the right to apply to work flexibly and their employers the duty to consider their requests seriously.

Research findings from the British Workplace Employee Relations Survey (Stevens et al, 2004) suggested that there was a significant increase, since the first survey was carried out in 2000, in the reported availability and take-up of several flexible working practices. However, with regard to the right to request flexible working, the survey found that only 41% of employees were aware of the duty on employers to consider requests (Stevens et al, 2004). With regard to take-up rates, the survey found that working mothers were more likely than working fathers to take up practices that reduced their working hours. For example, 59% of working mothers worked during term time only, compared with 24% of working fathers. Men were more likely than women to consider that flexible working practices would damage their career prospects, particularly in the case of working reduced hours and leaving on time. In addition, 48% of men thought that working fewer hours would negatively affect their job security compared with 38% of women (Stevens et al, 2004).

As can be seen above, a family-friendly framework of employee rights and practices has been promoted through various forms of family leave entitlements, flexible working arrangements and childcare development and financial support.

New strands and strengthened EO&D legislation

In addition to introducing European and nationally driven family-friendly policies, the UK has enacted other changes to EO&D legislation outlawing discrimination in the areas of religion or belief, sexual orientation and age. In addition, EO&D legislation in the areas of race, disability and gender has been substantially strengthened.

As Dickens (2007) showed, EU influence was instrumental in the development of family-friendly rights in the UK and in the widening and broadening of the substantive scope of British anti-discrimination law, especially following the Treaty of Amsterdam in 1997 and the subsequent racial equality directive (2000/43/EC) and the employment equality directive (2000/78/EC). British law has now been extended to cover three other areas of EO&D, again as a direct result of EU influence. Both the Employment Equality (Sexual Orientation) Regulations and the Employment Equality (Religion or Belief) Regulations were passed in 2003, and the Employment Equality (Age) Regulations in 2006 (see Chapter Five). As a consequence of this EU-driven widening of the EO&D remit, the three separate enforcing bodies that had been set up to oversee the legislation – the EOC, CRE and the Disability Rights Commission – were replaced in 2007 by the new Equality and Human Rights Commission (EHRC), which had a remit to oversee all EO&D legislation and the 1998 Human Rights Act (see Chapter Six).

2007 European Year of Equal Opportunities for All

In May 2006, the EU decided to make 2007 the European Year of Equal Opportunities for All, subtitled Towards a Just Society. The decision was made after a long process that had started in 2004 with a Green Paper on equality and non-discrimination in an enlarged Europe (EC, 2004). The following information is drawn from official documents about the ideas behind, and the goals and objectives of, the year.

2007 was chosen because:

- the EU considered it to be a transitional year between former action programmes and the new action programme (PROGRESS) started in 2008;
- at the end of 2007 all the anti-discrimination directives as a result of the Amsterdam Treaty needed to be transposed into national legislation;
- it was 10 years since the European Year against Racism.

During the Year of Equal Opportunities for All, it was envisaged that all sorts of awareness-raising initiatives should be taken in the member states for two reasons:

- to challenge discriminatory attitudes and behaviour that still existed; and
- to inform people about their legal rights and obligations.

The starting point was that it would be difficult to achieve the EU Lisbon strategic objectives if large groups of the EU's population were excluded from jobs, training and other opportunities. It was felt that eliminating discrimination in order to reap the benefits of EO&D was an important element in the development of a more competitive and dynamic economy and society. Also the Commission's Communication on the Social Agenda for 2005-10 emphasised the importance of promoting EO&D for all in order to achieve a more cohesive society. The EU perceived that despite numerous existing directives and action programmes too many people were still being discriminated against in society. It wanted to focus more and more on an EO&D policy to reach social and labour goals and to stimulate European economic growth.

So, according to the EU, there were two big political challenges for Europe in the coming years:

- **To tackle persistent inequalities and discrimination.** In spite of more than 30 years of legal protection and actions against discrimination, women were still paid on average 15% less than men for comparable work, and most leading roles in society, where policy decisions affecting women were made, were filled by men. Other groups of people such as migrants faced the risk of being socially excluded (for example, the Roma people, who constituted the most disadvantaged minority ethnic group in Europe).
- **To work on social cohesion because of the ageing of society and bigger migration movements that had started in the labour market.** Potential future demographic effects had made it necessary for more participation in the labour market by groups that were now excluded: 'building social cohesion is a key challenge for the Union. This implies allowing all members of Europe's diverse society to realise their potential and to participate fully in economic, social and political life'. (CEC, 2005: 5)

Four specific goals

Four specific goals were identified for the year and given the nickname of the 'four Rs': rights, representation, recognition, and respect and tolerance.

- **Rights:** raising awareness on the right to equality and non-discrimination, and the problems of multiple discrimination: 'Europe has one of the most advanced legislative frameworks in the world in these areas but there appears to be limited public awareness of the rights and obligations that this legislation confers' (CEC, 2005: 10). During the year, the six strands of EO&D identified in the Amsterdam Treaty were to be highlighted to show that people are entitled to equal treatment.

- **Representation:** stimulating debate on ways to increase participation in society of under-represented groups, in particular groups that are victims of discrimination: 'Debate and dialogue should be engaged as appropriate to promote greater participation of under-represented groups in all sectors and at all levels of society ... this means promoting full and equal participation of all' (CEC 2005: 10). Policies and actions were needed to secure this end.

- **Recognition:** celebrating and accommodating diversity and equality. 'The EU Year will acknowledge the diversity of Europe as a source of socio-economic vitality which should be harnessed, valued and enjoyed because it enriches the social fabric of Europe and is an important component of EU economic prosperity'. (CEC, 2005: 10)

- **Respect and tolerance:** promoting a more cohesive society. 'Raise awareness about the importance of promoting good relations between the various groups in society, and in particular among young people ... the key will be to work on eliminating stereotypes and prejudices.' (CEC, 2005:10)

Actions at EU Level

The total budget for the project at EU level amounted to 15 million euros, of which 7.65 million were allocated for national actions in member states.

The half of the budget retained at EU level was spent on three types of activities:

- meetings and events;
- an information and promotion campaign;
- two Eurobarometer surveys of disadvantage and the perception of disadvantage across the EU.

With Germany holding the EU presidency at the time, the year was officially launched in Berlin on 31 January 2007 with a two-day ministerial conference.

Guidelines for national actions

In order to receive a grant for undertaking national actions under the auspices of the project, each member state had to set up a National Implementation Body (NIB) with guidelines on how this would be composed. There could only be one proposal for a national action plan per country. Each action plan had to be a coherent document containing a national strategy and priorities and addressing the following points:

- the objectives of the year;
- the national context and specific challenges to be met;
- consultation with civil society and stakeholders;
- implementation of the national strategy;
- expected results and impact;
- monitoring.

Actions at local, regional or national level could include:

- meetings and events, including at least one national event to launch the year and to raise awareness to provide a forum for information, promotional and educational campaigns and measures, including the organisation of awards and competitions;
- surveys and studies to create a debate on the key issues of the year.

Once funding was awarded, the NIB was in charge of both coordinating and monitoring the implementation of the selected activities.

UK response

The UK response to the EU initiative is fully documented on the EHRC's website (EHRC, 2008). In summary, the year began with a launch event in Manchester in May 2007 and was followed by a series of conversation events, including regional seminars across the UK with speakers from government, the EHRC and the EU. The main focus was on what could be done to help create a society more at ease with its diversity. In Manchester, Meg Munn MP, the then Minister for Equalities, and the EHRC Chair Trevor Phillips visited local EO&D projects in the city. The regional roadshows brought together local community and voluntary groups, advice and support experts, local councillors, businesses and employers, academics and researchers, and the general public.

Five tailored events also took place aimed at specific groups:

- A conference on youth and issues affecting young people in Exeter in October 2007. This was aimed at young people in the 16–25 age range and at people who worked with, on behalf of, or cared for young people, or those with an interest in youth issues.

- A conference held in Birmingham in November 2007 focusing on challenges for local government and introducing Barbara Follett, the new Minister for Equality.
- A conference in Birmingham in November 2007 on the voluntary and community sector and how it could tackle inequality and the promotion of human rights.
- A forum held in London in December 2007 identifying men's inequalities and focusing on engaging men and boys in gender equality.
- A conference in London in December 2007 on older people and EO&D issues.

The UK closing event took place at the House of Commons in December 2007. It is fair to say that the year was treated in a relatively low-key way and received very little if any media coverage in the UK.

Conclusion

The extent of UK receptiveness to EU influence on EO&D has varied over time, reflecting different governments and their ideological positions. There was marked hostility and opposition under Conservative governments in the 1980s and early 1990s, but there has been a more receptive stance under New Labour governments since 1997. This chapter's analysis of progress on EO&D since the 1970s demonstrates how varied the impact of EU initiatives on EO&D in the UK has been.

Despite this, it can be claimed that the influence of the EU legislation on EO&D in the UK has been considerable. Its initial impact was in the area of gender, requiring certain amendments to the British sex discrimination legislation in order to comply with EU regulations, including equal pay for work of equal value, analytical job evaluation, transparent pay structures and the removal of the small-firm exemption from the legislative duty not to discriminate on grounds of sex.

The original scope of EU competency and influence on gender policies across the EU has gradually widened and broadened over the decades. Having signed up in 1997 to the Social Charter of the 1992 Maastricht Treaty, the New Labour government strengthened work–family reconciliation legislation and introduced many new measures in the UK, bringing Britain in line with other member states. It also strengthened the existing EO&D legislation in the areas of gender, race, and disability, and introduced new legislation in the areas of religion or belief, sexual orientation and age. Other EU-driven initiatives were the removal of monetary ceilings on compensation awards in discrimination cases, a shift in the burden of proof to employers, and the improved treatment of part-time and other 'non-standard' workers.

These national political developments can also be set in the context of the stages of EU legislation and its changing agenda. Largely during the 1970s, the EU introduced hard law associated with the equal treatment of women and men in paid work. During the 1980s, soft law in the area of work and family reconciliation policies moved on to the agenda. Finally, in the 1990s, the EU began to address social policy and returned to the issue of strengthening national gender legislation. It also assumed and enforced competency in new areas such as race, religion or belief, disability, sexual orientation and age, and began to pass legislation in these areas. Prior to this, race equality and disability had been largely ignored, with no hard legislation in either area.

Certainly, since 1997, the British government's record on implementation of EU EO&D policies has been good in relative terms, and the EU's competency and commitment to EO&D has strengthened and broadened. However, as Fagan et al (2006) have pointed out, the enlargement of the EU to 27 member states from January 2007 has raised questions over the feasibility of driving the EO&D agenda forward in the future, as indications suggest that it will be difficult to achieve the required unanimity for the implementation of new measures.

Summary

- The UK joined the European Economic Community in 1973. This was renamed the European Union (EU) by the Maastricht Treaty in 1992.
- The extent of UK receptiveness to EU influence on EO&D has varied over time, reflecting different governments and their ideological positions. There was marked hostility and opposition under Conservative governments in the 1980s and early 1990s, but there has been a more receptive stance under New Labour governments since 1997.
- The EU can be seen to be fundamentally grounded in the issue of EO&D, and gender equality policy is considered to be one of the EU's major success stories.
- However, the EU gender policy agenda has shifted from equal treatment to positive action; from 'hard' directives on equality to 'softer' legislation reconciling the competing demands of paid work and family life.
- While the issue of gender has always been prominent at EU level, the same is not true for race. EU law was not as developed in the area of race discrimination as it was in sex discrimination.
- However, since the late 1990s the EU has begun to accept and enforce its competency in other areas of EO&D, with the introduction of legislation on

additional strands of equality including race, disability, religion or belief, sexual orientation and age.

Questions for discussion

* Why did the EU concentrate on EO&D in the area of gender?
* Has this inhibited development in the other areas of EO&D in the UK?
* Will the EU continue to have an impact on EO&D and if so, how?

Further reading

Fagan, C., Grimshaw, D. and Rubery, J. (2006) 'The subordination of the gender equality objective: the National Reform Programmes and "making work pay" policies', *International Relations Journal Annual European Review*, pp 571-92.

Hantrais, L. (ed) (2000) *Gendered policies in Europe: Reconciling employment and family life*, London: Macmillan.

Hervey, T. K. (1995) 'Migrant workers and their families', in J. Shaw and G. More (eds) *New legal dynamics of the European Union*, Oxford: Clarendon Press.

Roelofs, E. (1995) 'The European equal opportunities policy', in A. van Doorne-Huiskes, J. van Hoof, and E. Roelofs (eds) *Women and the European labour markets*, London: Open University/Paul Chapman Publishing.

Cross-national, comparative approaches to equal opportunities and diversity in other EU member states

Overview

This chapter:
- contains a cross-national, comparative examination of some of the other EU member states and their interpretation and implementation of EU EO&D directives;
- examines gender policies in particular, this being the area where the EU began its venture into EO&D and where most of its legislation exists;
- interrogates the possibility of categorising the differing approaches across member states into ideal types.

Key concepts

Cross-national comparative analysis; ideal types

Despite EU attempts to unify social policy in general and EO&D policy in particular across the member states, a great variety of interpretation and differing levels of implementation of the legislation persists. It is important to note that up until the end of the 1990s, the term EO&D in the EU member states was generally assumed to apply to issues concerning women.

Although every EU member state government is formally committed to gender equality, discrimination remains. In all the EU member states, women:

* are under-represented in political institutions;
* are paid less than men for similar occupations; and
* continue to take the primary responsibility for unpaid work in the home.

If we look at just one of these dimensions – the representation of women in political institutions – Scandinavian countries, given their long history of radical, proactive gender policies, unsurprisingly rank the highest. In Sweden, 46% of Members of the Parliament (MPs) are women, while in Finland the proportion is 41%. In the UK, the proportion is 22%, while in Greece, there is only one woman MP (6%) and in Romania there are none. The mean for the 27 member states is around 23%. The EU's own institutions are no exception: of the 27 commissioners in the European Commission, eight are women, and 30% of the European Parliament is female (Pruvot et al, 2008).

The nature of feminists' political engagement has changed since the 1990s. There is an increasing awareness that discrimination in societies is not restricted to gender and that different types of discrimination can operate at the same time – in other words, multiple discrimination. For example, race, disability, age, religion or belief and sexuality can all be factors of the same process of discrimination. Yet the problem remains that, on average, women tend to come off worse than men regardless of other forms of discrimination they may face. Legislation has ensured the institutionalisation of gender EO&D policies in EU member states, and this legislation has certainly predominated in the attempt to achieve the equal participation of women in the labour market. For example, measures have been taken to:

* promote women's training;
* provide women with better opportunities to access jobs;
* promote women to decision-making posts;
* overcome horizontal segregation;
* reconcile work in paid employment with family responsibilities through better conditions for parental leave and childcare facilities.

The results vary among the member states, but overall, and in the context of most countries having had more than 20 years to develop their policies, success has been limited, with women's situation in employment continuing to be one of inequality and traditional gender roles having changed very little. Fagan et al (2006) noted that in certain EU member states measures to tackle work–life conflict are driven by a concern with increasing women's employment rate rather than promoting employment equality. This has led to policies that still assume women to be primary carers and that their participation in the workplace can and should be promoted on a different basis from that of men.

There has been a progressive increase in women's employment, coupled with a decrease in single-earner households throughout the EU (see Bagilhole, 2002b), but this does not mean that women have achieved occupational equality. Despite the rapid integration of women into paid work and the implementation of EO&D laws throughout the EU, gender inequality prevails. Throughout the EU, women remain horizontally and vertically segregated in the labour market in less secure, more low-paid jobs, essentially in the service sector, which accounts for over 80% of female employment across the EU. Gender pay gaps persist, and there is a strong relationship between sex segregation and low pay in every member state.

Women in most EU countries have maintained a high profile in service-related employment. In Denmark, France and the UK, women constitute over 50% of workers in this field. Statistics also indicate that the numbers of women in industry have risen or declined less sharply than the numbers of men, but that they are concentrated in administrative posts. Men continue to monopolise jobs in manufacturing and construction. Between 35% and 48% of all male employment is concentrated in these areas, and 84% of production workers in the EU are men. In most countries, the proportion of production jobs held by women has remained constant or declined. However, significant pockets of women workers do exist in these male-dominated occupational groups. In Portugal, for example, 23% of women work in production jobs, and only in the Netherlands and Luxembourg does the figure fall below 10%. However, while it is common for women to drive cars for domestic reasons, between 95% and 99% of driving jobs are done by men (Bagilhole, 2002b).

While the dominant view may be one of strong similarities in patterns of gender segregation in employment between EU countries, closer inspection reveals important national differences, as the following examples show.

In France, occupational segregation changed slightly in the 1980s in two ways: women gained a greater presence in the more technical and skilled occupations; and the proportion of women in some of the most highly female-dominated occupations stabilised or even decreased, while more women gained access to traditionally male occupations (Gonas and Lehto, 1999). Despite this slight attenuation of segregation, however, the general pattern has not been dramatically transformed, and now, in fact, there is evidence of increasing occupational segregation. For example, policies in the form of benefits and tax deductions, designed to enable parents to share their obligations towards their dependants more equitably by using the services of childminders, have led to the creation of more domestic service jobs. These jobs are almost exclusively done by women, which has had the unintended consequence of exacerbating labour market segregation: 'The domestic services sector was increasingly feminised, thereby reinforcing some forms of inequality in the labour market' (Lanquetin et al, 2000: 87).

Many southern European countries show a different pattern of employment segregation to other countries. In places such as Italy and Spain, men appear more willing to take jobs traditionally held by women (for example, catering, waiting at tables and childcare), whereas in northern European countries men are less willing to do these jobs (see Cross and Bagilhole, 2002; Bagilhole and Cross, 2006). However, in Italy, very few inroads have been made into equalising pay for women and men. Even when women have the same skills and qualifications as men, they tend to be employed in less well-paid jobs. Women are also frequently excluded from schemes involving bonus payments or allowances, and they tend to work shorter hours than men and to avoid overtime because of their family responsibilities and the absence of publicly provided child and eldercare services. More than two-thirds of the women employed in the service sector, for example, work reduced hours, even though part-time work is poorly developed in Italy (Del Re, 2000).

Sweden, like other Nordic states, has a strong public sector that funds and runs most childcare and eldercare. Under its parental insurance scheme, either parent can take paid leave to look after young children. Despite this, gender segregation in the labour market remains. Patterns of segregation in the labour market are clearly reflected in the divisions between typically female and male occupations, and even in mixed occupations women and men seldom do the same jobs. Men still earn more and are in the majority in higher-status positions. There has been little change in the gender composition of different occupations during the 1990s, despite an underlying political intention to breakdown segregation patterns (Bergqvist and Jungar, 2000).

The Netherlands has the lowest female employment participation rate of all western countries, if the volume of the female labour force is taken into account. There is no other country in the EU where more women work in part-time jobs (over 60% of Dutch women). This is partly due to the lack of sufficient childcare facilities. The traditional gender arrangements are institutionalised in a breadwinner–caretaker model. In the Netherlands, the usual practice is for women to work part-time to enable them to combine paid work and childcare, while men work full-time, providing the greater part of the family income (Benschop et al, 2001).

Looking at vertical segregation, it is difficult to ascertain the true number of women managers in the EU because different countries use different classifications and some countries do not collect these data at all. Depending on how management jobs are defined in the first place, the proportion of women managers varies, although it is clear that men have close to a monopoly on the most senior positions and greatly outnumber women in middle-level managerial jobs in virtually every country. Throughout the EU, women's advance into senior management positions has been very slow. In EU countries, fewer than 5% of women are in senior management roles and this percentage has barely changed since the early 1990s (Davidson and Burke, 2000). 'Years after the EU adopted equal opportunity laws, European management is still a man's enclave' (Vinnicombe, 2000: 9).

It might be assumed that female managers would have the greatest chance of success in Nordic countries where family and EO&D policies are strongly enforced by legislation. Yet the number of women managers is not significantly higher in these countries than in the rest of the EU. For example, in Denmark, a high level of labour force participation is no assurance of women's representation in management. Women make up 47% of the salaried labour force, but only 14% of managers and 5% of top management. In southern EU countries, the situation for women managers is more complex. There are signs of strong growth in the number of women in the workforce and in management, especially young women. However, their numbers still remain low; in Italy. women hold 3% of upper management positions and in Spain 5% of private sector management jobs (Bagilhole, 2002b).

Today, the EU perspective can help feminists identify and challenge the processes that maintain these gender inequalities. Comparing one country's situation with others is the first step in assessing changes that have happened and the barriers that remain. For instance, working women in the German Democratic Republic used to have access to good childcare, but these facilities partly disappeared after reunification, highlighting one of the reasons why West German mothers had been prevented from working. Other policy differences between east and west in the area of gender equality are likely to come under the spotlight with the recent accession of more Eastern European countries to the EU.

One of the key objectives of the EU is to eliminate inequalities and promote gender equality throughout the member states, using a comprehensive approach that includes legislation, mainstreaming and positive action. At least four articles of the Treaty of Amsterdam set out gender equality objectives for the EU. Articles 2 and 3 focus on 'gender mainstreaming'. This means that the gender equality objective is to be integrated into all EU policies. Article 141 focuses on equality between women and men in matters of employment and occupation and Article 137 on sex discrimination within and outside the workplace. Confirming this commitment, all member states approved the European Pact for Gender Equality in March 2006, and the EU Commission designed a 'roadmap for equality between women and men' for 2006-2010. Therefore the legal commitments of the EU set a very useful context for comparison of member states' approaches and commitment to gender equality.

Comparisons between women (particularly mothers) in paid work in different EU countries reveal the importance of different forms of national EO&D policy. For example, in France the provision of state childcare is a major factor in women's greater continuity in employment and in their greater tendency to work full-time. The impact of the role of family policy can be extended to part-time work. In some countries, such as the UK and the Netherlands, it is used to reconcile professional and family life. Of particular significance is the role of tax and benefit systems in influencing participation decisions. A comparative study of Flanders and the Netherlands considered the impact of fiscal systems, social security systems and labour market systems on the divisions of paid and unpaid labour (Rubery, 1999). Comparative research revealed how policies other than those strictly concerned with EO&D also influence behaviour.

Formal mechanisms of EO&D

EU decisions are binding on individual member states, and many of the steps taken towards national EO&D initiatives, especially those enshrined in legislation, have developed to a great extent from EU directives, resolutions, recommendations and action plans (see Chapter Seven). However, the process and extent of the institutionalisation of EO&D is marked by the historical and political context of different EU countries and their dates of accession to the EU (Suarez and Suarez, 2003). A fundamental issue for the implementation of EO&D is the close relationship between its development and the attitude of the political parties in power (see Chapter Seven for an analysis of this in the UK).

Silius (2002) detected differences in the level of institutionalisation of EO&D in each of nine EU member states that she studied, which she categorised as high, medium or low.

- Countries with a **high** level of institutionalisation were the UK, the Netherlands and Germany, which have long histories of EO&D development and democracy, as well as a long relationship with the EU.
- Italy, Spain and Finland had **medium** levels of institutionalisation, which reflected their pre-EU entry ideologies towards EO&D, but in very different ways. In the case of Italy and Spain, there had been very little state intervention in measures to reconcile work and family matters for women, so they had a lot of catching up to do. Finland, despite a long history of state provision in this area, bore the legacy of the 'gender-neutral' character of Finnish EO&D, which was antipathetic to women-only policies.
- Slovenia and Hungary, both among the most recent entrants to the EU, and France, one of the longest-standing members, all scored **low** levels of institutionalisation. Slovenia and Hungary are working towards achieving the EU-led EO&D initiatives. Prior to EU membership, they had been developing EO&D in their own legislative bodies and institutions, although to a low degree. France was a peculiar case, since its levels of institutionalisation might have been expected to be higher. The universalism of its equality discourse, however, seems to have been an obstacle to the development of EO&D policies directed specifically to women.

We can see, therefore, that there is not necessarily a consistent approach to the institutionalisation of EU-led EO&D initiatives, even in long-standing member states, and it is often national socio-political factors that influence EO&D development.

Socio-political factors

One of the most relevant socio-political factors that affects the way that member states interpret and implement EU-led EO&D initiatives in the area of gender is what Le Feuvre and Andriocci (2003) called their 'gendered culture'. They suggested that EU member states could be categorised by their attitude to the allocation of childcare and other forms of care responsibility, either to individuals and families or to the state. They drew on and developed Pfau-Effinger's (1999) work to enable a typology of different 'gender cultural models' to be drawn up. Four of these are particularly appropriate for categorising EU member states:

- **Male breadwinner/female home-carer model.** This model is based on differentiation between the public and private spheres individuals are assigned according to their sex. Men are considered to be the main breadwinners, whereas women are primarily assigned those activities that are connected with the home.

- **Male breadwinner/female part-time worker model.** In this model, both men and women are expected to work, but the arrival of children redefines the pattern of women's labour market participation. Women's reconciling of paid work with family obligations usually takes the form of reduction in women's paid working time.
- **Dual breadwinner/state carer model**. In this model, both men and women are again expected to work. The reconciliation of work and family is facilitated by the collective organisation of household services, in particular childcare. The state is regarded as more competent for fulfilling this task than private households, but nevertheless women tend to still use the policy measures directed at 'reconciliation' to a greater extent than their men.
- **Dual breadwinner/dual carer model.** Men and women are not seen as complementary but 'interchangeable' both in the labour market and in unpaid caring activities. The burden of caring activities connected with children does not revert directly to the state; rather, fathers' investment in domestic activities is expected.

This leads to the idea of a continuum, with men and women assigned to 'specific spheres' at one end (as in many southern EU member states) and both sexes expected to articulate their professional, parental and personal commitments to society at the other (as in Nordic EU member states). The rest of the member states fall somewhere in between, where women are granted formal equality in the labour market but are also expected to carry most of the burden of unpaid family and domestic work. A fuller analysis will now be made of individual EU member states to show where they fall in this continuum.

Italy: male breadwinner/female home-carer model

Vingelli's (2006) analysis of the Italian approach to gender equality seems to fit well with this model. She argued that in Italy gender policy is about women, and women are about the family. She identified a strong emphasis on reconciliation of women's time, 'policies to reconcile the multiple roles of women in the family and at work' or 'to reconcile the family role of women with their professional responsibilities'. The government's view is that this reconciliation is a problem for women.

In Italy, the workforce is still characterised by gender-based segregation, both vertical and horizontal. According to government estimates, there is a 20-25% pay gap between women and men. In addition, there are more women than men in part-time employment, which reinforces traditional roles. The increase in the economic activity rate of women with children has not been followed by a more equal distribution of family responsibilities. Unpaid tasks in the private sphere rest almost entirely with women. Vingelli (2006) pointed out that 35.2% of employed men admit to devoting no hours to family related tasks at all. However, the unequal distribution of tasks inside families is never stressed as an issue. The main solution is seen as better management of women's time through reconciliation tools.

On the other hand, Barazzetti et al (2001) identified two important laws passed in 2000 that may have a more positive impact on gender equality in the future. One of these laws was aimed at enforcing positive action for women. It introduced specific positive action plans in the public sector designed to remove obstacles preventing EO&D policies for women in the workplace from fully taking effect. It promoted the admission of women into sectors and levels in which they were under-represented, with the objective of favouring an equal female presence in all hierarchical positions. If public sector organisations failed to comply, they were prevented from employing new personnel. The second new law promoted parental leave and provided grants to those firms allowing flexible working for both women and men.

However, Barazzetti et al (2001) argued that in terms of Italian gender policy the main question that still needs to be addressed is whether policies should focus on the protection of women or on parity for them. The current approach demonstrates a mixture of two different cultures, resulting in a contradiction in policies aimed at women. On the one hand, there is a culture founded on bringing out gender differences and on making the most of women's conditions, leading to protective policies. On the other hand, an equality culture driven by EU EO&D initiatives aims at general transformation policies for women and men.

Certainly, the rising female presence in the labour market has been one of the most significant transformations in the labour force in the last two decades in Italy. Women took up 66% of the newly created jobs between 1998 and 2001. In the past decade in particular, the activity rate of women with children has been rising constantly, but the majority of jobs created have been temporary ones. Overall, women's employment rate in Italy has only reached 54.6%, a figure that lags behind that of other EU member states. It is 9% under the average rate in EU, and over 15% lower than the target the EU has set for 2010 (Vingelli, 2006).

The Netherlands: male breadwinner/female part-time worker model

Women's participation in paid labour in the Netherlands is low compared with neighbouring EU member states, and many married women only have part-time jobs. As Van der Sanden and Waaldijk (2002) pointed out, both the social security and taxation systems in the Netherlands were shaped by the principle of the male breadwinner who was to provide all the income for 'his' family. Verloo (2006) argued strongly that without the catalyst and at times enforcement powers of the EU, EO&D policies for women in the Netherlands would have been much weaker. For example, the abolition of the law against employing married women civil servants was only achieved when EU directives on equal pay, in 1975 (75/117/EEC, commonly known as the Equal Pay Directive) and the directive on equal treatment, in 1976 (76/207/EEC, commonly known as the Equal Treatment Directive) were implemented in 1979. The 1975 Equal Pay Act in the Netherlands applied only to the private sector until enforcement measures by the EU in 1980 resulted in the inclusion of the public sector. In response to the EU Equal Treatment Directive (1976), the Dutch government eventually established an Equal Treatment Act (ETA) in 1980. The effectiveness of the EPA and the ETA have been called into question, as they contained no provisions for the prohibition of indirect discrimination, limited possibilities for sanctions and no possibilities for group action (Van der Sanden and Waaldijk, 2002). The EPA and ETA were combined in a new Equal Treatment Act in 1989. Generally, regulations for women and men were equalised, which meant that protective measures for women, such as the prohibition of women working on Saturday afternoons, Sunday and at night, were abolished.

Significantly, it was not until the 1990s that several Acts aimed at improving the possibilities of combining paid work and unpaid household and care activities came into effect. Until then, the Dutch government's intervention in the area of childcare was minimal, and despite increasing the quantity of childcare facilities, provision is still inadequate. Thus, the predominant model in the Netherlands of mothers working part-time continues.

France: dual breadwinner/state carer model

Picq (2006) argued that gender equality in France is viewed by the state as concerning both women and men, and as a democratic value. Gender inequality is perceived to stem from out-of-date attitudes historically founded on traditional gender norms and attitudes. Le Feuvre and Andriocci (2001) argued that although the principle of gender equality has been recognised in law for 30 years, its actual application has been thwarted by a consistent lack of political will and financial resources.

They argued that in France the level of state intervention to facilitate the reconciliation of professional life and family life is high, as in many Nordic countries, but comes from a very different political ideology. In France, a national preoccupation with maintaining birth-rates translated into measures aimed at protecting the family in general and working mothers in particular. Policy measures have played a major role in promoting levels of state-funded childcare that are far higher than in most EU member states. This explains the historically high levels of women's employment rates in France, particularly in full-time jobs. However, it has been argued that this state intervention focuses on issues of family welfare and has in fact reinforced the social functions of wife and mother that are the basis of much gender discrimination.

On the other hand, Le Feuvre and Andriocci (2001) argued that the so-called 1983 Roudy Act on EO&D in employment seems to have moved French law from an approach based on the idea of protecting women as wives and mothers to one that aimed at promoting gender equality in all spheres of French society. However, there has not been a complete shift in French policy from 'the protective perspective centred on women as wives and mothers to an egalitarian perspective centred on women as individuals and citizens' (Le Feuvre and Andriocci, 2001: 35). On the contrary, they argue, much of the EO&D legislation introduced in France over the past few years reflects successive French governments' commitment to both these objectives. State interventions aimed at protecting working mothers have not been superseded by clear-cut positive action measures.

A significant upsurge in the number and range of EO&D legislative measures in France in the 2000s has resulted from pressure from the EU to implement their EO&D directives. For example, the 2001 law on professional equality requires companies to produce annual reports comparing women's and men's situations in their enterprises, and temporary positive action for women is allowed. In 2004, a law on equality and desegregation of the labour market was passed, and in 2006, a law aimed at achieving wage equality in five years (Picq, 2006).

Finland: dual breadwinner/dual carer model

The Nordic countries – that is, Sweden, Denmark, Norway, Finland and Iceland – are often envisaged as representing one model. However, in the context of the EU, it is important to remember that there are some differences between them. Neither Norway nor Iceland are members of the EU; Denmark became a member in 1973, Finland and Sweden in

1995. However, in terms of EO&D measures, the Nordic countries usually collaborate with each and develop their policies in tandem. Before Finland and Sweden entered the EU, there was a lot of discussion within these two countries as to whether or not EO&D would weaken because of their membership. However, it was also recognised that these countries could contribute to the development of EO&D in the EU (Lehto, 1999). In fact, joining the EU has for the most part had a positive impact on EO&D in Finland and Sweden, even if cases do exist to the contrary.

Post-war social policies in Finland were guided by a firm belief in economic independence as the prerequisite for women's emancipation. Women participated in the labour market even before any state childcare system. In 1950, the employment rate for women was 57% (Silius, 1996). The first EO&D measure accepted in Finland was the principle of equal pay for equal work in 1951. New legislation on day care in 1973 supported mothers in work, but it was not without opposition and did not produce the radical changes in the gendered division of labour that were expected. However, it did acknowledge that waged work for mothers of small children was morally acceptable (Julkunen, 1999). In 1990, home-care allowance was made available as an option for taking care of children under three years. At the same time, all children under three years old were guaranteed a day-care place. Even if the popular image of childcare in Finland is that children spend all day in 'institutions' and parents work full-time, the reality is that many children are cared for at home even when both parents work. The solutions are diverse: relatives care for the children and parents choose shiftwork or a combination of the two (Silius and Tuori, 2002).

The labour market in Finland is sharply segregated by gender; only 10% of occupations have roughly the same number of men and women. Female-dominated fields are less well paid than male-dominated fields. During the 1970s and 1980s, there was a 'mark and penny policy' – pay increases were awarded in amounts of money and not in percentages. This benefited low-income earners and was particularly favourable to women. However, in the 1990s, the system was changed back and wage increases were again rewarded in percentages. Differences between women's and men's wages grew a little, and women's salaries are now around 80% of men's salaries (Women and Men in Finland, 2001).

Silius and Tuori (2002) argued that Finnish notions of equality are strongly 'gender neutral' and laws in Finland are generally written in gender-neutral terms. Mothers and fathers are referred to as 'parents', women and men as 'persons'. Gender neutrality, or in some cases 'gender blindness', is seen as characteristic of the whole EO&D discourse in Finland. Its 1987 Act on equality between women and men focused on equality from three angles:

- promotion of equality between women and men;
- prohibition of gendered discrimination; and
- improvement of the position of women.

The first two were gender neutral but the third one implied that the aim of the law was women's advancement. An employer who had two equally well-qualified candidates could choose a woman if women were in a minority at the workplace. It was also possible to organise special training for women in order to promote their progress in careers, if men were in the majority of managerial roles. Positive action became part of the Equality Act in 1995. Quotas in municipal and state decision-making bodies were introduced. According to the Equality Act, there should always be a minimum of 40% of women and men in state administration committees, consultative committees, working groups and other preparatory, planning and decision making and municipal bodies. In the municipal councils, the effect was dramatic; the number of women increased from around 20% to over 40% (Silius and Tuori, 2002).

As part of the influence of the EU, gender mainstreaming became an issue in Finnish EO&D politics in 1997. However, Silius and Tuori (2002) argued that mainstreaming had been the de facto practice in Finnish EO&D work before this, even if the term was first used at the end of the 1990s. The Finnish Government's Action Plan for Gender Equality 2004-2007 was more comprehensive and tangible than before. It aimed to:

- promote gender equality in working life;
- facilitate the reconciliation of work and family life;
- increase the number of women in economic and political decision making;
- alleviate labour market segregation;
- reduce stereotyped gender images in the media;
- combat violence against women;
- increase men's participation in gender equality;
- encourage shared responsibility for home and children;
- enhance gender equality in regional development, international and EU co-operation (Heikkinen, 2005).

Heikkinen (2005) pointed out that the government's list of equality issues was getting longer, and, while equality in working life and equal pay remained, important additions were equality issues from men's point of view and encouraging men to take family leave.

Eastern Europe: a special case

Hungary: dual breadwinner/state carer model in the past reverting to male breadwinner/female home-carer model

After the Second World War, Eastern European countries came under a socialist-type industrial regime, based on the Soviet Union model. Two of the main pillars of the socialist ideology were that 'all people, regardless of sex or race, were equal politically, economically and socially' and that 'all those capable of working in the paid labour market should do so and rewards in the new society were to be based on this form of worker participation' (Makkai, 1997: 189). Female labour was necessary to the economy and 'paid employment was seen as the major avenue through which women's equality should be achieved' (Crompton and Harris, 1999: 131). To this end, a widespread state childcare system was set up (Makkai, 1997). However, Crompton and Harris (1999: 132) argued that 'despite an official ideology that privileged paid, rather than domestic or caring, work, support for mothers was linked to the biological maternal role'. The measures aimed at integrating women into the labour market did not question the gender inequalities that continued in the family: 'The domestic division of labour has remained highly conventional, despite women's long-term labour-force participation' (Crompton and Harris, 1999: 135). Although they were encouraged and supported in the labour market, women also carried the 'double burden' of domestic unpaid work.

The 1949 Hungarian Constitution contained general provisions on the right to work, on the freedom to choose employment and on the equal rights of men and women. At the same time, it stated that 'mothers shall receive support and protection before and after they give birth to a child in accordance with separate provisions' (Makkai, 1997: 189). Gazsi et al (2001) argued that this indicated that the state took a stand according to which tasks related to children and expected the caring role to be shouldered by women, essentially signing the parental role over to women. Furthermore, by strengthening women's traditional role, it contributed to the evaluation of women as second-rate citizens in the world of paid work. Nevertheless, an extensive state maternity and childcare system and a guarantee of full employment was established that remained for over 40 years.

Le Feuvre and Andriocci (2003) documented the significant impact that the transition of socialist regimes to market economies had on women's employment during the 1990s. There were restrictions on the rights concerning abortion, many childcare facilities closed, and female unemployment rates were high. Le Feuvre and Andriocci (2003) argued that the congruence of all these factors underpinned a patriarchal ideology based on the male breadwinner/female home-carer model, which despite 60 years of women's participation in the labour market remained ideologically strong.

In 1995, in line with the change of politics and move to a market economy, new legislation dismantled and transformed state maternity provision, with the state withdrawing from a range of maternity benefits and services. In 1998, different forms of childcare assistance were introduced, but as Gazsi et al (2001) argued, they were not complemented by a change in the patriarchal attitude towards women. They argued that the new policy was not meant to promote female equality, but to promote childbirth and restore the traditional family, and predicted that some better-off women may choose to leave employment, and others may be pushed out by a combination of two factors:

- the revitalised 'stay at home' ideology;
- the closure of crèches and kindergartens or the introduction of high fees to use them.

The current system of Hungarian labour law enacted after the political changes in 1992 provides the basic framework for the legal guarantees of EO&D for women and men and prohibition of discrimination on grounds of sex in both the private and public sector. The principle of 'equal pay for equal work' is defined in the Hungarian Constitution and in labour law:

> Everyone has the right to equal compensation for equal work, without any discrimination whatsoever. All persons who work have the right to an income that corresponds to the amount and quality of work they carry out. Everyone has the right to rest time, free time and to regular paid vacation. (Gazsi et al, 2001: 21)

The Hungarian Constitution and the EU Treaty of Rome had become compatible, and Hungary joined the EU in 2004.

Conclusion

It would seem that across the EU labour market inequalities for women persist despite the growth of EO&D policy. Various barriers to the efficiency and effectiveness of EU-led EO&D policies can be identified. Although member states are required to adopt EU policy measures, final responsibility for elaborating a policy programme for gender equality lies firmly with individual countries. Thus, socio-political factors produce a variation in the 'gendered cultural contexts' that persist in the different countries. In addition, there is a lack of post-hoc evaluation of EU-led EO&D policy measures, and an absence of analysis of the wider social mechanisms preventing change.

The suggested categorisations of male breadwinner/female home carer, male breadwinner/female part-time worker, dual breadwinner/state carer and dual breadwinner/dual carer utilises different models of family and paid work reconciliation. This is helpful in understanding the differences in the application of EO&D policies across EU member states.

It is striking that, after decades of EO&D legislation and policies, women still need to negotiate between the public and the private sphere. This testifies to the fact that traditional gender role cultures persist in society, and confirms that EO&D legislation on its own is not effective enough to promote social change unless accompanied by other kinds of measures. This should be taken into account when developing policies for conciliating work and family life, which mostly seem to try to help women to shoulder more easily the double burden of domestic and public life. The ineffectiveness of EO&D measures in the context of employment does not stem only from this contradiction, but also from the structure of the labour market itself.

Summary

- Despite EU attempts to unify EO&D policy across the member states, a great variety of interpretation and differing levels of implementation of the legislation persists.
- Until the end of the 1990s, the term EO&D in the EU member states was generally assumed to apply to issues concerning women.
- Although every EU member state government is formally committed to gender equality, discrimination remains, with women's situation in employment continuing to be one of inequality and traditional gender roles having changed very little.
- There is not a consistent approach to the institutionalisation of EU-led EO&D initiatives, and it is often national socio-political factors that influence EO&D development.
- One of the most relevant socio-political factors that affects the way that member states interpret and implement EU-led EO&D initiatives in the area of gender is their specific 'gendered culture'. This leads to the idea of a continuum, with men and women assigned to 'specific spheres' at one end and both sexes expected to articulate their professional, parental and personal commitments to society at the other.

Questions for discussion

- What type of gender culture persists in the UK?
- How is this reinforced by UK EO&D policies?

Further reading

Bagilhole, B. (2002) *Women in non-traditional occupations: Challenging men*, London: Palgrave Macmillan.

Benschop, Y., Halsema, L. and Schreurs, P. (2001) 'The division of labour and inequalities between the sexes: an ideological dilemma', *Gender, Work and Organization*, vol 8, no 1, pp 1-18.

Hantrais, L. (ed) (2000) *Gendered policies in Europe: Reconciling employment and family life*, London: Macmillan.

Silius, H. (2002) 'Women's employment, equal opportunities and women's studies in nine European countries – a summary', in G. Griffin (ed) *Women's employment, women's studies and equal opportunities 1945-2001*, Hull: University of Hull, pp 470-514.

Future agenda for equal opportunities and diversity

Overview

This chapter:
- critiques equal opportunities and diversity (EO&D) as a limited liberal concept;
- examines how EO&D legislation and policies are likely to develop in the future;
- investigates how relevant the concepts of EO&D are likely to remain in social policy and where the main issues are likely to arise;
- takes a deeper look at how the terrain of EO&D is changing;
- considers the future of EO&D in the context of important questions such as how a balance is to be struck between the need to treat people equally, the need to treat people differently and the need to maintain shared values and social cohesion, and how to handle negotiations over contested issues.

Key concepts

Liberalism; equal treatment; social cohesion; contestation

Failure of EO&D legislation?

British EO&D legislation preventing discrimination against women and minority ethnic people has been in place for over 30 years, and disabled people have been protected against discrimination for over ten years, and yet these measures have proved insufficient to eliminate inequality. Various explanations for this have been put forward, including the following:

- *Personal choice:* much of what is identified as discrimination or inequality reflects different personal choices or tastes (Hakim, 2003).
- *Double burden:* women's inequality in the labour market is a consequence of their extra domestic burden in the family (Bagilhole, 1994a).
- *Resistance and backlash:* policies to reduce inequality are actively resisted by groups other than those who benefit from EO&D policies (Bagilhole, 2006).
- *Economic:* by providing a source of flexible labour, women and minority ethnic people in particular help employers reduce their labour costs (Beechey, 1977).
- *Long agenda:* the elimination of inequality requires a radical transformation of all institutions that is unlikely to take place – the 'long' rather than the 'short agenda' for EO&D (Cockburn, 1991).
- *Political exclusion:* the under-representation of women, minority ethnic and disabled people in the political process and in decision making in the economy results in only limited and partial commitment of the state when EO&D laws involving positive action plans are launched (Rubery and Fagan, 1994).
- *Heterogeneity of groups:* the rejection of the notion of talking about, for example, women as a group renders problematic the question of whether specific policies act in the interest of a group, or how the interests of that group can be conceptualised (McCall, 2005).

It has been argued that legislation alone is not sufficient to change some of the deep-seated disadvantage and inequalities experienced by women, minority ethnic and disabled people, gay men, lesbians and bisexuals, those who hold certain religious beliefs, and older and younger people. Action is called for on many fronts, but legislation has an important role to play as part of wider comprehensive strategies for tackling inequality, discrimination and disadvantage. As the Runnymede Trust Commission (2000) argued, it has:

- helped to curb the worst kinds of discrimination in employment and provision of services; and
- made an invaluable impact on the general climate of opinion.

Dickens (2007: 104) maintained that:

Putting legislation into a necessary perspective as one of many measures should not be allowed to underplay the importance of achieving an appropriate, effective, legal framework. What law can achieve is necessarily limited but the legislative framework for equality is important both symbolically and practically.

It could be argued that EO&D legislation (with the exception of the public sector equality duties for gender, race and disability) is fairly limited and that the full potential of what the spirit of the law requires is not being realised in practice. It is therefore not particularly surprising that the impact of the legislation appears to have been limited (Owen at al, 2000; Hibbert and Meager, 2003; Cabinet Office, 2005).

In the past, British EO&D legislation in general, and in its practical operation, has fostered an individual rather than an organisational focus. A different focus on changing organisations could push beyond the 'deficit' model, seen as requiring 'special' provisions to overcome 'disadvantage', for example, helping women and minority ethnic groups adapt to and get on within structures as they currently are. This would mean a long agenda (Cockburn, 1989), requiring changes in male-gendered, culturally bound (but presumed to be neutral) organisational and occupational structures, practices, norms and value systems in order to accommodate those other than men.

Until relatively recently British legislation had not moved very far in this direction. The 1995 Disability Discrimination Act (DDA) did include an important positive duty on employers to make 'reasonable adjustment' to assist disabled people, but none of the other discrimination legislation contains such a duty (Doyle, 1997). This requirement, although limited and hedged around with business needs, acknowledges that the way in which work and workplaces are structured poses barriers for people with disabilities. Nonetheless, requiring organisations rather than the individual to adapt was a positive move in the direction of a social model of disability with its emphasis on attitudinal, physical and institutional barriers in the creation and persistence of a disabling society (Roulstone and Warren, 2006).

EO&D legislation has been accused of merely encouraging a compliance approach. However, it does seem that compliance with the legislation can act as a catalyst to taking further action beyond minimum legislative requirements (Dickens, 1999). Although it only prohibits or in some cases encourages certain behaviours, it can also bring about changed understandings, values and attitudes. For all its limitations, it is clear that the anti-discrimination and family-friendly legislation has had a positive impact and that strengthening the legislation, including the equality duties for gender, race and disability in the public sector, could help deliver greater impact.

There is no shortage of well-researched, evidence-based recommendations for change from the former equality commissions and from independent commentators (for example, Hepple et al, 2000). This has been the case since the legislation was first enacted, but what was often lacking was the political will to act on the recommendations. Since 1997, successive New Labour governments have strengthened the DDA, imposed positive duties in gender, race and disability on the public sector, shifted the burden of proof in discrimination cases from employees to employers, introduced and strengthened family-friendly policies, and introduced anti-discrimination legislation on the grounds of sexual orientation, religion or belief, and age. A seminal year in the EO&D project, 2007 provided the basis for future development. It was the EU Year of Equal Opportunities for All (see Chapter Seven), the three existing equality commissions were amalgamated into the Equality and Human Rights Commission (EHRC) (see Chapter Six), the former commissions gave their last reports on what still needed to be done, and a new single Equality Act was promised for 2009. Dickens (2007: 145) argued that the single equality body, and proposed single Equality Act 'can be cast as a trajectory (albeit a hesitant and uneven one) from a piecemeal and patchwork approach to the legislative tackling of inequality towards inclusiveness, integration and intersectionality (recognizing a person's membership in more than one marginalized group)'.

The creation of a single commission was not without controversy (see Chapter Six). Potentially, however, a single body will allow issues of multiple disadvantage and discrimination to be better addressed through an intersectional approach (see Chapters Three and Chapter Six). An Equal Opportunities Commission (EOC) review showed that in other countries opinion remained strongly supportive of a single body (O'Cinneide, 2002). Certainly, the government presented the EHRC as a 'step change in how we promote, enforce and deliver equality and human rights' (DTI, 2004: 12). Having a single Equality Act will be important in avoiding some problems experienced by single agencies elsewhere but the nature of that legislation is crucial.

The EU has had a positive influence on EO&D policies in member states (see Chapters Seven and Eight). However, the enlargement of the EU to 27 member states from January 2007 has raised questions over the feasibility of driving the EO&D agenda forward in the future, as indications suggest that it will be difficult to achieve the required unanimity for the implementation of new measures. There has also been a changing emphasis on equality objectives and how to pursue them within the EU economic policy and employment strategy. EO&D for women was included as a key pillar in the 1997 European Employment Strategy, constituting an important commitment to advancing gender equality and gender mainstreaming in particular. Member states were required to report to the EU annually on progress towards gender equality. However, in 2003, with the reform of the Lisbon process and the introduction of the new strands of EO&D, the equality pillar disappeared and the reporting requirements changed from 2005, with the visibility of gender issues fading as a result (Fagan et al, 2006). Verloo (2006: 211) identified a tendency at EU level to assume an unquestioned similarity of inequality across different groups. Looking at race and ethnicity, sexual orientation and gender, she argued that a '"one size fits all" approach to addressing multiple discrimination is based on an incorrect assumption of sameness or equivalence of the social categories connected to inequalities and of the mechanisms and processes that constitute them'. Political and policy practice in the EU claims to address multiple inequalities but has seldom referred to intersectionality when dealing with them.

An extra complication is the heterogeneity of groups. For example, there are broad economic inequalities in the way in which gender is experienced in the UK labour market. There have been high compensatory awards made to some women professionals for sexism in the City of London, while other, low-paid women in local government are struggling to secure equal pay for work of equal value. In terms of race and ethnicity, the Runnymede Trust Commission (2000: 28) pointed out that there is 'substantial divergence, and the earnings and educational achievements of some groups compare favourably with the national average. For example, Indians and Chinese are proportionately better qualified than the rest of the population'. Moreover, while young African-Caribbean men are notably disadvantaged in employment and education, African-Caribbean women's earnings and social mobility are growing at a faster rate than those of white women.

Feminist theory has tackled this with the concept of **intersectionality**, which stresses how the various types of discrimination can overlap. Intersectionality as a theory and methodology for research and policy making could be a springboard for the operationalisation of a social justice agenda based on EO&D mainstreaming (see Chapters Three and Five).

The single Equality Act will need more teeth than the current legislation possesses and the EHRC will need the powers and resources to scrutinise this process and to take legal action where necessary. EO&D requires the recognition and inclusion of differences, which could provide a framework for creating an imaginative and proactive piece of legislation that recognises both the common and diverse interests of women, minority ethnic and disabled people, gay men, lesbians, people of certain religious beliefs, and older and younger people. For example, if employers were required to prove that their recruitment procedures were fair, it would make sense for this to be done for all groups at the same time. Recognition of diversity does not necessarily lead to political paralysis, but it may do so. Intersectionality as a theory and policy-making tool may be the remedy.

As Davis (2008: 79) argued: 'Intersectionality initiates a process of discovery, alerting us to the fact that the world around us is always more complicated and contradictory than we ever could have anticipated'. It encourages us to keep in mind the various strands of equality when collecting EO&D data and proposing measures to alleviate disadvantage and counter discrimination. Importantly, it demonstrates the weakness in the current EO&D legislation of treating people the same. Most forms of positive action to aid disadvantaged groups are prevented by the legislation, which is concerned with preventing current and future discrimination but does nothing to overcome the effects of past discrimination. The extent to which positive action is permitted under the legislation is very limited (for example, it allows some outreach recruitment and training to improve the position of currently under-represented groups under sex and race legislation or to prevent or compensate for disadvantages linked to sexual orientation, religion or belief, or age) and no positive (or reverse) discrimination is allowed. As Barnes and Ashtiany (2003) argued, the equal treatment formulation of much of the legislation acts as a barrier to any employer wishing to implement more progressive EO&D policies. In the preface to a report by Hepple et al (2000: i), Lord Lester claimed that: 'The defective state of the UK's current anti-discrimination law helps no one except lawyers'.

As the Runnymede Trust Commission (2000) argued:

• there is too much law;
• it is inaccessible;
• it places too much emphasis on state regulation;
• it places too little emphasis on organisations and individuals to generate change;
• it is inconsistent.

The whole legislative framework needs a substantial overhaul (Hepple et al, 2000). In some countries, for example, Australia, Canada, Ireland, New Zealand and the US, single Equality or Human Rights Acts exist. There are several advantages to this approach:

• The principle of equality is recognised as indivisible.
• Solidarity is promoted among people facing discrimination.

- Inconsistencies between different statutes cannot arise.
- It is easier to incorporate further grounds of unlawful discrimination.

A shifting terrain for EO&D?

The need for changes to the EO&D legislation must be set in the context of old and stubborn problems that have not been satisfactorily dealt with and new issues that are shifting the terrain for EO&D.

Old problems

Equal pay

The gender pay gap remains stubbornly resistant to change under current legislation. Underlying the 1970 Equal Pay Act (EPA) was the assumption that women workers were the same as men; this is what made equal pay such a powerful and influential issue (Fraser, 1999). However, the individualised nature of this legislation, which does not allow class actions, has come under attack. Over 17,000 equal pay claims entered the system in 2005/06, more than double the previous year, itself a sharp increase from the year before that. There are in fact many multiple claims against the same employer, many against local authorities that have been very slow to enact equal pay for work of equal value after their extensive equal pay audits. Without a collective dimension, a successful claim under the EPA does not alter anything beyond the individual claimant's case.

An alternative would be to allow EHRC-supported or initiated class action suits (Deakin and Morris, 2005). Class action would allow embedded organisational practices to be challenged and might result in more substantial penalties for discriminators. It acknowledges that discriminatory practices affect people by virtue of their membership of a group (Hepple et al, 2000). There are existing alternative models for tackling pay inequalities that do not rest on individual complaints-based approaches, which could inform a fundamental rethink that is needed in this area. The proactive approach taken in Ontario, Canada, could provide a model. It requires employers, in consultation with trade unions, to take staged action to address pay inequality, with pay equality plans monitored and progress reviewed by an equality agency (McColgan, 1997). The Canadian experience informed the recommendations of Hepple et al's (2000) review of the EPA, which argued for changes to overcome present weaknesses in the law. Since that review, other inquiries have advocated mandatory pay reviews (Equal Pay Task-force, 2001).

Family-friendly policies

Lewis and Lewis (1996) demonstrated the dominant approach of family-friendly policies of giving women perks to support them in their childcare role within families. This has a limited effect on gender equality. Such policies have failed to challenge workplace cultures that may act to restrict not just what is available, but also the extent to which it can be used in practice (Bagilhole, 2006). Such policies fail to challenge the uneven domestic division of labour, as parental leave is predominantly provided for and taken by women. For example, unlike maternity leave, paternity leave is very short, the right to take it is subject to service qualifications and the level of payment is not earnings-related, its low level affecting take-up (Dickens and Hall, 2006). Liff and Cameron (1997) classify this as part of a 'woman's problems' approach to equality. Liff and Ward (2001) pointed out that the danger is that such initiatives make women look inadequate and as if they are the recipients of special treatment. They argued that this is likely to create resentment and a belief that those women who do succeed have not done so on merit.

In addition, Dickens (2007) argued that, although flexible work arrangements may be valued as an aid to combining domestic responsibilities and paid work, the quality of such 'non-standard' work is critical. Too often this work is in low-grade, low-paid, stereotypically women's jobs. She argued that the right of certain carers to request arrangements to work flexibly in their current job is progress, as when women sought part-time jobs in the past this commonly led to downward occupational mobility. On the other hand, the UK government's implementation of the EU Working Time Directive (93/104/EC) has not been helpful for the pursuit of gender equality. The provision allowing individuals to opt out of the maximum 48-hour working week sits uneasily alongside the avowed concern with work–life balance, and restricts the potential of the directive to tackle men's long hours of work (Barnard et al, 2003). Dickens (2007) argued that what was needed was a focus not on the parent as the problem, but rather on the problems posed for parents by the organisation in combining paid work with domestic responsibilities.

Future issues and trends

The Equalities Review (2007) identified particular trends that it felt would change the future terrain of EO&D: an ageing population, increasing ethnic diversity, changed patterns of migration and changes in the prevalence and types of disability. These indicate that there will be more people facing disadvantage, simply because there will be more people in the groups that traditionally experience prejudice and inequality in the population.

Ageing population

There were 9.4 million adults over the age of 65 in 2005 (16% of the population) and this figure is predicted to rise to 12.4 million by 2021 (20%). By the middle of this century, the number of people aged 80 or over will be double what it is today. In 2005, London was the only region where there were more people aged under 16 than people aged 60 and over. In every other region, especially in Scotland, Wales, the South West and North East of England, there were more people aged 60 and over than children (SEU, 2006). The growth in the ageing population means that existing pressures on healthcare services, the social care system and the informal care provided by families will intensify. It has been estimated that by 2026 the demand for informal care will rise by 45% (Wanless, 2006). Poverty intensifies with longevity, and this differentially affects women, some minority ethnic people and disabled people. Thus, as the Equalities Review (2007: 38) pointed out, 'without effective strategies in place, the danger is that increasing longevity will create greater inequalities within the older population'.

Increasing ethnic diversity

The minority ethnic map of the UK is changing. The minority ethnic population of Britain is forecast to grow from 9% to around 11% by the end of the next decade, although there are different patterns of growth within this overall figure. The number of 'mixed-race' births in 2003-04 greatly exceeded the number of births within any other minority ethnic group. The highest future increases will be among Black Africans, Pakistanis and Bangladeshis, as a result of their younger demographic profile. The employment rates of new immigrant communities vary widely. For example, the employment rate among Somalis is just 12%, compared with 62% for all other new immigrants (Kyambi, 2005). The Equalities Review (2007) argued that the high levels of unemployment in some minority ethnic groups posed a real threat to social cohesion.

In the UK, we are used to classifying people by their skin colour and point of origin, although white people usually largely escape such scrutiny, apart from the Irish in the past and now Eastern Europeans. The mixed-race group demonstrates that things are more complicated than that, and always have been. Interestingly, many of the historical figures now cited as black heroes, for example, Mary Seacole and Bob Marley, were actually mixed race. Today, mixed-race people in the public eye are often described as black, for example, former MP Oona King, racing driver Lewis Hamilton and author Zadie Smith.

Box 9.1: Statistics for mixed-race people

- 677,000 people in the UK define themselves as mixed race.
- Mixed-race people account for 1.2% of the total population.
- 14.6% of the minority ethnic population are mixed race, a larger group than people of Bangladeshi, African Caribbean, African or Chinese origin.
- 47% of mixed-race people in England and Wales are under 16.
- 3.5% of school-age children and 4% of all under-fives are mixed race.

Source: Equalities Review, 2007.

In 1991, the national census began to monitor the population's racial make-up but a mixed-race category was not supplied until the 2001 Census. Projections show that this group could become the largest minority ethnic group in Britain within the next 25 years (Equalities Review, 2007). More than a quarter of minority ethnic children under five are mixed race. Analysis shows that people with one African Caribbean and one white parent make up the majority, followed by Asian/white and African/white. Those of 'any other mixed background' make up nearly a quarter. The Equalities Review (2007) argued that such figures are useful in so far as they show that, for many, notions of people from different ethnic backgrounds living separate lives are outdated. However, there remains a big gap in knowledge about what this means for EO&D policy. Mixed-race children may feel they are not recognised in the curriculum, and may feel family or peer pressure to identify with one group or the other.

New forms of migration

The Equalities Review (2007: 40) predicted that 'migration will be increasingly polarised between highly-skilled migrants and those with low skills, and also between short-term migrants and those who come to stay'. Enlargement of the EU to include Eastern European countries in 2007 introduced some new questions for the EO&D agenda and migration from the enlarged EU increases diversity. An international report on the progress of EU candidate countries from Eastern Europe in implementing EU discrimination policies made it clear that for most the issue of race, let alone sexuality and the other 'diversities', was still very abstract if not totally absent from their agendas. On a transnational European scale, many candidate countries had only limited ethnic diversity and no 'racial' issues apart from those concerning the Roma (European Industrial Relations Review, 2003) (See Chapter Eight). EU enlargement allowed millions of Eastern Europeans access to the UK, changing the nature of immigration. Since 2004, 683,000 Eastern Europeans have registered to work in UK. The figure originally estimated was around 13,000 annually, leading to well-publicised fears about some local services being overwhelmed.

Box 9.2: Open access

- Eight Eastern European nations were given access to the UK's jobs market in 2004: the Czech Republic, Estonia, Hungary, Latvia, Lithuania, Poland, Slovakia and Slovenia.
- The highest proportion of approved workers in the UK are Polish (66%), followed by Lithuanians (10%) and Slovaks (10%).
- More than 80% of approved workers are aged between 18 and 34, and 59% are male.
- The most common jobs among Eastern Europeans in the UK are factory workers (163,000), packers (37,000), kitchen assistants (36,000), cleaners (33,000) and waiters (27,000).
- Many Eastern Europeans carry out much-needed work mainly in public services – around 2,400 are bus or lorry drivers, 5,100 are care workers and 1,000 are doctors or nurses. In Nottingham, the local bus company recruited in Poland because of Polish workers' 'terrific work ethic'; one-third of its workforce is now Polish.
- A 20,000-a-year quota system was introduced for unskilled Bulgarians and Romanians in January 2007; about 9,000 applied to work in the UK in the first six months of the year.

Source: Kirby, 2007.

A study by the Joseph Rowntree Foundation (JRF) (Kirby, 2007) found that many of these new migrants did not try to integrate; one in four never socialised with British people and only four in 10 thought they were treated as equals. Nick Johnson, Commission for Racial Equality (CRE) Director of Policy, was reported in the *Guardian* as saying:

> We often see Eastern European men working together and living together; yet they need to integrate more to understand our cultural norms. For example, people drinking in the street – they (Poles) don't see anything wrong with that but for

people here it is associated with loutish behaviour and it breeds hostility. (Kirby, 2007:5)

The JRF study (Kirby, 2007: 4) reported 'little understanding' by some migrants that Britain was a multicultural society and cited instances of prejudice among migrants towards Asian people as well as a traditional hostility towards travellers or Roma people, increasing numbers of whom have come to the UK from Eastern Europe.

Most Eastern Europeans who come to the UK are young – 80% are under 34 – and come alone. Another comment from Nick Johnson, CRE Director of Policy, reported in the *Guardian*, was:

> This is a very different type of migration. In the past people were coming with their families to stay and make a new life in the UK. But these migrants already have rights as EU citizens and many are only coming for a short time without their families. (Kirby, 2007)

However, those who prophesied an endless stream of Eastern Europeans may be wrong. In August 2007, figures showed that numbers had begun to fall; around 50,000 Eastern Europeans registered to work between April and June 2007, 6,000 down over the same period in 2006. This seems partly to have been caused by wage rises in Poland, tempting some workers back.

Increasing disability

The proportion of disabled people in the population is set to rise. This increase is the result of an ageing population and medical advances and other improvements for disabled people. There has also been an increase in the number of conditions classified as disabilities; these now include, for example emotional and behavioural disorders. The fastest growth in the numbers of people reporting a disability has occurred among children aged under 16. According to the 2002 General Household Survey, the number of disabled children under 16 in Britain was 770,000 out of a population of 11.8 million children (6.5%). It is predicted that if disability among this age group continues to increase at the same rate, there will be over 1.25 million children reporting a disability by 2029 (IPPR, 2006). This will have important consequences for women. The mothers of disabled children are twice as likely not to be working as women with non-disabled children. Russell (2003) argued that the increasing incidence of childhood disability points to the need for more measures to ensure family-friendly working to increase the ability of family and carers to support disabled children.

Conflicts of interest between disadvantaged groups

There is a need to acknowledge and consider, in our ever more diverse and complex society, the likelihood of conflicts of interest between disadvantaged groups. We need to recognise the ways in which the interests of women, minority ethnic and disabled people, lesbians and gay men, people of different and no religious beliefs, and the old and the young may conflict and even encourage continuing negative discrimination.

Policy issues are complex. An illustration of this is the way in which Morris (1992) took issue with feminist analysis that viewed the care of disabled people as an oppression of women. This approach was taken to its limit by Finch's (1984: 16) statement that: 'On balance it seems to me that the residential route is the only one which ultimately will offer us a way out of the impasse of caring'. Morris (1992) saw this as disabilist and erroneously based on the assumption that women were all non-disabled, totally denying the existence and numerical dominance of women among disabled people:

Such definitions ignore, and thus perpetuate the oppression of, impaired people, the majority of whom, in Britain today at least, are women. (Morris, 1992: 73)

Another example of conflicts of interest between disadvantaged groups is the commentary disabled people use to critique the professional, medicalised model of disability. Much of that model, in terms of health and social services provision, is actually delivered by women. In turn, the women delivering the services are generally managed by men, and although management within health and social care organisations is changing, it sometimes has unexpected results. For example, while some women and minority ethnic people have achieved managerial positions within such organisations, they may, as managers, perpetuate the unequal opportunities they themselves faced (Bagilhole, 1997).

Contentious issues concerning conflicting views around the rights of women to abortion, the campaigns for the introduction of legalised assisted death and the disabled people's movement continue. Moreover, the introduction of new strands of EO&D has prompted new conflicts to emerge. As Filby (2007) pointed out, some religious groups can themselves promote and defend inequalities. Catholic groups, for example, continue to play an important role in certain EO&D issues. In the interwar years, they successfully opposed public funding of birth-control advice. They opposed the legalisation of abortion in 1967, supported subsequent unsuccessful attempts to amend the Abortion Act and are prominent in anti-abortion lobby groups. Some faith groups within Islam and Christianity openly refuse to accept that homosexuals should have equal rights with heterosexuals.

Issues around religious beliefs and civil partnerships and gay adoption persist. Porter (2007: 144) argued that the debate in 2007 over measures to extend the prevention of discrimination in the provision of goods and services to gay men and lesbians 'demonstrated that the government can find itself trapped between competing interest groups. In this case the Church of England and Roman Catholic Church claimed that their members' rights to practice their faith would be infringed if they were forced to provide adoption services to Gay and Lesbian couples'. In education, national curriculum guidelines on anti-discrimination in gender, race, and disability are clear but no mention is made of sexual orientation so as not to offend certain religious communities. The 1998 Human Rights Act attempts to address these issues, 'stipulating that faith groups should be allowed to exercise their beliefs and practice their religion, but not to the point where this infringes the rights of other groups' (Filby, 2007: 58).

Multiculturalism or universal human rights?

In terms of minority ethnic immigration, the first strategy of policy makers in the UK centred on **assimilation**. This meant the merging of minority ethnic differences into the so-called majority culture. As the Runnymede Trust Commission (2000, 37) put it, 'people were expected to give up everything in order to belong'. Eventually cultural difference began to be recognised and valued, leading to the strategy of **multiculturalism**, or the assumption that by understanding different minority ethnic cultures the majority would be tolerant and accepting of these groups. However, this led to arguments about how tolerant the majority society should be if some minority cultural values went against the majority view. In the UK, debate arose in particular around issues of multiculturalism and women's rights. This centred on the 2003 Genital Mutilation Act, 'forced' versus arranged marriages and so-called 'honour killings'. The Runnymede Trust Commission (2000: 52) confronted some of these issues, arguing that 'there are disputes both between communities and within them in which the state cannot remain neutral'. It identified four possible ways of resolving such disputes:

- appealing to the principles of moral universalism;
- referring to the majority's values and customs;
- adhering to the no-harm principle;
- achieving consensus through intercultural deliberation.

However, it admitted that although 'moral universalism' (for example, life, liberty and the pursuit of happiness) was at first sight an attractive approach, in practice it was too abstract a concept to guide decisions in particular cases. Referring to the 'majority's values and customs' denied the fact that a society 'continuously redefines its identity and modifies its customs and practices, including those it currently holds to be fundamental' (Runnymede Trust Commission, 2000: 52). It argued that the 'no-harm principle' is 'largely unproblematic when physical harm is involved, but it does not provide specific enough guidance on matters such as … moral and emotional harm … what constitutes harm is itself often a matter of deep disagreement' (Runnymede Trust Commission, 2000: 53). It ends by taking the view that in practice, 'consensus through intercultural deliberation' is frequently the only effective solution. Its advantage is that:

> … it shows respect for minority viewpoints, involves people in decisions that affect them, deepens understanding between communities, and leads to realistic and widely acceptable decisions. It requires ground rules, however. There must be a shared commitment to these rules, and more widely to the values of tolerance, readiness to compromise, and respect for the dignity of individuals and deliberative decision-making that underpins them. (Runnymede Trust Commission, 2000: 53)

The trust argued that underpinning this approach should be values embodied in international human rights standards. On the basis of these values, it argued, 'it is legitimate to ban female circumcision, forced marriages, cruel punishment of children, and repressive and unequal treatment of women, even though these practices may enjoy cultural authority in certain communities. (Runnymede Trust Commission, 2000: 54).

Conclusion

EO&D legislation and policy needs to move towards a multiple-focus approach and away from the current divided focus on gender, race, disability, religion or belief, sexual orientation and age exemplified by the separate Acts in each of these areas. An 'integrated/generic' approach to EO&D with one piece of proactive legislation and one enforcing agency could link EO&D issues common to the different strands into effective, coherent, proactive policies. What is needed is policies and practices to deal with 'shared disadvantage' across more than one group and 'specialist disadvantage' experienced within one group, and an intersectional perspective to deal with multiple disadvantage and discrimination, and conflicting interests between and within groups.

Some argue that cultural changes needed to create a fairer society cannot be achieved through laws. Certainly, legal reforms alone cannot resolve inequality. However, alongside political leadership, legislation does provide an impetus for change. Therefore, there is a need for the retention of an equal treatment legislative framework, plus proactive positive action measures. Approaches that recognise group-based disadvantage and inequality from an intersectional perspective should be favoured over approaches that focus on the individual and conceptions of individual merit that fail to recognise historical disadvantage, institutional discrimination and structural inequalities. There is a need to recognise both variations in experience between different groups and the way these intersect with, and are conditioned by, gender, ethnicity, disability and other sources of individual and collective identity.

All these issues are extremely challenging, and are complicated by the fact that while problems of the past persist, such as the gender pay gap, new issues are emerging that shift the EO&D terrain. In addition, as Verloo (2006: 213) argued, 'strategies on one axis of inequality are mostly not neutral towards other axes'. Negotiations over contested issues – for example, the content of the national curriculum, rights for gay men and lesbians and equality for women in the home and workplace – need to take place. The Runnymede Trust Commission (2000) argued that ground rules for these necessary negotiations are provided in part by international human rights standards enshrined in the European Convention on Human Rights and the UN Convention on the Rights of the Child:

> The fundamental need, both practical and theoretical, is to treat people equally and with due respect for difference…. Neither equality nor respect for difference is a sufficient value in itself. The two must be held together, mutually challenging and supportive. (Runnymede Trust Commission, 2000: xvii)

The infamous Tebbit test of judging a person's commitment to Britain as to which cricket team they support when England is playing the West Indies, Indian or Pakistani team, is not only racist but also seriously out of date. People today are constantly juggling different, not always wholly incompatible, identities. As the Runnymede Trust Commission (2000: 36) reported: 'South Asians and African-Caribbeans support India, Pakistan and the West Indies against England but England against Australia, especially when the English team includes Asian and black players'. New approaches such as intersectionality may point the way forward for EO&D policy making in a sensitive and effective way that recognises and acknowledges these emerging complex identities and our increasingly complex and diverse society. This is not to suggest that the way forward is easy, but that it must be attempted in the light of the theoretical and practical policy insights we have managed to gain thus far.

Summary

- For various reasons British EO&D legislation has proved insufficient to eliminate inequality.
- However, legislation has an important role to play as part of wider comprehensive strategies for tackling inequality, discrimination and disadvantage.
- It can be argued that EO&D legislation is fairly limited and that the full potential of what the spirit of the law requires is not being realised in practice.
- Since 1997, successive New Labour governments have strengthened, developed and increased EO&D legislation, and created a single equality commission, which holds the potential for an intersectional approach to EO&D policy.
- The EU has had a positive influence on EO&D policies in member states. However, the enlargement of the EU to 27 member states and the development of policy initiatives across six strands of equality has raised questions over the feasibility of driving the EO&D agenda forward in the future.
- An extra complication is the heterogeneity of groups covered by EO&D legislation. Feminist theory has tackled this with the concept of intersectionality, which stresses how the various types of discrimination can overlap.
- There remain 'old' and stubborn problems for EO&D including unequal pay for women and men, and assumptions about women being the main carers underpinning family-friendly policies.
- Alongside the 'old' issues are new issues that are shifting the terrain for EO&D, such as an ageing population, increasing ethnic diversity, new forms of migration and increasing disability.
- There is a need to acknowledge and consider, in our ever more diverse and complex society, the likelihood of conflicts of interest between disadvantaged groups.

Questions for discussion

- Does the main weakness in EO&D legislation arise from its conceptualisation of equality as treating people the same?
- The race and sex discrimination legislation embody a symmetrical approach to an asymmetrical social problem (that is, men and white people are not discriminated against to the extent that women and minority ethnic workers are, yet they are equally protected). Should this be so?

- Are some disadvantages more substantial than others?
- What is the best way to resolve contentious issues of conflicting interests?

Further reading

Davis, K. (2008) 'Intersectionality as buzzword: a sociology of science perspective on what makes a feminist theory successful', *Feminist Theory*, vol 9, pp 67-85.

Dickens, L. (1999) 'Beyond the business case: a three-pronged approach to equality action', *Human Resource Management*, vol 9, pp 9-20.

Dickens, L. (2007) 'The road is long: thirty years of equality Legislation in Britain', *British Journal of Industrial Relations*, vol 45, no 3, pp 463-94.

Hepple, B., Coussey, M. and Choudury, T. (2000) *Equality: A new framework. Report of the Independent Review of the Enforcement of UK Anti-Discrimination Legislation*, Oxford: Hart Publishing.

Roulstone, A. and Warren, J. (2006) 'Applying a barriers approach to monitoring disabled people's employment: implications for the Disability Discrimination Act 2005', *Disability and Society*, vol 21, pp 115-31.

Runnymede Trust Commission (2000) *The future of multi-ethnic Britain*, London: Profile Books Ltd.

Verloo, M. (2006) 'Multiple inequalities, intersectionality and the European Union', *European Journal of Women's Studies*, vol 13, no 3, pp 211-28.

References

Abbott, P. and Wallace, C. (1990) *An introduction to sociology: Feminist Perspectives*, London: Routledge.

Adams, D. and Houston, D.M. (2006) *Equalities, diversity and prejudice in Britain: Results from the 2005 National Survey*, Report commissioned by the Equalities Review, Centre for the Study of Group Processes, University of Kent.

Adams, L., Carter, K. and Schafer, S. (2005) *Equal Pay Reviews Survey*, Manchester: Equal Opportunities Commission.

Adorno, T., Frenkel-Brunswick, E., Levinson, D. and Sanford, N. (1950) *The Authoritarian Personality*, New York: Harper.

Age Concern (2006) *How ageist is Britain?* London: Age Concern.

Amos, V. and Ouseley, H. (1994) 'Foreword', in M. Cheung-Judge and A. Henley (eds) *Equality in action. Introducing equal opportunities in voluntary organisations*, London: NCVO Publications.

Anker, R. (1998) *Gender and Jobs. Sex Segregation of Occupations in the World*, Geneva: International Labour Office.

Anthias, F. and Yuval-Davis, N. (1993) *Racialized boundaries: Race, nation, gender, colour and class and the anti-racist struggle*, London: Routledge.

Audit Commission (2004) *The journey to race equality: Delivering improved services to local communities*, London: Audit Commission.

Bagilhole, B. (1993) 'Managing to be fair: implementing equal opportunities in a local authority', *Local Government Studies*, vol 19, no 2, pp 163-75.

Bagilhole, B. (1994a) *Women, work and equal opportunities*, Aldershot: Avebury.

Bagilhole, B. (1994b) 'A tale of two counties: implementation of equal opportunities and race relations policies', *Local Government Policy Making*, vol 21, no 2, pp 41-8.

Bagilhole, B. (1996a) 'Tea and sympathy or teetering on social work? An analysis of the boundaries between voluntary and professional care', *Social Policy and Administration*, vol 30, no 3, pp 189-205.

Bagilhole, B. (1996b) 'Kith not kin: women as givers and receivers of voluntary care', *European Journal of Women's Studies*, vol 3, pp 39-54.

Bagilhole, B. (1997) *Equal opportunities and social policy: Issues of gender, race and disability*, Harlow: Addison Wesley Longman.

Bagilhole, B. (2002a) 'Divide and be ruled? Multiple discrimination and the concept of social exclusion', in E. Breitenbach, A. Brown, F. Mackay and J. Webb (eds) *The changing politics of gender equality in Britain*, Houndmills: Palgrave.

Bagilhole, B. (2002b) *Women in non-traditional occupations: Challenging men*, London: Palgrave Macmillan.

Bagilhole, B. (2004) 'Equality and human rights: A new equality framework for Britain', Paper presented at the Athena European Network Conference, Helsinki, Finland, 27-30 May (www.rosadoc.be/site/rosa/english/european%20projects/athena/introduction.htm).

Bagilhole, B. (2005) 'From equal treatment to positive action: the influence of the European Union on equal opportunities in the UK', *Construction Information Quarterly, Journal of the Chartered Institute of Building, Special Issue*, vol 7, no 3, pp 79-83.

Bagilhole, B. (2006) 'Family-friendly policies and equal opportunities: a contradiction in terms?', *British Journal of Guidance and Counselling*, vol 34, no 3, pp 327-43.

Bagilhole, B. (2008 forthcoming) 'Applying the lens of intersectionality to UK equal opportunities and diversity policies', *Canadian Journal of Administrative Sciences*.

Bagilhole, B. and Byrne, P. (2000) 'From hard to soft law and from equality to reconciliation in the United Kingdom', in L. Hantrais (ed) *Gendered policies in Europe: Reconciling employment and family life*, London: Macmillan.

Bagilhole, B. and Cross, S. (2006) 'It never struck me as female: investigating men's entry into female-dominated occupations', *Journal of Gender Studies*, vol 15, no 1, pp 35-48.

Bagilhole, B. and White, K. (2008) 'Towards a gendered skills analysis of senior management positions in UK and Australian universities', *Tertiary Education and Management* (Journal of the European Association for Institutional Research), vol 14, no 1, pp 1-12.

Baird, V. (1992) 'We've only just begun', *New Internationalist*, January, no 227, pp 4-7.

Bamber, D. (2001) 'Labour's U-turn over cash for asylum seekers', *Telegraph*, 19 June, p 10.

Barazzetti, D., Leccardi, C., Leone, M. and Maraggia, S. (2001) *Employment and women's studies: The impact of women's studies training on women's employment in Europe*, HPSE-CT2001-00082, Background Data Report, Italy (www.hull.ac.uk/ewsi).

Barnard, C., Deakin, S. and Hobbs, R. (2003) 'Opting out of the 48-hour week: employer necessity or individual choice? An empirical study of the operation of Article 18(1)(B) of the Working Time Directive in the UK'. *Industrial Law Journal*, vol 32, pp 223-52.

Barnes, C. (1991) *Disabled people in Britain and discrimination*, London: Hurst and Co.

Barnes, L. and Ashtiany, S. (2003) 'The diversity approach to achieving equality: potential and pitfalls', *Industrial Law Review*, vol 32, pp 274-96.

Beauchamp, K. (1979) *One race, the human race*, London: Liberation.

Beechey, V. (1977) 'Some notes on female wage labour in capitalist production', *Capital and Class*, vol 3, pp 45-66.

Begum, N. (1994) 'Mirror mirror on the wall', in N. Begum, M. Hill and A. Stevens (eds) *Reflections: The views of black disabled people on their lives and community care*, London: Central Council for Education and Training in Social Work.

Benabou, R. (1997) *Inequality and growth*, National Bureau of Economic Research Working Paper 5658, Cambridge, MA: National Bureau of Economic Research.

Benedict, R. (1968) *Race and racism*, London: Routledge and Kegan Paul.

Benhabib, S. (1994) 'From identity politics to social feminism: A plea for the nineties', *Philosophy of Education* (www.ed.uiuc.edu/EPS/PES-Yearbook/94_docs/BENHABIB.HTM, accessed 8 January 2008).

Benn, S.I. and Peters, R.S. (1959) *Social principles and the democratic state*, London: George Allen and Unwin.

Benschop, Y., Halsema, L. and Schreurs, P. (2001) 'The division of labour and inequalities between the sexes: an ideological dilemma', *Gender, Work and Organization*, vol 8, no 1, pp 1-18.

Bergqvist, C. and Jungar, A.C. (2000) 'Adaptation of diffusion of the Swedish gender model?', in L. Hantrais (ed) *Gendered policies in Europe: Reconciling employment and family life*, London: Macmillan.

Berthoud, R. and Blekesaune, M. (2006) *Persistent employment disadvantage, 1974 to 2003*, Institute for Social & Economic Research Working Paper 2006-9, Colchester: ISER, University of Essex.

Beynon, R. (2006) 'Race and immigration: is it the end of the affair?', *Joint Council for the Welfare of Immigrants Bulletin*, Spring.

Birkett, K. and Worman, D. (eds) (1988) *Getting on with disabilities. An employer's guide*, London: Institute of Personnel Management.

Blair, T. (2004) 'Foreword' in *Fairness for all: A new Commission for Equality and Human Rights* (Cm 6185), Norwich: The Stationery Office.

Blakemore, K. and Drake, R. (1996) *Understanding equal opportunity policies*, Hemel Hempstead: Prentice Hall/Harvester Wheatsheaf.

Bourne, C. and Whitmore, J. (1993) *Race and sex discrimination*, London: Sweet and Maxwell.

Brah, A. (1992) 'Women of South Asian origin in Britain: issues and concerns', in P. Braham, A. Rattansi, and R. Skellington (eds) *Racism and antiracism: Inequalities, opportunities and policies*, London: Sage Publications.

Brandt, G. (1986) *The realisation of anti-racist teaching*, Lewes: Falmer Press.

Breitenbach, E., Brown, A., Mackay, F. and Webb, J. (eds) (2002) *The changing politics of gender equality in Britain*, Basingstoke: Palgrave.

Breitenbach, E. and Galligan, Y. (2006) 'Measuring gender equality: reflecting on experiences and challenges in the UK and Ireland', *Policy & Politics*, vol 34, no 4, pp 597-614.

Brown, C. (1984) *Black and white Britain*, London: Heinemann.

Buchanan, A. and Mathieu, D. (1986) 'Philosophy and justice', in R.L. Cohen (ed) *Justice: Views from the social sciences*, New York, NY: Plenum Press.

Cabinet Office (2005) *Improving the life chances of disabled people. Final report*, London: Cabinet Office and Prime Minister's Strategy Unit.

Cameron, C., Moss, P. and Owen, C. (1999) *Men in the nursery: Gender and caring work*, London: Sage Publications.

Carter, T. (1986) *Shattering illusions: West Indians in British politics*, London: Lawrence Wishart.

CEC (Commission of the European Communities) (1995) *Fourth Medium-Term Community Action Programme on Equal Opportunities for Women and Men (1996-2000)*, COM (95) 381, Brussels: Commission of the European Communities.

CEC (2005) *Decision of the European Parliament and Council on the European Year of Equal Opportunities for All (2007)*, Brussels: Commission of the European Communities.

Center for Women's Global Leadership (2001) *A Women's Human Rights Approach to the World Conference Against Racism*, www.cwgl.rutgers.edu/globalcenter/policy/gcpospaper.html

Chaney, P. (2004) 'The post-devolution equality agenda: the case of Welsh Assembly's statutory duty to promote equality of opportunity', *Policy and Politics*, vol 32, no 1, pp 37-52.

Cheung-Judge, M. and Henley, A. (1994) *Equality in action. Introducing equal opportunities in voluntary organisations*, London: NCVO Publications.

Cholewinski, R. (1998) 'Enforced destitution of asylum seekers in the UK: the denial of fundamental human rights', *International Journal of Refugee Law*, vol 10, no 3, p 462.

Choudhury, T. (2006) 'The Commission for Equality and Human Rights. Designing the big tent', *Maastricht Journal of European and Comparative Law*, vol 13, pp 311-22.

Cockburn, C. (1989) 'Equal opportunities: the short and long agenda', *Industrial Relations Journal*, vol 20, no 3, pp 45-62.

Cockburn, C. (1991) *In the way of women: Men's resistance to sex equality in organizations*, London: Macmillan.

Cohen, R.L. (1986) (ed) *Justice: Views from the social sciences*, New York, NY: Plenum Press.

Collins, H. (1992) *The equal opportunities handbook*, Oxford: Blackwell.

Cook, J. and Watt, S. (1987) 'Racism, women and poverty', in C. Glendinning and J. Millar (eds) *Women and poverty in Britain in the 1990s*, Hemel Hempstead: Harvester Wheatsheaf.

Cook, S.W. (1978) 'Interpersonal and attitudinal outcomes in co-operating interracial groups', *Journal of Research and Development in Education*, 12.

Crawley, C. and Slowey, J. (1995) *Women and Europe, 1985-1995*, Birmingham: Crawley.

CRE (1989) *The race relations code of practice in employment: Are employers complying?*, London: Commission for Racial Equality.

CRE (1991) *Annual report*, London: Commission for Racial Equality.

CRE (2007) *A lot done: A lot to do*, London: Commission for Racial Equality.

Crenshaw, K. (1989) 'Demarginalizing the intersection of race and sex: a black feminist critique of antidiscrimination doctrine, feminist theory, and antiracist politics', *University of Chicago Legal Forum*, vol 1989, pp 139-67.

Crenshaw, K. (1991) 'Mapping the margins: intersectionality, identity, politics, and violence against women of color', *Stanford Law Review*, vol 43, pp 1241-99.

Crewe, I. (1983) 'Representation and the ethnic minorities', in N. Glazer and K. Young (eds) *Ethnic pluralism and public policy*, London: Heinemann.

Crompton, R. and Harris, F. (1999) 'Attitudes, women's employment, and the changing domestic division of labour: a cross-national analysis', in R. Crompton (ed) *Restructuring gender relations and employment: The decline of the male breadwinner*, Oxford: Oxford University Press, pp 128-49.

Cross, S. and Bagilhole, B. (2002) 'Girls' jobs for the boys? Men, masculinity and non-traditional occupations', *Gender, Work and Organization*, vol 9, no 2, pp 204-26.

Cunningham, S. (1992) 'The development of equal opportunities theory and practice in the European Community', *Policy & Politics*, vol 20, no 3, pp 177-89.

Dale, A. (2006) 'A life-course perspective on ethnic differences in women's economic activity in Britain', *European Sociological Review*, vol 22, no 4, pp 67-82.

Dale, J. and Foster, P. (1986) *Feminists and state welfare*, London: Routledge and Kegan Paul.

Daunt, P. (1991) *Meeting disability: A European response*, London: Cassell.

Davidson, M. and Burke, R. (2000) 'Women in management: current research issues', in M.J. Davidson and R.J. Burke (eds) *Women in management*, London: Sage Publications, pp 1-7.

Davis, A. (1981) *Women, race and class*, London: The Woman's Press.

Davis, K. (2008) 'Intersectionality as buzzword: a sociology of science perspective on what makes a feminist theory successful', *Feminist Theory*, vol 9, pp 67-85.

Deakin, S. and Morris, G. (2005) *Labour law*, Oxford: Hart Publishing.

de Burca, G. (1995) 'The language of rights and European integration', in J. Shaw and G. More (eds) *New legal dynamics of the European Union*, Oxford: Clarendon Press.

Del Re, A. (2000) 'The paradoxes of Italian law and practice', in L. Hantrais (ed) *Gendered policies in Europe: Reconciling employment and family life*, London: Macmillan.

DEMOS (2000) *Family business*, DEMOS Collection, Issue 15, Trowbridge: Redwood Books.

Department of Employment (1995) *Equality pays. How equal opportunities can benefit your business. A guide for small employers*, London: Department of Employment.

DfEE (Department for Education and Employment) (2000) *Evaluation of the Code of Practice on Age Diversity in Employment*, London: Department for Education and Employment.

Dickens, L. (1999) 'Beyond the business case: a three-pronged approach to equality action', *Human Resource Management*, vol 9, pp 9-20.

Dickens, L. (2006) 'Equality and work life balance: what's happening at the workplace?', *Industrial Law Journal*, vol 35, pp 445-49.

Dickens, L. (2007) 'The road is long: thirty years of equality legislation in Britain', *British Journal of Industrial Relations*, vol 45, no 3, pp 463-94.

Dickens, L. and Hall, M. (2006) 'Fairness – up to a point. Assessing the impact of New Labour's employment legislation', *Human Resource Management Journal*, vol 16, pp 338-56.

Doyle, B. (1997) 'Enabling legislation or dissembling law: the Disability Discrimination Act 1995', *Modern Law Review*, vol 60, pp 64-78.

DTI (Department of Trade and Industry) (2003) *Press Release*, P/2003/537, 29 October.

DTI (2004) *Fairness for all: A new Commission for Equality and Human Rights* (Cm 6185), Norwich: The Stationery Office.

DTI (2005) *Full Regulatory Impact Assessment for Sexual Orientation*, London: Department of Trade and Industry.

DTI (2006) *Success at work. Protecting vulnerable workers and supporting good employers*, London: Department of Trade and Industry.

DTI and DCA (2004) *White Paper on Equality and Human Rights: A new framework for Britain*, London: Department of Trade and Industry and Department of Constitutional Affairs.

Dummett, A. (1991) 'Europe? Which Europe?', *New Community*, vol 18, no 1, pp 167-75.

EC (1994) *European social policy. A way forward for the Union. A White Paper*, COM (94) 333, Brussels: Office for Official Publications of the European Communities.

EC (2004) *Equality and non-discrimination in an enlarged European Union. Green Paper*, Luxembourg: Office for Official Publications of the European Commission.

EHRC (2008a) *Sex and power*, London: Equality and Human Rights Commission www.equalityandhumanrights.com

EHRC (2008b) *Single Equality Bill*, www.equalityandhumanrights.com

EOC (2006a) *Moving on up? Bangladeshi, Pakistani and Black Caribbean women and work. Early findings from the Equal Opportunities Commission's investigation in England*, Manchester: Equal Opportunities Commission (www.theequalitiesreview.org.uk).

EOC (2006b) *Facts about women and men in Great Britain*, Manchester: Equal Opportunities Commission (www.EHRC.com).

EOC (2007) *Sex and power: Who runs Britain?*, Manchester: Equal Opportunities Commission (www.EHRC.com).

EOR (*Equal Opportunities Review*) (1992) Equal Opportunities Review, no 41, January/February, pp 20-5.

EOR (1994) 'Taking the cap off discrimination awards', *Equal Opportunities Review*, no 57, September/October, pp 11-13.

EOR (1996) 'EC fourth equality action programme', *Equal Opportunities Review*, no 67, May/June, pp 34-5.

Equalities Review (2007) *Fairness and freedom: The final report of the Equalities Review*, London: Equalities Review.

Equality Institutions Review (2002) *Equality and diversity: Making it happen*, Norwich: The Stationery Office.

Equal Pay Task-force (2001) *Just wages*, Manchester: Equal Opportunities Commission.

Etkowitz, H., Kemelgor, C. and Uzi, B. (2000) *Athena unbound: The advancement of women in science and technology*, Cambridge: Cambridge University Press.

European Industrial Relations Review (2003) 'International: Report on equality, diversity and enlargement', no 358, November, pp 24-31.

Evans, M. (1994) 'Introduction', in M. Evans (ed) *The woman question*, London: Sage Publications.

Fagan, C., Grimshaw, D. and Rubery, J. (2006) 'The subordination of the gender equality objective: the National Reform Programmes and "making work pay" policies', *International Relations Journal Annual European Review*, pp 571-92.

Faludi, S. (1991) 'Blame it on feminism', *Mother Jones Magazine*, September/October, pp 5-6.

Fekete, L. (2001) 'The emergence of xeno-racism', *Race and Class*, vol 43, no 2, pp 23-40.

Filby, L. (2007) 'Religion and belief' in P. Thane, T. Evans, L. Filby, N. Kimber, H. McCarthy, S. Millar, M. Porter and B. Taylor (eds) *Equalities in Great Britain, 1946-2006*, Report commissioned by the Equalities Review, London: Centre for Contemporary British History, Institute of Historical Research, University of London.

Finch, J. (1984) 'Community care: developing non-sexist alternatives', *Critical Social Policy*, vol 9, no 4, pp 5-19.

Finger, A. (1992) 'Forbidden fruit', *New Internationalist*, no 233, July, pp 8-10.

Finkelstein, V. (1980) *Attitudes and disabled people: Issues for discussion*, London: Royal Association for Disability and Rehabilitation.

Finkelstein, V. (1981). 'Disability and the helper-helped relationship' in A. Brechin, P. Liddiard and J. Swain (eds) *Handicap in a Social World*, London: Hodder and Stoughton.

Foot, P. (1969) *The rise of Enoch Powell*, Harmondsworth: Penguin.

Forbes, I. (1991) 'Equal opportunity: radical, liberal and conservative critiques', in E. Meehan and S. Sevenhuijsen (eds) *Equality, politics and gender*, London: Sage Publications.

Forbes, I. and Mead, G. (1992) *Measure for measure. A comparative analysis of measures to combat racial discrimination in the member countries of the European Community*, Research Series No 1, Sheffield: Department of Employment.

Ford, G. (ed) (1992) *Fascist Europe: The rise of racism and xenophobia*, London: Pluto Press.

Frankena, W.K. (1962) 'The concept of social justice', in R.B. Brandt (ed) Social Justice, Engle Cliffs, NJ: Prentice-Hall Inc.

Fraser, K.M. (1999) *Same or different: Gender politics in the workplace*, Aldershot: Ashgate.

Fredman, S. (2002a) *Future of equality in Britain*, Manchester: Equal Opportunities Commission.

Fredman, S. (2002b) *Discrimination law*, Oxford: Oxford University Press.

Fredman, S. (2005) 'Double trouble: multiple discrimination and the EU Law', *European Anti-Discrimination Law Review*, vol 2, pp 13-21.

Fredman, S. and Spencer, S. (2006) 'Equality: towards an outcome-focused duty', *Equal Opportunities Review*, vol 156, pp 14-19.

Gale, A. (1995) 'Women in construction', in D. Langford, M.R. Hancock, R. Fellows and A. Gale (eds) *Human resources in the management of construction*, Harlow: Longman.

Gazsi, J., Hars, A., Juhasz, B., Peto, A. and Szabo, S. (2001) *Employment and women's studies: The impact of women's studies training on women's employment in Europe*, HPSE-CT2001-00082, Background Data Report, Hungary, (www.hull.ac.uk/ewsi).

George, V. and Wilding, P. (1994) *Welfare and ideology*, Hemel Hempstead: Harvester Wheatsheaf.

Gibbon, P. (1993) 'Equal opportunities policy and race equality', in P. Braham, A. Rattansi and R. Skellington (eds) *Racism and anti-racism: Inequalities, opportunities and policies*, London: Sage Publications.

Gilroy, P. (1987) *There ain't no black in the Union Jack*, London: Hutchinson.

Gilroy, R. (1993) *Good practices in equal opportunities*, Aldershot: Avebury.

Godwin, K. (2006) 'Race equality: an ongoing obligation', *Equal Opportunities Review*, vol 154, pp 13-20.

Gonas, L. and Lehto, A. (1999) 'Segregation of the Labour Market', in European Commission, *Women and Work: Equality between women and men*, Luxembourg: Office of the Official Publications for the European Communities.

Gooding, C. (1994) *Disabling laws, enabling Acts: Disability rights in Britain and America*, London: Pluto Press.

Gooding, C., Hasler, F. and Oliver, M. (1994) *What price civil rights?*, London: Rights Now Campaign.

Grainger, H. and Fitzner, G. (2006) *The Fair Treatment at Work Survey 2005: Executive summary*, Employment Relations Research Series No 63, London: Department of Trade and Industry.

Guardian (2000) 12 March, p 15.

Hakim, C. (2003) *Models of the family in modern societies: Ideals and realties*, Aldershot: Ashgate.

Hall, L.A. (2001) 'Sexuality', in P. Addison and H. Jones (eds) *A companion to contemporary Britain 1939-2000*, Oxford: Oxford University Press.

Hall, S. (1983) 'The great moving right show', in S. Hall and M. Jacques (eds) *The politics of Thatcherism*, London: Lawrence and Wishart.

Hantrais, L. (1993) 'Women, work and welfare in France', in J. Lewis (ed) *Women and social policies in Europe. Work, family and the state*, Aldershot: Edward Elgar Publishing Ltd.

Hartmann, P. and Husbands, C. (1974) *Racism and the mass media: A study of the role of the mass media in the formation of white beliefs and attitudes in Britain*, London: Davis-Poynter.

Hatten, W., Vinter, L. and Williams, R. (2002) *Dads on dads: Needs and expectations at home and at work*, London: MORI Social Research Institute.

Hattersley, R. (1965) 'Defending the White Paper', *The Spectator*, 20 August, p 20.

Heikkinen, M. (2005) *Gender equality in Finland: Recent developments*, www.rosadoc.be/site/rosa/english/pdf/athena/swot_quations_finland.pdf

Hepple, B. (1983) 'Judging equal rights', *Current Legal Problems*, vol 36, pp 71-90.

Hepple, B. (2006) 'The equality commissions and the future commission for equality and human rights', in L. Dickens and A. Neal (eds) *The changing institutional face of British employment relations*, Utrecht: Kluwer Law International, pp 101-14.

Hepple, B., Coussey, M. and Choudury, T. (2000) *Equality: A new framework. Report of the Independent Review of the Enforcement of UK Anti-Discrimination Legislation*, Oxford: Hart Publishing.

Hervey, T. K. (1995) 'Migrant workers and their families', in J. Shaw and G. More (eds) *New legal dynamics of the European Union*, Oxford: Clarendon Press.

Hesse, B., Dhanwant, K., Bennett, C. and Gilchrist, P. (1992) *Beneath the surface: racial harassment*, Aldershot: Avebury.

Hibbert, A. and Meager, N. (2003) 'Key indicators of women's position in Britain', *Labour Market Trends*, vol 110, pp 503-11.

Hilgard, E.R., Atkinson, R.L. and Atkinson, R.C. (1979) *Introduction to psychology*, New York: Harcourt Brace, Jovanovich Inc.

Hill Collins, P. (2000) *Black feminist thought: Knowledge, consciousness and the politics of empowerment* (2nd edn), New York, NY: Routledge Press.

Holden, A. (2005) *Makers and manners: Politics and morality in post-war Britain*, London: Politicos.

Holroyd, J. (1999) 'Racially aggravated offences', *New Law Journal*, 14 May, p 722.

Home Office (1998a) *Fairer faster and firmer: A modern approach to immigration and asylum*, White Paper, London: Home Office.

Home Office (1998b) *Supporting families*, London: Home Office.

Home Office (2001) *Community cohesion: A report of the Independent Review Team*, London: Home Office.

Home Office (2004) *Strength in diversity: Towards a community cohesion and racial equality strategy*, London: Home Office Community Directorate.

hooks, b. (1981) *Ain't I a woman? Black women and feminism*, Boston, MA: South End Press.

Howard, M. and Tibballs, S. (2003) *Talking equality: What men and women think about equality in Britain today*, London: Future Foundation.

Humm, M. (1995) *The dictionary of feminist theory* (2nd edn), London: Prentice Hall/Harvester Wheatsheaf.

Independent (1992) 18 February, p 12.

Indian Mail (1993) 14-20 December.

Institute for Employment Studies (2006) *Barriers to employment for Pakistanis and Bangladeshis in Britain*, DWP Research Report 360, London: Department of Work and Pensions.

IPPR (Institute for Public Policy Research) (2006) *Disability 2020*, London: Institute for Public Policy Research.

James, G. (2006) 'The Work and Families Act 2006: legislation to improve choice and flexibility?', *Industrial Law Journal*, vol 35, pp 272-8.

Jencks, C. (1988) 'What must be equal for opportunity to be equal?', in N.E. Bowie (ed) *Equal opportunity*, Boulder, CO: Westview Press.

Jewson, N. (1990) 'Inner city riots', *Social Studies Review*, vol 5, no 5, pp 170-4.

Jewson, N. and Mason, D. (1986) 'The theory and practice of equal opportunities: liberal and radical approaches', *Sociological Review*, vol 34, no 2, pp 307-34.

Jewson, N. and Mason, D. (1993) *Equal employment opportunities in the 1990s: A policy principle come of age?*, Leicester: University of Leicester.

Jewson, N., Mason, D., Dewett, A. and Rossiter, W. (1995) *Formal equal opportunities policies and employment best practice*, Department for Education and Employment Research Series No 69, Sheffield: Department for Education and Employment.

Joseph, G. and Lewis, J. (1981) *Common differences*, London: South End Press.

Julkunen, R. (1999) 'Gender, work and welfare state. Finland in comparison', in M. Gonroos (ed) *Women in Finland*, Helsinki: Otava.

Kandola, R. and Fullerton, J. (1998) *Diversity in action: Managing the mosaic*, London: Chartered Institute of Personnel and Development.

Kandola, R., Fullerton, J. and Ahmed, Y. (1995) 'Managing diversity: succeeding where equal opportunities has failed', *Equal Opportunities Review*, 59, January/February, pp 31-6.

Kanter, R.M. (1977) *Men and women of the corporation*, New York, NY: Basic Books.

Kimber, N. (2007) 'Race and equality', in P Thane, T. Evans, L. Filby, N. Kimber, H. McCarthy, S. Millar, M. Porter and B. Taylor (eds) *Equalities in Great Britain, 1946-2006*, Report commissioned by the Equalities Review, London: Centre for Contemporary British History, Institute of Historical Research, University of London.

Kirby, T. (2007) 'The evolving face of Great Britain', *Race for Change, Special Report on Race Relations in Britain*, Guardian Professional Special edition, 26 September.

Konrad, A.M. and Mangel, R. (2000) 'The impact of work-life programs on firm productivity', *Strategic Management Journal*, vol 21, pp 1225-37.

Konrad, A.M., Prasad, P. and Pringle, J. K. (2006) *Handbook of workplace diversity*, London, Thousand Oaks, CA: Sage Publications.

Kyambi, S. (2005) *Beyond black and white: Mapping new immigrant communities*, London: Institute for Public Policy Research.

Laczko, F. and Phillipson, C. (1990) 'Defending the right to work: age discrimination in employment', in M. McEwen (ed) *Age: The unrecognised discrimination*, London: Age Concern.

Lanquetin, M.T., Laufer, J. and Letablier, M.T. (2000) 'From equality to reconciliation in France?', in L. Hantrais (ed) *Gendered policies in Europe: Reconciling employment and family life*, London: Macmillan.

Law, I. (1996) *Racism, ethnicity and social policy*, Hemel Hempstead: Prentice Hall/Harvester Wheatsheaf.

Le Feuvre, N. and Andriocci, M. (2001) *Employment and women's studies: The impact of women's studies training on women's employment in Europe*, HPSE-CT2001-00082, Background Data Report, France (www.hull.ac.uk/ewsi).

Le Feuvre, N. and Andriocci, M. (2003) *Comparative Data Report 3: Employment opportunities for women in Europe (France)*, Report of the EU-funded project Employment and Women's Studies: The Impact of Women's Studies Training on Women's Employment in Europe, HPSE-CT2001-00082 (www.hull.ac.uk/ewsi)

Lehto, A.-M. (1999) 'Women in working life in Finland', in *Women in Finland*, Helsinki: Otava.

Leng, R., Taylor, R. and Wasik, M. (1998) *Blackstone's guide to the Crime and Disorder Act 1998*, London: Blackstone.

Leonard, A. (1987) *Pyrrhic victories: Winning sex discrimination and equal pay cases in industrial tribunals*, Manchester: Equal Opportunities Commission.

Lester, A. (2007) 'Catalyst article CRE magazine', *Guardian* special issue, 26 September.

Lester, A. and Bindman, G. (1972) *Race and law*, Harmondsworth: Penguin.

Lewis, S. and Lewis, J. (eds) (1996) *The work-family challenge: Rethinking employment*, London: Sage Publications.

Liff, S. and Cameron, I. (1997) 'Changing equality cultures to move beyond "women's problems"', *Gender, Work and Organization*, vol 4, no 1, pp 35-46.

Liff, S. and Ward, K. (2001) 'Distorted views through the glass ceiling: The construction of women's understandings of promotion and senior management positions', *Gender, Work and Organization*, vol 8, no 1, pp 19-36.

Lombardi, E. and Meier, P. (2006) 'Gender mainstreaming in the EU', *European Journal of Women's Studies*, vol 13, pp 151-66.

Lorde, A. (1984) 'Age, race, class and sex: women redefining difference, in Lorde, A. (ed) *Sister outsider*, Freedom, CA: The Crossing Press.

Lovenduski, J. (1986) *Women and European politics: Contemporary feminism and public policy*, London: Harvester Wheatsheaf.

Lunt, N. and Thornton, P. (1993) *Employment policies for disabled people: A review of legislation and services in fifteen countries*, Employment Department Research Series no 16, Sheffield: Employment Department.

Mackay, F. (2006) 'Descriptive and substantive representation in new parliamentary spaces. The case of Scotland', in M. Sawer, M. Tremblay and L. Trimble (eds) *Representing women in parliament. A comparative study*, Abingdon: Routledge.

Mackay, F. and Bilton, K. (2000) *Learning from experience: Lessons in mainstreaming equal opportunities*, Edinburgh: University of Edinburgh/The Governance of Scotland Forum.

Mackay, F., Myers, F. and Brown, A. (2003) 'Towards a new politics? Women and the constitutional change in Scotland', in A. Dobrowolsky and V. Hart (eds) *Women making constitutions: New politics and comparative perspectives*, New York, NY: Palgrave.

Maes, M.E. (1990) *Building a people's Europe: 1992 and the social dimension*, London: Whurr Publishers.

Makkai, T. (1997) 'Social policy and gender in Eastern Europe', in D. Sainsbury (ed) *Gendering welfare states*, London: Sage Publications, pp 188-205.

Manning, A. and Swaffield, J. (2005) *The gender gap in early-career wage growth*, LSE Discussion Paper No 700, London: Centre for Economic Performance, London School of Economics.

Marshall, J. (1994) *Women managers: Travellers in a male world*, Chichester: Wiley.

Mason, D. (1990) 'Competing conceptions of fairness and the formulation and implementation of equal opportunities policies', in W. Ball and J. Solomos (eds) *Race and local politics*, London: Macmillan.

McCall, L. (2001) 'Sources of racial wage inequality in metropolitan labor markets: racial, ethnic, and gender differences', *American Sociological Review*, vol 66, no 4, pp 520-42.

McCall, L. (2005) 'The complexity of intersectionality', *Signs: Journal of Women in Culture and Society*, vol 30, pp 1771-1800.

McCarthy, H. (2007) 'Gender equality', in P Thane, T. Evans, L. Filby, N. Kimber, H. McCarthy, S. Millar, M. Porter and B. Taylor (eds) *Equalities in Great Britain, 1946-2006*, Report commissioned by the Equalities Review, London: Centre for Contemporary British History, Institute of Historical Research, University of London.

McColgan, A. (1997) *Just wages for women*, Oxford: Clarendon Press.

McColgan, A. (2005) *Discrimination law: Text, cases and materials*, Oxford: Hart Publishing.

McCrudden, C. (1987) 'The Commission for Racial Equality: formal investigation in the shadow of judicial review', in R. Baldwin and C. McCrudden (eds) *Regulation and public law*, London: Weidenfield and Nicholson, pp 222-66.

McCrudden, C. (1996) 'The "merit principle" and fair employment in Northern Ireland', in A. Magill and S. Rose (eds) *Fair employment in Northern Ireland: Debates and issues*, Belfast: Standing Advisory Commission of Human Rights.

McEwen, E. (ed) (1990) *Age: The unrecognised discrimination*, London: Age Concern.

Meehan, E. (1990) 'British feminism from the 1960s to the 1980s', in H. Smith (ed) *British feminism in the 20th century*, London: Edward Elgar.

Meehan, E. (1993) *Citizenship and the European Community*, London: Sage Publications.

Miles, R. (1989) *Racism*, London: Routledge.

Millar, S. (2007) 'Disability', in P Thane, T. Evans, L. Filby, N. Kimber, H. McCarthy, S. Millar, M. Porter and B. Taylor (eds) *Equalities in Great Britain, 1946-2006*, Report commissioned by the Equalities Review, London: Centre for Contemporary British History, Institute of Historical Research, University of London.

Miller, D. (1976) *Social justice*, Oxford: Clarendon Press.

Morley, L. (1994) 'Glass ceiling or iron cage: women in UK academia', *Gender, Work and Organization*, vol 1, no 4, pp 194-204.

Morris, A.E. and Nott, S.M. (1991). *Working Women and the Law: Equality and Discrimination in Theory and Practice*, London: Routledge.

Morris, J. (1992) 'Personal and political: a feminist perspective on researching physical disability', *Disability, Handicap and Society*, vol 7, no 2, pp 157-66.

Norris, P. and Lovenduski, J. (2001) 'Blair's babes: critical mass theory, gender and legislative life', Faculty Research Working Paper Series 20, John F. Kennedy School of Government, Harvard University, Cambridge, MA, available at www.ksg.harvard.edu/wappp/research/working/blairs_babes.pdf (accessed February 2008).

O'Brien, M. and Shemit, I. (2003) *Working fathers: Earning and caring*, Research Discussion Series, Manchester: Equal Opportunities Commission.

O'Cinneide, C. (2002) *A single equality body: Lessons from abroad*, Working Paper Series 4, Manchester: Equal Opportunities Commission.

Observer (1968) 21 April, p 10.

Offen, K. (1992) 'Defining feminism: a comparative historical approach', in G. Bock and S. James (eds) *Beyond equality and difference*, London: Routledge.

Office of Public Sector Information (1998) Scotland Act, www.opsi.gov.uk

Office of Public Sector Information (1998) Government of Wales Act, www.opsi.gov.uk

Oliver, M. (1990) *The Politics of Disablement*, London: Macmillan.

Oliver, M. (1996) *Understanding disability. From theory to practice*, London: Macmillan.

ONS (Office for National Statistics) (2004) Annual Population Survey, January 2004 to December 2004, Office for National Statistics, www.statistics.gov.uk

Opportunity Now (2001) *Equality and excellence: The business case*, London: Opportunity Now.

Osborne, R.D. (2003) 'Progressing the equality agenda in Northern Ireland', *Journal of Social Policy*, vol 32, no 3, pp 339-60.

Owen, D., Green, A., Maguire, M. and Pitcher, J. (2000) 'Patterns of labour market participation in ethnic minority groups', *Labour Market Trends*, vol 108, pp 505-10.

Parekh, B. (1992) 'A case for positive discrimination', in B. Hepple and E.M. Szyszak (eds) *Discrimination: The limits of law*, London: Mansell Publishing.

Parekh, B. (2006) *Rethinking multiculturalism: Cultural diversity and political theory* (2nd edn), Basingstoke: Palgrave MacMillan.

Parmar, P. (1981) 'Young Asian women: a critique of the pathological approach', *Multiracial Education*, vol 9, no 3, pp 19-29.

Paul, R. (1991) 'Black and Third World people's citizenship and 1992', *Critical Social Policy*, vol 32, pp 52-64.

Pfau-Effinger, B. (1999) 'The modernization of the family and motherhood in Western Europe', in R. Crompton (ed) *Restructuring gender relations and employment: The decline of the male breadwinner*, Oxford: Oxford University Press, pp 60-79.

Picq, F. (2006) *Athena 2 Project 3B, SWOT Analysis for France* (www.rosadoc.be/site/rosa/english/pdf/athena/swot_france.pdf)

Pitt, G. (1992) 'Can reverse discrimination be justified?', in B. Hepple and E.M. Szyszak (eds) *Discrimination: The limits of law*, London: Mansell Publishing.

Porter, M. (2007) 'Gender identity and sexual orientation', in P Thane, T. Evans, L. Filby, N. Kimber, H. McCarthy, S. Millar, M. Porter and B. Taylor (eds) *Equalities in Great Britain, 1946-2006*, Report commissioned by the Equalities Review, London: Centre for Contemporary British History, Institute of Historical Research, University of London.

Powell, A., Bagilhole, B. and Dainty, A. (2006) 'The problem of women's assimilation into UK engineering cultures: can critical mass work?', *Equal Opportunities International, Special Issue, Gender Equality in Science, Engineering and Technology*, vol 25, no 8, pp 688-99.

Prasad, P. and Mills, A. (1997) 'From showcase to shadow: understanding the dilemmas of managing workplace diversity', in P. Prasad, A. Mills, M. Elmes and A. Prasad (eds) *Managing the organizational melting pot: Dilemmas of workplace diversity*, Thousand Oaks, CA: Sage Publications.

Pruvot, S., Miller, S., Koeman, A.M. and Ambrosini, F. (2008) *Where are all the European feminists?*, London: European Alternatives Future of European Feminism Project (www.euroalter.com/article_subpages/article28europea.html).

Rake, K., Davies, H., Joshi, H. and Alami, R. (eds) (2000) *Women's incomes over the lifetime. A report to the Women's Office*, London: Cabinet Office.

Rattansi, A. (1992) 'Changing the subject? Racism, culture and education', in J. Donald and A. Rattansi (eds) *Race, culture and difference*, London: Sage Publications/Open University.

Rawls, J. (1971) *A theory of justice*, Oxford: Oxford University Press.

Rayman, P., Davis, C.-S., Ginorio, A.B. and Hellenshead, C.S. (1996) *The equity equation: Fostering the advancement of women in science, mathematics and engineering*, San Francisco, CA: Jossey Bass.

Rees, T. (1998) *Mainstreaming equality in the European Union: Education, training and labour market policies*, London: Routledge.

Renton, D. (2006) *We touched the sky: A history of the Anti-Nazi League, 1977-1981*, London: New Clarion Press.

Rex, J. (1992) 'Race and ethnicity in Europe', in J. Bailey (ed) *Social Europe*, London: Longman.

Rigg, J. (2007) 'Disabling attitudes? Public perspectives on disabled people', in A. Park, J. Curtice, K. Thomson, M. Phillips and M. Johnson (eds) *British social attitudes: The 23rd report – Perspectives on a changing society*, London: Sage Publications.

Rivers, I. (2001) 'The bullying of sexual minorities at school: its nature and long term correlates', *Educational and Child Psychology*, vol 18, no 1, pp 32-46.

Roelofs, E. (1995) 'The European equal opportunities policy', in A. van Doorne-Huiskes, J. van Hoof and E. Roelofs (eds) *Women and the European labour markets*, London: Open University/Paul Chapman Publishing.

Ross, R. and Schneider, R. (1992) *From equality to diversity: A business case for equal opportunities*, London: Pitman.

Roulstone, A. and Warren, J. (2006) 'Applying a barriers approach to monitoring disabled people's employment: implications for the Disability Discrimination Act 2005', *Disability and Society*, vol 21, pp 115-31.

Rubery, J. (1999) 'Overview and comparative studies', in European Commission (eds) *Women and work: Equality between women and men*, Luxembourg: Office for the Official Publications of the European Communities.

Rubery, J. and Fagan, C. (1994) *Wage determination and sex segregation in the European Community. Supplement to Social Europe*, Luxembourg: Office for Official Publications of the European Community.

Runnymede Trust Commission (2000) *The future of multi-ethnic Britain*, London: Profile Books Ltd.

Russell, P. (2003) *Bridging the gap: Developing policy and practice in child care options for disabled children and their families*, London: Council for Disabled Children.

Ryan, M.K. and Haslam, S.A. (2005) 'The glass cliff: evidence that women are over-represented in precarious leadership positions', *British Journal of Management*, vol 16, pp 81-90.

Saggar, S. (1991) *Race and public policy*, Aldershot: Avebury.

Sargeant, M. (2006) 'The Employment Equality (Age) Regulations 2006: A legitimization of age discrimination in employment', *Industrial Law Journal*, vol 5, pp 209-44.

Savoie, Ernest J. and Sheehan, Maureen (2001) 'Highlights of the Conference Diversity in the Workplace: Challenges and Opportunities', in *Diversity in the Workplace: Challenges and Opportunities*, Michigan: Wayne State University Press.

SEU (Social Exclusion Unit) (2006) *A sure start to later life: Ending inequalities for older people*, London: Office of the Deputy Prime Minister.

Sheehan, M. (1995) 'Fair employment: an issue for the peace process', *Race and Class*, vol 37, no 1, pp 71-82.

Sheffield Hallam University (2005) *We care, do you?*, ACE National Action for Carers and Employment, London: Carers UK.

Shukra, K. (1998) *The changing patterns of Black politics in Britain*, London: Pluto Press.

Silius, H. (1996) 'Finnish gender contracts', in C. Kartik, C. Roy, A. Clement, A. Tisdell and C. Blomqvist (eds) *Economic development and women in the world community*, London: Praeger, pp 139-154.

Silius, H. (2002) 'Women's employment, equal opportunities and women's studies in nine European countries – a summary', in G. Griffin (ed) *Women's employment, women's studies and equal opportunities 1945-2001*, Hull: University of Hull, pp 470-514.

Silius, H. and Tuori, S. (2002) 'Finland', in G. Griffin (ed) *Women's employment, women's studies and equal opportunities 1945-2001*, Hull: University of Hull, pp 69-121.

Singh, V. and Vinnicombe, S. (2005) *The female FTSE report*, Cranfield: Centre for Developing Women Business Leaders, Cranfield School of Management.

Sivanandan, A. (1976) *Race, class and the state: The Black experience in Britain*, London: Institute of Race Relations.

Sivanandan, A. (1982) *A different hunger*, London: Pluto Press.

Sivanandan, A. (1985) 'RAT and the degradation of the Black struggle', *Race and Class*, vol xxvi, no. 4, pp 1-33.

Sivanandan, A. (1988) 'The new racism', *New Statesman and Society*, 4 November, pp 4-6.

Sivanandan, A. (2001) 'Poverty is the new black', *Race and Class*, vol 43, no 2, pp 1-5.

Smeaton, D. and Marsh, A. (2006) *Maternity and paternity rights and benefits: Survey of parents*, Employment Relations Report no 50, London: Department of Trade and Industry.

Soper, K. (1994) 'Feminism, humanism and postmodernism', in M. Evans (ed) *The woman question*, London: Sage Publications.

Spelling, P. (1995) *European Commission legislation, policy and funding on equal opportunity and education*, Equal Opportunities Higher Education Network conference proceedings, University of Warwick.

Squires, J. (1999) *Gender in political theory*, Cambridge: Polity.

Squires, J. (2004) 'The new equalities agenda: recognising diversity and securing equality in post-devolution Britain', in A. Dobrowolsky and V. Hart (eds) *Women, politics and constitutional change*, Basingstoke: Palgrave Macmillan.

Squires, J. (2007) *The new politics of gender equality*, Basingstoke: Palgrave Macmillan.

Steele, C.M. and Aronsen, J. (1995) 'Stereotype threat and the intellectual test performance of African Americans', *Journal of Personal Social Psychology*, vol 69, no 5, pp 797-811.

Stevens, J., Brown, J. and Lee, C. (2004) *The Second Work-Life Balance Study: Results from the Employees' Survey*, Employment Relations Research Series No 27, London: Department for Trade and Industry.

Stonewall (2003) *Profiles of prejudice: Detailed summary of findings* (www.stonewall.org.uk/documents/long_summary_no_logo.doc)

Stonewall (2008) *Workplace Equality Index 2008: The top 100 employers for lesbian, gay and bisexual people in Britain*, London: Stonewall.

Suarez, I.C. and Suarez, L.V. (2003) *Comparative Data Report 1: The institutionalization of equal opportunities*, Report of the EU-funded project Employment and Women's Studies: The Impact of Women's Studies Training on Women's Employment in Europe, HPSE-CT2001-00082 (www.hull.ac.uk/ewsi/CR1%20Comparative%20Report%20(Spain)htm).

Symington, A. (2004) 'Intersectionality: a tool for gender and economic justice. Women's rights and economic change', *Facts and Issues*, vol 9, pp 1-8.

Thane, P. (1996) *The foundations of the welfare state*, Harlow: Longman.

Thane, P. (2007) 'Age and equality' in P Thane, T. Evans, L. Filby, N. Kimber, H. McCarthy, S. Millar, M. Porter and B. Taylor (eds) *Equalities in Great Britain, 1946-2006*, Report commissioned by the Equalities Review, London: Centre for Contemporary British History, Institute of Historical Research, University of London.

Thane, P., Evans, T., Filby, L., Kimber, N., McCarthy, H., Millar, S., Porter, M. and Taylor, B. (eds) (2007) *Equalities in Great Britain, 1946-2006*, Report commissioned by the Equalities Review, London: Centre for Contemporary British History, Institute of Historical Research, University of London.

The Stephen Lawrence Inquiry (1999) *Report of an Inquiry by Sir William MacPherson of Cluny, Cm 4262-I*, London: The Stationery Office.

Tomlinson, S. (1990) *Multicultural education in white schools*, London: Batsford.

Travis, A. (2004) 'Drive to redefine British pride', *Guardian*, 19 May, p 2.

UNESCO (United Nations Educational, Scientific and Cultural Organization) (1997) *The Economic and Social Council of the United Nations*, E/1997/L.30, Para adopted by ESCO, 14 July.

Van der Sanden, J. and Waaldijk, B. (2002) 'Netherlands', in G. Griffin (ed) *Women's employment, women's studies and equal opportunities 1945-2001*, Hull: University of Hull, pp 122-76.

Verloo, M. (2006) 'Multiple inequalities, intersectionality and the European Union', *European Journal of Women's Studies*, vol 13, no 3, pp 211-28.

Vingelli, G. (2006) *Review of the implementation of the Beijing platform for action, and the outcome documents of the 23rd special session of the General Assembly, Italy* (www.rosadoc.be/site/rosa/english/european%20projects/athena/introduction.htm).

Vinnicombe, S. (2000) 'The position of women in management in Europe', in M.J. Davidson and R.J. Burke *Women in management: Current research issues, volume II*, London: Sage Publications.

Virdee, S. (2006) '"Race", employment and social change: Critique of current orthodoxes', *Ethnic and Racial Studies*, vol 29, pp 605-28.

Walby, S. (1990) *Theorising patriarchy*, Oxford: Blackwell.

Walking in my shoes: Personal experiences of inequality in Britain (2007) Crown copyright, commissioned by the Equalities Review, London: Equalities Review.

Wanless, D. (2006) *Securing good care for older people: Taking a long-term view*, London: King's Fund.

Ware, V. (1985) 'Growing up in black and white', *New Internationalist*, no 145, March,21.

Weeks, J. (1981) *Sex, politics and society: The regulation of sexuality since 1800*, Harlow: Longman.

Weeks, J. (1990) *Coming out: Homosexual politics in Britain from the nineteenth century to the present*, London: Quartet.

Weeks, J. (2007) 'Wolfenden and beyond: the remaking of homosexual history' (www.historyandpolicy.org/archive/policy-paper-51.html).

Weller, P., Feldman, A. and Purdam, K. (2001) *Religious discrimination in England and Wales*, Home Office Research Study 220, London: Home Office.

Wilkinson, R.G. (2005) *The impact of inequality*, London: Routledge.

Williams, C.L. (1992) 'The glass escalator: hidden advantages for men in the "female" professions', *Social Problems*, vol 39, no 3, pp 253-67.

Williams, F. (1989) *Social policy: A critical introduction*, Cambridge: Polity.

Williams, L.S. and Villemez, W.J. (1993) 'Seekers and finders: male entry and exit in female-dominated jobs', in C.L. Williams (ed) *Doing women's work: Men in non-traditional occupations*, London: Sage Publications.

Wilson-Kovacs, D.M., Ryan, M. and Haslam, A. (2006) 'The glass-cliff: women's career paths in the UK private IT sector', *Equal Opportunities International*, vol 25, no 8, pp 674-87.

Women and Men in Finland (2001) *Gender statistics 2001:002*, Helsinki: Statistics Finland.

Women and Work Commission (2006) *Shaping a fairer future*, London: Women and Equality Unit. (www.womenandequalityunit.gov,uk/publications/wwc_shaping_fairer_future06).

Woodward, A. (2004) 'Diversity? The Europeanization of difference and the influence of the United States on conceptualizations of equality policy', Paper presented at the Fifth European Feminist Research Conference, Lund, 20-24 August.

Young, K. (1990) 'Approaches to policy development in the field of equal opportunities', in W. Ball and J. Solomos (eds) *Race and local politics*, London: Macmillan.

Index